NIXON'S HEAD

NIXON'S HEAD

by

Arthur Woodstone

ST. MARTIN'S PRESS
New York

PREFACE

When President Eisenhower had his first heart attack, for the next several days the Vice-President, next in line of succession, was mentioned in every conceivable context but one. The media dredged up the Hiss case and the campaigns of 1946, 1950, 1952 and 1954; political analysts said that Richard Milhous Nixon was admired (never loved) and hated (never pitied) as a politician (never as a man); the overnight biographers, pulled off city desks to summarize his life, said he was the father of two girls, a Californian of humble origins and a Quaker. But no newspaper, wire service or broadcaster defied the conventions for examining important public figures, as if having achieved prominence entitled Nixon to less probing as a human being rather than more. So when they asked what made Dick Nixon "tick," it was a gesture; the answers were skin-deep. They did write that he had a strong desire to win. However, so do football heroes and corporation presidents. Nobody asked (in the presence of the public) why the desire in Nixon sometimes seemed so overwhelming.

The next year, 1956, during the period when he was seeking re-election, the Vice-President's eccentric moments so multiplied in number, intensity and even type that to more observant reporters covering the campaign, it seemed the man was begging them to spell it out. Still, correspondents limited what they reported to diffident hints that public figures were not always coldly rational men. For example, a star reporter for *The New York Times* wrote that late one night, when he and others covering the Nixon campaign had nothing better to do, they sat around psychoanalyzing the Vice-President without reaching any conclusions. Of course, he couldn't very well have written of the conclusions they had not reached, but the reporter never even mentioned the facts that prompted these professional journalists to play amateur analysts.

In 1960 and again in 1968, during the Presidential campaigns, some professional skeptics in the press convinced themselves that by stressing Nixon, the shady political animal, they were winning a tough battle against press hand-outs and other packaged news. But in addition to its familiar ring, such reportage camouflaged the possibility that something besides cold political judgment made candidate Nixon tick. The image of the calculating politician, encouraged by Nixon's boasts of his own cunning, was so strong that it made his "last" press conference in 1962 after the California gubernatorial race seem an isolated emotional aberration.

Once Nixon was President, many White House correspondents felt that his peculiarities should concern no one but the man, his God and—if he had one—his analyst. Evoking "objectivity" as their goal, they limited themselves to taking down Nixon's words. And insofar as they played any personal role in the process, they provided neat language and a logical order to official statements—which made them little more than illustrious stenographers. In fact, these correspondents were often such fine writers that they gave the President a clarity and a logic that, at the moment of observation, he may not have truly possessed.

The better journalists covering Richard Nixon at the start of his term, knowing they were unqualified to sit behind "the couch," felt they had no right to speak in print of the aspects of the President's behavior which often disturbed them most. But more inhibiting than the knowledge of their own deficiencies as clinicians was their fear that once you've probed the quality or stability of a man's mind—especially if you are suspicious of his politics—you have opened the door to thought control and tyranny by the press.

By 1970, however, enough had happened to make it difficult for honest observers of the White House scene to report comforting certainties that frequently did not exist: Many of the President's assaults on his opponents to win votes or legislative programs no longer seemed reasoned or pragmatic—any more so than Lyndon Johnson's scalding treatment of his own aides or his discomfort among northern intellectuals. Urged on by at least two successive Administrations in which expediency and politics often seemed to play smaller roles than ego and emotion, these few journalists stopped nodding incessantly at Machiavelli and began talking more in public of Freud.

Because prefaces tend to "cop" pleas before trial to minimize the judge's sentence, I point out now that I am not a psychiatrist, a clinical psychologist or an analyst. I am a journalist and researcher who believes in the admonition of academicians Jacques Barzun and Henry Graff: "The facts *never* speak for themselves," which may be the simplest recorded refutation of the myth of objectivity. Helene Deutsch, considered within her own profession one of the world's outstanding psychoanalysts, has put it another way: "The ultimate goal of all research is not objectivity, but truth."

Not every claim made for President Nixon is truthful, nor are many made against him. Seeing no sense in balancing one argument against another in order to appear objective, I have selected only the facts that I think significant and linked them together to offer a hopefully accurate if somewhat pointed view of Richard Nixon.

Among other things, this book stresses his practical errors. One reason is that there have been so many in his life. The other is, as Bertrand Russell said in *Sceptical* [sic] *Essays*, a man's mistakes are so frequently "the key" to his personality.

For some people, *Nixon's Head* will serve only as a categorical insult. They will fight the idea that any man can stumble to the top of the system on faulty and possibly dangerous equipment. And they will fight because that allegation reflects as poorly on their collective wisdom to choose leaders as on the automatic dignity of the Presidency, itself.

For other people, the book will only reinforce their worst suspicions. For the remainder, *Nixon's Head* will set them to thinking in new directions, for if the book raises more questions than the author can answer, it at least raises them.

Because the point of view is provocative and because I pursue it relentlessly—though resorting as little as possible to "the language of the consulting room"—I figure that many Washington sources will not appreciate my using their names. But as *Nixon's Head* is based in large measure on material which has been published but never pulled together in such a way, there are names I do mention, and to those few I mention often, because of their perception and honesty, I owe the debt of gratitude. They are journalism's hope.

A. J. W.

The title of this book is based on something Averell Harriman said on television in 1970, fourteen years after he had sought the Presidential nomination: "I think anyone who wants to be President should have his head examined."

CHAPTER ONE

On December 1, 1969, the President's former internist, Arnold A. Hutschnecker, M.D., left the White House with an advance copy of a national commission's statement "on the causes and prevention of violence." Though Hutschnecker was not a recognized expert in the field, Richard M. Nixon had asked him to render his own "philosophy" on a report about a massive social problem, which a thirteen-man panel chaired by Milton Eisenhower, Ph.D., had spent eighteen months attempting to comprehend and solve.

Seven days later, Hutschnecker returned with a recommendation that would turn educators and psychologists alike on their ears: "Mass testing of *all* [his emphasis] six to eight-year-old children." Crime could be prevented, Hutschnecker alleged, by preventing a child with "delinquent tendencies" from growing into a "full-fledged delinquent." Soon after, with the apparent encouragement of Nixon, the doctor left for Mexico to initiate stage two of his scheme. He met there with Robert Hartman, whom he described as a "research professor of philosophy" at the National University of Mexico with a method for predicting delinquency in intelligent children of age ten or older and of all children over twelve. That method was a test which could not predict "actual violent behavior but," said Hutschnecker, "[could] detect the tendency or proneness to such behavior."

Weaving in Hartman's theories, Hutschnecker worked more deliberately on a second draft of his report, which he delivered to the White House several weeks after returning from Mexico. Meanwhile, three and a half months had passed since the day Nixon laid eyes on the Commission's statement on violence, but he had done nothing about it. Even though the report had been authored by Dwight Eisenhower's brother; it cited haphazard urbanization, the disfigurement of the environment and dislocations in the human identity as the sources of violence in America. And Nixon's distaste for those conclusions was evident in Milton Eisenhower's cautious announcement which the White House authorized for release so that it would be buried in the traditional dumping ground—the weekend editions: "The President authorized me to say that he is gravely concerned about the problems we have studied."

Because the President thought more of Hutschnecker's work, he tried to keep it alive. Nixon bucked the report through John Ehrlichman, his chief of domestic programs, to Robert Finch, Secretary of Health, Education and Welfare, asking for information about the feasibility of "pilot projects embodying some of these approaches." He also sent Daniel Patrick Moynihan, intellectual, charming, witty and important, to New York to tell Hutschnecker how things were going. Moynihan proved a flattering emissary. Hutschnecker later wrote an article for *The New York Times* in which he crowed: "The President sent his counselor . . . to see me."

Looking back on the sequence of events, Hutschnecker explained that on April 6, 1970, he began receiving calls from newspapers and broadcasters who "demanded" details about "your testing of children." But the doctor figured he was as crafty as any professional politician: " 'It was a confidential report,' I replied evasively." Nonetheless the press, apparently relying on sources within HEW, described the plan as one which "has won the President's personal interest."

That could only have pleased the physician, but the consequences did not. The American Sociological Association (ASA) instantly called a press conference in partnership with the American Psychological Association (APA) to charge that the Hutschnecker–Hartman tests were as absurd to contemplate as they were impossible to carry out. The APA's Dr. Kenneth Little scored Hutschnecker for revealing "a complete lack of understanding as to what psychological tests can or cannot do, or even what they were meant to do." Dr. Little calculated that the possible margin of error in measuring "deviant" behavior could run as high as fifty percent and cause incalculable damage to children if cures were attempted for diseases they did not have. Seconding

Little's attack, Dr. Edmund H. Volkart of ASA went right back to the conclusions reached by the Eisenhower panel: social environment—not personality—was the principal source of American violence. Then the sociologist added that the so-called deviant behavior, the very thing Hutschnecker sought to measure and curb, could lead as easily to creativity as it could to violence. Other psychiatrists and psychoanalysts joined in. Medical director of the American Psychiatric Association, Dr. Walter Barton, declared, "Not to the best of our knowledge does his proposal have any potential support whatsoever within the profession of psychiatry."

Hutschnecker fought back, alleging that, among others, Dr. Louise Bates Ames, associate director of the Gesell Institute of Child Development, believed in the efficacy of testing juveniles for delinquent proclivities. But the chief message now reaching the White House's number one occupant was that Hutschnecker's ideas about violence and its origins were perhaps more incorrigible than America's army of potential juvenile delinquents.

Even more discomforting, however, was the fact that people all around the country had the impression that Hutschnecker's theories had the President's endorsement. Hutschnecker ceased to receive important and glamorous emissaries sent all the way from Washington. The President's former doctor was left to fight his own battles in New York.

While ridicule was heaped on Hutschnecker, no one publicly questioned why Nixon chose him in the first place to pass judgment on someone else's work in a field where he was not a recognized expert. Privately, reporters speculated: Harlem, the most famous ghetto in the world, where crime abounds, begins pressing into shape eleven or twelve blocks north of Hutschnecker's elegantly furnished Park Avenue office; and "that," said one reporter, "is just the kind of ominous geography that will make him an expert in Nixon's eyes." Still, if Nixon wanted an expert on ghettos, there were doctors who lived *in* Harlem. If he wanted an expert on criminal behavior or on ordinary child behavior, the President of the United States could have called upon hundreds of professionals who specialize in either area. But he had chosen Hutschnecker.

3

Nixon met Hutschnecker in 1951 or 1952, after the physician had published a book, *The Will to Live*, "a layman's guide to psychosomatic illness." On the book jacket is the message, "Mind and body are one." One chapter title is "It's Easier to Hate, but Healthier to Love"—or Ivan Pavlov Meets Norman Vincent Peale. From the time Harry Emerson Fosdick decided to challenge Freud for influence over human emotions, this is the type of information which has appealed to people who find a self-help psychology, a *philosophy*, less exhausting, costly or threatening than psychoanalysis. One of Hutschnecker's readers, Nixon soon came to New York for a visit. Hutschnecker recalls that Nixon came about five times in 1952, once in 1953 and a "couple of times" in 1954. The visits, taking the Vice-President 210 miles from Washington to New York, continued until at least 1956.

"The discovery of this fact," Hutschnecker explained in 1969, in order to silence speculation over those visits, "had been a comparatively easy matter because on several of his visits to me, the Secret Service men accompanying the then Vice-President were in evidence in front of my Manhattan office."

On the Saturday before Election Day, 1960, the Associated Press, Hutschnecker says, tracked him down at his home in Connecticut to ask for a statement on candidate Nixon's health: "Avoiding the ambiguous 'no comment,' I made it clear to the press that while it was true that I had treated the Vice-President, it was at a time when I was still engaged in the practice of internal medicine." The answer seems more ambiguous than the one he shunned in the name of clarity, but it served to send the AP man away and, so far as is known, no reporter bothered Hutschnecker with questions about Nixon for eight years.

On November 13, 1968, when Richard Nixon had been President-elect for a week, the late columnist Drew Pearson told the National Press Club he had called Dr. Hutschnecker just before the election, on October 31, to inquire about "reports that Mr. Nixon had been under the care of a psychiatrist." Hutschnecker admitted, according to Pearson, that while it was a "delicate matter," candidate Nixon "did have a problem—not standing up under great pressure."

4

Because he had a patient in his office, Hutschnecker asked Pearson to call back that afternoon. Also that morning, Pearson had his assistant Jack Anderson call Herbert G. Klein, communications director, and ask about the case: "We mentioned the name of Dr. Hutschnecker to get comment, confirmation or denial." At 4 p.m., Pearson called back Hutschnecker in New York, but this time the physician said that Nixon had consulted him "but this was for problems of internal medicine and it was not psychotherapy."

Having failed to substantiate the rumor "to my full conviction," Pearson explained, somewhat mournfully, he did not think he ought to write the story on October 31. He was sorry he hadn't. Why, he wondered, had the Vice-President of the United States, billed by his party as the busiest in history, wasted time travelling all the way to New York regularly "when we have some excellent [internists] here in Washington." In the two weeks that had elapsed since speaking to Hutschnecker, Pearson had satisfied himself that Nixon was not Hutschnecker's patient for a strictly physical illness. He told the Press Club that "Dr. Hutschnecker had told others and confirmed the fact."

The columnist shared President Eisenhower's opinion that all details of any candidate's health and well being should be available to the public. "Perhaps I'm wrong"—Pearson was remorseful—"perhaps I was not courageous enough. I don't know."

Newsweek concluded that "L'affaire Hutschnecker proved little more than Nixon had once consulted a Park Avenue specialist"; that it is "all but impossible to draw the line on gossiping about Presidents" and finally, that Pearson, "that ancient bane of the men in the White House, will manage to get Presidential scuttlebutt into print one way or the other."

So will *Newsweek*, which repeated the scuttlebutt, and then without confessing to a similar affliction of doubt, blinked its eyes at the contradictions in Hutschnecker's story and reached the conclusion that no conclusion could be reached: "He refused to discuss Nixon's problem" with the magazine, "except to say that it was physical and 'Nixon wondered if there could be some emotional cause for it.'" One of the visits in the 1950's, said the doctor, came after Vice-President Nixon returned from "a very rough trip overseas."

Thus *Newsweek*, when Nixon was President-elect, faithfully recorded Hutschnecker's internally conflicting statement without dissecting it: Did Hutschnecker mean that his patient had wondered whether his problem had mental or emotional roots, while the doctor whose own work sought to "help allay daily anxieties and stresses that cause serious illness" blithely didn't wonder at all? Or did Hutschnecker give in to curiosity and ask Nixon questions no physical examination would have covered? How does a doctor decide that his patient's complaint has no psychosomatic roots without asking first what might properly be labelled *psychological* questions? (It might take a psychiatrist several interviews to reach such a finding.) When Hutschnecker mentioned that one of Nixon's visits resulted from a "very rough trip overseas," what did he mean? Did Nixon bruise his shins when his plane hit an air pocket? Was his right hand paralyzed from shaking hands with all those foreign dignitaries? Or was there, in the doctor's reluctant opinion, a correlation between rough trips and anxiety?

In 1969, eight months after Hutschnecker spoke to *Newsweek*, *The New York Times* and Pearson, *Look* published an article written by Hutschnecker suggestively titled: "President Nixon's Former Doctor Writes About THE MENTAL HEALTH OF OUR LEADERS." From his previous statements, one might assume he meant all leaders but Nixon. But Hutschnecker couldn't seem to stop talking about his former patient, now President of the United States. Anticipating that raising the "health issue," as he called it, might appear arbitrary after so many months, the physician gave his reasons. The article provided the opportunity to deny the "assumption," he said, of a "leak from my office. This challenge, and I must state this categorically, is without foundation. There was no leak, and there was no violation of the sacred obligation a doctor has to safeguard the privacy of all of his patients."

The second reason (the selfless one) for writing the article was to still, as he put it, the "anxiety about Mr. Nixon's emotional stability," which he must have thought continued to trouble some Americans. He said the rumors which began a week after Nixon's election were based on "distortion of facts and . . . falsifications" by a certain "columnist" Hutschnecker appeared too contemptuous to name.

Beginning with his evasively "clear" response to AP that he "had treated the Vice-President . . . at a time when I was still engaged in the practice of internal medicine" (suddenly making room again for the inference that he might have had a secondary practice in psychosomatic medicine), he wrote this revealing passage: "Naturally, no specific diagnosis can be given even now. What I as a physician am allowed to say is that Mr. Nixon came for physical checkups, none of which showed evidence of any illness. Because of rumors that the Vice-President was seeing a New York psychiatrist, we had come to an understanding, *years before the 1960 elections* [emphasis added] that we should discontinue our doctor-patient relationship. The rumors may have resulted from the fact that in 1951 I had published a book on psychosomatic medicine, which made some people assume that I had always been a psychoanalyst. Whatever the reasons," he continued in *Look*, "after my election-eve explanation (in 1960), the press dropped the health issue.

"By 1960, I had largely changed my medical practice to psychotherapy . . ."

Hutschnecker's story had changed in small, fascinating details between the time of Pearson's publicity on November 13, 1968, and eight months later when the doctor's piece appeared in *Look*. After Pearson's remarks, a reporter of *The New York Times* was among the first to reach Hutschnecker. The physician told the reporter that he blamed "the Kennedy camp" for circulating reports brought forth by Pearson *as long ago as 1960*, and that Walter Winchell had carried a "malicious, nasty note" in his column. "*At that time*," the *Times* reported of Hutschnecker, "*he said he advised Mr. Nixon to seek another doctor* [emphasis added] so as to forestall 'further rumors.' "

"1960" in the *Times* became "years before 1960" in *Look*.

A doctor is entitled to such mistakes but an author whose aim is to clear the air once and for all of dark rumors about his former patient's mental state should, one imagines, reconcile his own discrepancies. When did Hutschnecker and Nixon sever their doctor-patient relationship? In 1960? or before?

Harriet Van Horne, another columnist and a former neighbor of Hutschnecker's Park Avenue office, recalls seeing Nixon enter the building in 1962. She asked the doorman there about it. "He comes to see the shrink," was the answer. Maybe the doorman was jumping to conclusions: Hutschnecker admits to "only largely" changing to psychotherapy after 1960; maybe Nixon was there to consult that segment of Hutschnecker which was still internist. Maybe it means absolutely nothing that this particular visit occurred shortly after Nixon's defeat by Edmund (Pat) Brown in the race for Governor of California—for Nixon manifestly one of the roughest trips of all.

Hutschnecker, who was not, as he has said so often, Nixon's analyst nor even his psychosomatic specialist, but his internist, said in *Look* that he "detected no sign of mental illness in him." Nixon, he continued in a less clinical vein, always impressed him as a man of "superior intellect and keen perception. He was an intense listener . . ."

Dr. Hutschnecker is not the man to avoid a forum and is, as demonstrated in his plan to save the children, a man of strong opinions. *Newsweek* observed that "once, he startled Nixon by interjecting in a nonprofessional chat: 'I don't know how long it will take the world to recover from the policies of [John Foster] Dulles.' " The internist-psycho-somaticist-psychiatrist-cum-psychoanalyst apparently didn't consider the late Secretary of State a stable leader. Because of his fear that irrational men can ruin the world, not only does Hutschnecker want to test all the children of the United States for their criminal tendencies, but he also wants to test the stability of any man seeking to become a President of the United States. Toward this end, he would use, he explains, the Pavlovian scale: Type-one, for example, would be "strong" and "excitatory," type-two comprised of "the lively," type-three "the calm-imperturbable" and type-four "the weak, inhibitory." Type-two leaders represent for Hutschnecker the most desirable of choices because they manifest a "controlled reaction when exposed to stress": men who stand up under pressure. In *Look*, when the Nixon

8

Administration was six months old, Dr. Hutschnecker stated that, as President, Nixon "may [emphasis added] turn out to be a type-two."

Hutschnecker explained that Nixon's behavior at the famous press conference following his defeat in California seven years before was nothing to worry about because it was a "subjective reaction to a personal traumatic experience." Already, in his first three months of office, Nixon had shown he was able to handle a stress situation when the American reconnaissance plane was shot down by North Korean Communists in April, 1969. Nixon, Hutschnecker analyzed, "exercised restrained judgment and control," because the destruction of the plane constituted an "impersonal" crisis and hence did not have the same emotional impact on Nixon as the California defeat. Moreover, said Hutschnecker, Nixon would continue making wise judgments so long as he continued to rely "on the help of time and advisers." It was an extraordinary article and not the least extraordinary aspect of Hutschnecker's pronouncements, as will be shown, was his misreading of the Korean situation. The article had about it the air of a teacher telling his pupil, or a psychiatrist telling his patient, that he had his problems, but that he'd make it just fine if he held his temper in check and continued to take advice. And within a few months Nixon asked for it. There may have been more than one reason why he did.

Nixon had gone to Hutschnecker in the early 1950's, after the doctor had written a book on psychosomatic illness, because the politician was worried that his physical pains (which included sore throats that disappeared when he was cheered by enough people) had an emotional root. That had led to gossip in 1960 and again in 1968 about his "emotional instability" and weakness under pressure, and now, after nearly a year as President, Nixon did not need further public analyses, even favourable ones, of his mental health. So, in effect, he bribed the doctor by involving him in the processes of government. The other possible explanation for his inviting Hutschnecker to the White House in late 1969 was that the President, who was under pressure at the time, had recognized the beginning of another of his many emotional

9

crises and was, in his own way, asking his doctor for help.

The public outcry against Hutschnecker's plan presumably made it useless to Nixon. The charge, for example, that his friend the physician had proposed "detention camps" for potential delinquents, exaggerated the truth, but it was the kind of dramatic misstatement which, as Nixon knows, sticks in impressionable heads. (Hutschnecker had asked for day-care centers, more or less, which welfare experts have long sought out of different motives.) Nixon didn't need any more problems than he already had as President of the United States. Nor did it matter that he had pretty much brought this problem on himself by asking the ill-defined help of an outsider with an ill-defined role in White House affairs and an equally ill-defined role in Nixon's private affairs. It seems now that, as a result, the revolutionary Hutschnecker plan was relegated by the President to the same obscurity held by the Eisenhower panel.

Hutschnecker took this fate somewhat unhappily; he'd obviously heard about the way bureaucracies manage to lose things they can't cope with. So he spanked the Administration in print a second time. "Officially the President has not as yet rejected my plan," he wrote in a special editorial in *The New York Times*. However, he would not wait for a formal rejection. Instead he would pursue his plan through a private foundation, which would give him the money. "Such a project," Hutschnecker declared, "may convince the Government of the effectiveness of crime prevention and motivate it to adopt this or a similar plan. If we are seriously determined to cure the cancer of crime which costs this nation billions of dollars, to say nothing of lives, then the early detection of delinquent tendencies seems not only the most effective action available to us but an inescapable responsibility of the Government."

Quite coincidental, one supposes, to all of this activity was the re-release in 1970 of a book Dr. Hutschnecker first issued in 1964. Titled *The Will to Happiness*, his third book contains the following line: ". . . Unhappy people are dangerous people." As things turned out badly for both, one wonders who was the unhappier—Arnold Hutschnecker or Richard Nixon?

CHAPTER TWO

There is an intuitive reaction to Nixon, and the harder he tries to overcome it, the more intense the feeling grows. "Fatty ham frying in oil" is how one severe detractor describes his style, and even Bela Kornitzer, a friendly biographer, acknowledged that, as a politician "subconsciously alert to public opinion," he is always on stage, acting. And Stewart Alsop, who admires Nixon's toughness and fundamental decency, says Nixon is hammy, because he was raised on the outskirts of Hollywood where "hamminess" symbolizes a "highly respected" life style. That Nixon is like other Southern Californians or that they all become hammy by osmosis is debatable; but his wariness, slickness and theatrical excesses are too well established to debate. He will even pretend to be angry when he honestly is.

One remark apropos of Nixon was: "He was much too careful . . . much too smooth . . . for one who purported to be telling the whole truth without qualifications. I felt he had put on a show . . . his statement . . . seemed to me to be overacted." Nonetheless, this insight can be distinguished from the usual feeling about Nixon, because it is Richard Nixon's very own insight—into Alger Hiss.[1] And although it would not stand up as evidence in any American court of law, it was on the basis of his intuition that Nixon would hound Hiss all the way to jail. It is a fascinating revelation of the man's thought patterns.

Nixon claims he first heard of Hiss, a former State Department official who had moved on to the presidency of the prestigious fund, Carnegie Endowment for Peace, on August 3, 1948, from a former Communist named David Whittaker

[1] In 1950, Nixon said Helen Gahagan Douglas (who had been an actress and a good one) overacted and shouldn't be allowed to get away with it. Nixon cohorts made her the object of an insidious smear campaign, implying she was a Communist ("The Pink Lady") when she was not.

Chambers, who testified that he and Hiss had belonged to the same underground Communist organization ten years earlier. (In fact, Hiss's name had been mentioned eighteen months earlier, but in passing.) Nixon, who was a junior member of the House Un-American Activities Committee, had not been impressed with Chambers as a witness. He considered him "lackluster," had doubts about his sanity and, on top of all that, was aware that Chambers had offered no evidence supporting his charge against Hiss. Hiss immediately telegraphed to request time to clear his name, and he appeared before the Committee in Washington two days later, on August 5. In contrast to Chambers, who had recently been under psychiatric care and was unsure of himself, Hiss was a lucid, self-confident and effective witness. The other committee members, including Karl Mundt, acting HUAC chairman and Nixon's frequent ally, were favorably impressed by Hiss and believed that Chambers, on the other hand, was either mistaken in his identification or a madman given to vicious fantasies.

The reaction of outsiders was similar. Mary Spargo of *The Washington Post* came up to Nixon at the end of the hearing, he recalls in *Six Crises*, and bluntly predicted that if the Committee did not prove its charges against Hiss, it would be the end of the Committee. Then Ed Lahey of *The Chicago Daily News* accused the Committee of character assassination for placing Chambers on the stand without first checking his story. Nixon observed Lahey carefully and says he saw the reporter "literally shaking with anger" and his eyes "blazing." Although Miss Spargo and Lahey were both angry, Nixon slyly implies they were angry at the Committee rather than at him. He does not acknowledge that failure to prove a case against Hiss might damage him worse than it damaged the Committee, since that day he had been the only member, a junior one at that, who was patently after Hiss's hide.

But humiliation at the hands of outsiders seemed to be the least of his problems that day. He learned from his fellow members of the Committee that they were anxious to drop the Hiss matter, and he would soon discover that the Democratic Administration was planning to bring perjury charges against Chambers, who, in effect, had become Nixon's property. But, having invested too much of himself already, Nixon was not prepared to surrender now.

He admits his reputation was on the line. He talked to the other Committee members at length, finally winning the majority of them over to his side. Although there was no evidence to prove Hiss guilty of any crime, Nixon calculated that if they stuck to it maybe they could nail him for perjury. Long after, Nixon recalled that after winning the argument, he felt suffused with an enormous sense of achievement; he also felt, somewhat contradictorily, that he was still *the Committee's* sole "defender."

Nixon, years later, admitted he had no "real facts" to prove Hiss guilty of any crime; he obviously had less than the wholehearted support of the Committee, and, as it turned out, he had his private doubts about accepting Chambers's word against Hiss's. All of this made his pursuit of Hiss extraordinary and, for many, inexplicable, unless they held to the theory that Richard Nixon was ruthlessly ambitious, so much so that he would put an innocent man into prison to gain power for himself and, incidentally, for the Republican Party three months before a Presidential election against Harry S. Truman, who would label the investigation a "red herring."

William A. Reuben prepared a short account of the Hiss investigation which he facetiously entitled *The Honorable Mr. Nixon.* Reuben, making his observations eight years later, thought "most remarkable of all" was Nixon's clairvoyance: "Nixon's judgment came first and *then* evidence was produced to support it."

Reuben had tremendous doubts as to the value of the evidence. For example, at the outset of the hearings, Nixon gave the general public the impression that "Chambers's disclosures dealt with 'Communist espionage activities' when no such testimony . . . was offered until November, three months later. There was also on Nixon's part the same uncanny knack of deciding that Hiss was guilty of perjury long before a grand jury possessed sufficient evidence to return an indictment . . .

Pre-judging the guilt as a traitor of an American citizen

would be highly censurable, were it not for the fact that Hiss subsequently *was* convicted." The conviction, alone, "obliterated all of Nixon's excessive zealousness in acting as a one-man judge, jury, prosecutor, witness, detective and press agent . . ." Reuben posed an overriding question about Nixon's conduct: "What made Nixon so absolutely certain that Chambers was telling the truth and that Hiss was a liar?" Although the answer remained out of reach in 1956, the year Reuben's book was published, the potential explanation had assumed "disturbing proportions" in Reuben's mind.

Several people speculated in 1948, and for years after, that Richard Nixon had come to his conclusion before the hearings began on August 3, accusing him of the most vile kind of politics, played coldly for personal and partisan gain, even if it meant sending an innocent man to prison. But it seems that Nixon didn't become convinced that Hiss, the former high-ranking State Department official, was a perjurer until the first hearing was several minutes old. *"He was rather insolent toward me from the time I insisted on bringing Frankfurter's*[1] *name in,"* Nixon wrote privately of Hiss, in a memorandum evidently unavailable to Reuben, *"and from that time my suspicions of him continued to grow."* (italics added)

The moment he thought Hiss was insolent to him, humiliating him in public, Nixon decided that Hiss was a liar, as the juxtaposition of two unrelated ideas, written down in an unguarded moment, so obligingly reveal. Thereafter, Nixon alone, among the nine members of the House Un-American Activities Committee, had no trouble intuitively penetrating Hiss's "virtuoso" cunning in order to discover that he was also a spy, a charge he never proved. Though he lent the memorandum of his first encounter with Hiss to Earl Mazo who published excerpts from it in 1959, Nixon seems to have regretted this indiscretion, for, by 1962, when his own *Six Crises* came out, it was as if a memorandum fixing the time and personal reason for his hostility had never

[1] Supreme Court Justice Felix Frankfurter. For reasons that remain unexplained even today, Nixon was *insistently* attempting to establish if the Justice had helped Hiss get a government job. Nixon says he had the feeling Hiss was trying to keep Frankfurter's name out of the record.

existed. Rather, he implants the idea that he did not become suspicious of Hiss until he had insulted *another* member of the Committee. Hiss told the Committee he did not know a man named Whittaker Chambers, so he was handed a photograph to stimulate his memory. According to Nixon, in *Six Crises*, Hiss made an "elaborate show" of examining the photograph before "innocently but also somewhat condescendingly" remarking that the face was not the least unusual. At that point Hiss "had planted in my mind," Nixon writes, "the first doubt about his credibility." Nixon did not spell out the condescending line in his book, but ten years earlier, during a 1952 interview with *U.S. News and World Report*, he remembered Hiss saying, "He might even look like you, Mr. Mundt." It's rather pathetic that Nixon should have pretended in *Six Crises* that he was Mundt's defender, when from all the evidence, including a comparison of his statements at various times, the only man who felt lastingly belittled by Hiss was Nixon; and when, at the hearing's conclusion, Mundt praised Hiss's "forthrightness," one can easily imagine it as a second humiliating slap in the face to Nixon.

Without serious support and uncertain of his case, Nixon's pursuit of Hiss quickly assumed the feverish intensity of a religious experience. Nixon was convinced that Hiss was a liar who, for all his breeding and lofty position, was no better at the core than he. In all of his public pronouncements about the investigation, then and later, Nixon vainly attempted to give an acceptable form to his intense loathing. Although he found that Hiss, the first time they met, had been "an amazingly impressive witness . . . he made a fatal error, and that was in overstating his case. He said, 'I have not been a Communist,' but he went further and said, 'I've never known a man by the name of Whittaker Chambers.'" That, of course, rendered Hiss, in Nixon's eyes, "just too slick" for his own good. In *Six Crises* Nixon insists that his "considerable experience" with witnesses taught him that whenever they have something to hide, they "overact" or "overstate" their defense. The behavioral essence of a liar, then, was his transparent trickiness. By this formula, Nixon pierced Hiss's slickness as easily as Hiss's arrogance pierced him.

Between August 5 and August 16, Nixon labored eighteen and twenty hours a day, preparing himself for the second meeting with Hiss. He re-examined Chambers and consumed all manner of background material on Hiss and Communism in order, he says, to plug up any holes through which Hiss could again slip away. Nixon was armed only with his instinct, enlivened by his animosity and a compulsion to be right. Strangely, the young Congressman was terrified he might be wrong; even he, Nixon confesses, found it difficult believing a "man like Chambers over a man like Hiss."[1] Nixon anxiously pinned his hopes on that second meeting, August 16, as if he could prove his case *mano a mano* or by staring into Hiss's eyes. But he met with more slipperiness and more contempt. Hiss sparred with Nixon for a quarter of an hour, and Edward Hebert, a southern Democrat on the Committee, got so mad, according to Nixon, that Hebert accused Hiss of hedging and then declared that either he or Chambers "is the greatest actor that America has produced." Nixon was momentarily delighted by this pronouncement from a member of the Committee. "Hiss was shaken to his toes by this blast," because, says Nixon, Truman had implied the hearings were a smear against the New Deal, but now, for the first time, here was a Democrat challenging Hiss, a fact that perhaps Nixon makes more of than he should, since all of the HUAC Democrats were conservatives and none supported the New Deal.

Evidently Hiss was not too badly shaken, for throughout the rest of the hearing he remained very much on his toes and Nixon came away with the same suspicions, the same two facts he started with eleven days before: Alger Hiss had

[1] The whole quotation touches on Nixon's shallow comprehension of the law as well as his deep emotions: "It was difficult back in 1948, before the scope of the Communist underground movement had become generally known, to believe a man like Chambers over . . ." After a little digestion, the implication lunges off the page. Unwittingly, Nixon was saying that 1948 was a year when the public did not automatically accept charges of Communism against a fellow American, without proof or due process; on the other hand, if he had gone after Hiss at the height of the McCarthy era, say 1952, the public would not have demanded proof of guilt.

been rude to him while Whittaker Chambers had been abjectly submissive.

On August 17, two weeks after Hiss's name had been introduced by Chambers, the Committee belatedly arranged a face-to-face meeting between accuser and accused. Hiss had been urging just such a confrontation since August 5 but was told by Nixon that the Committee first wanted "to be certain that there is no question of mistaken identity." The confrontation was arranged suddenly and took place in a closed hearing, in a rented New York hotel room, with Nixon in charge. A contretemps ensued over Nixon's tardiness in swearing Chambers as a witness: Chambers had been testifying for some minutes before Nixon interposed to suggest this routine procedure, and Hiss said sarcastically that it was a good idea.

Nixon was furious: "Mr. Hiss, may I say something? I suggested that he be sworn, and when I say something like that I want no interruptions from you." Hiss was furious too: ". . . I think there is no occasion for you to use that tone of voice in speaking to me, and I hope the record will show what I have just said." The record showed what both men said, a fact which merely increased Nixon's hypersensitivity. "The record fails to show just how the incident occurred," he told Mazo long afterwards, without quoting the record. "Hiss actually interrupted me as I made the suggestion, and of course his manner and tone were insulting in the extreme." To complete his vindication, and possibly imply that a man who has just been insulted in the extreme can retain his cool when he's on the side of the angels, Nixon hastily added this crucial observation: Hiss was "visibly shaken, losing his air of smoothness . . . In fact, this hearing, I think for the first and probably the last time [Hiss] showed the Committee *the real Hiss . . . he acted the part of a liar who had been caught*[1]

[1] If Nixon could be intuitive, so could Hiss. In his own book, *In the Court of Public Opinion*, Hiss reports that on August 16 he "sensed a proprietary attitude toward Chambers [not yet present], as though he were the Committee's witness and I am [sic] the outsider. I raised the topic frankly," Hiss explains, using a self-advertising adverb Nixon also leans on occasionally. He told Nixon (obviously the member of the Committee who was being the most proprietary) that he had read newspaper accounts that the California

[emphasis added], rather than the part of an outraged innocent man which he had so successfully portrayed before" —and which, ironically, Nixon was now portraying. But more vital than the revelation itself was the fact that *others*, according to Nixon (who presumably forgot the second hearing in which Hebert shook Hiss to his toes) had at last seen through Hiss too, but the glimpse was brief and the number of others small. Of the nine Committee members, only three were present in the hotel room—Nixon, John McDowell and, toward the end of the hearing, J. Parnell Thomas, all Republicans. However, Nixon continues to catch revealing traits no other is astute enough to catch: He watches as Hiss "stares stonily straight ahead" instead of at Chambers, whom he claims he does not know. For Nixon, this was the reaffirmation that Hiss was lying. Nixon had nothing to clutch at but straws, which may be why he now dipped those straws in curare. Nixon's tone, says Reuben, was "angry"—that of a prosecutor, not an investigator. Alistair Cooke, the English correspondent, had the same feeling.

The third hearing dragged on, and with Chambers now there to haunt him, Hiss, who had merely overacted and moved shiftily the first day, according to Nixon, now began twisting and turning, with his answers growing longer and ever more evasive. At long last, Nixon crows in *Six Crises*, Hiss was cracking under the pressure, reacting to the probes (Nixon's) like a "caged animal" and in the caged animal's eyes Nixon saw "cold hatred." Although he was furious, too,

---

Representative had spent the weekend with Chambers at the latter's farm in New Jersey. "Nixon replied: 'That is quite incorrect.' " Hiss adds his clincher: Bert Andrews (the one reporter who encouraged Nixon to continue the Hiss case and who became, in effect, Nixon's unofficial adviser) some years later wrote articles confirming that "Nixon had the day before, Sunday, August 15, driven to Chambers's farm in *Maryland* [emphasis added] and had spent several hours conversing with Chambers in Andrews's presence." Chambers also confirms this in *Witness*, adding that Nixon had not spent several hours; he had spent the "weekend." Nixon had told the truth in the technical sense only. It is not the least surprising that two men, as alike in certain respects as Hiss and Nixon, could sniff out each other's slippery evasions so readily, nor should it be the least surprising that they felt competitive.

although long, evasive answers reflect Nixon's own behavior under the pressure of probing questions (as almost any of his news conferences will attest), and although he had elsewhere boasted of his staginess and of the delicacy of some of those evasions, he doesn't make any connection between his traits and the ones in Hiss he so profoundly abhors. He admits to having seen such traits in other witnesses (obviously hostile in the legal sense) but, in *Six Crises*, never mentions his own behavior under similar circumstances. He has copped many a plea in his time, but not here, not on this point; he does not explain away habits for which he has been criticized. The astonishing impression left after reading Nixon's analysis of Hiss is that Nixon has totally and truly repressed the similarities between them. *Six Crises*, however, was written during a period of despair perhaps necessitating the burial of obviously undesirable thoughts.

Eventually Nixon found *his* evidence. In the dark of night on December 2, 1948, after four months of failure, Chambers walked out into a pumpkin patch on his Maryland farm, lifted the lid off a particular pumpkin and produced microfilm of twelve typewritten pages ("the pumpkin papers") allegedly connecting Hiss to Chambers in 1938. Informed that his witness had pulled evidence out of a pumpkin in a field at midnight, Nixon had another of his insights, one he'd evidently had before: he was afraid that he "*really might* have a crazy man on [his] hands." But the case had been dying, since nothing had happened in nearly four months he could use against his enemy, and Nixon rapidly overcame his fear. "For the first time we have documentary evidence," he announced to the press on December 5. "It is no longer just one man's word against another's."

Nixon and the microfilm received a tremendous amount of publicity, and remained the one tangible piece of evidence Nixon had, until, shatteringly, The Eastman Kodak Company reported the microfilm was not manufactured until seven years after Hiss and Chambers (whom Hiss had finally recognized as a man named Crosley he had known in 1937) allegedly ceased dealing with each other. This generated a crisis within the crisis; Nixon was pinning all his hopes on

19

that film. In *Six Crises* he confesses he was chagrined and embarrassed, hastily adding that Chambers felt worse, so much worse that during the night the witness tried unsuccessfully to commit suicide. Nixon thinks he can understand how Chambers felt: his career gone, reputation and family ruined, Nixon says, entirely because of a mistaken report on the age of a sliver of microfilm. But pity did not stop Nixon from attacking Chambers with "all of the fury and frustration that had built up within me," for although he does not say it, his own anger and reputation were also on the verge of ruin.

Earlier in the investigation, Nixon had declared that where you found a Communist (implying that Hiss was), you automatically found a spy. But with the case disintegrating and no way to improve the world's faith in himself or totally destroy its faith in Hiss, Nixon cried ferociously, "If the American people understood the real character of Alger Hiss, they would boil him in oil,"[1] emphasizing once more that Nixon's driving ambition all along was to destroy Hiss because of his character.

As history notes, Chambers's story and the microfilm eventually satisfied the members of HUAC and the Grand Jury, which indicted Hiss for perjury, although "the pumpkin papers" played no part in convicting Hiss, who was jailed on the narrow issue of whether he had lied to Congress in denying that he had seen Chambers after 1937. If Hiss had not raised the issue of knowing Chambers, Nixon thinks, he might never have gone to prison: ". . . He had to pay the price for his bold gamble."

Nixon reveals in *Six Crises* that he also had taken the big gamble, but *he* won. He had had a tremendous amount of difficulty arriving at his decision to take it, however. After talking the rest of HUAC into going ahead with the investigation on his word, he felt profound dread. What had he gotten himself into? he mused years later, when it was safe to muse. He was a freshman Congressman doing battle on his own against the Establishment and the President of the United States. (It was the populist emerging in him: he was the

[1] The quotation is from Chambers's own account in *Witness*.

country boy fighting the city boy, and for Nixon the city boys always seem to be the Establishment, at least a different Establishment from his own.) He had already been called callow and exceedingly ambitious, and that incensed him: They did not credit Nixon with deep feelings. But if he couldn't back up his feelings about Alger Hiss with facts—or at the very least, with popular support—he faced personal disaster. On the other hand, he notes, it would have been equally disastrous (for the security of the nation) if he did not pursue this evil character all the way to prison. Nixon, of course, had alternatives: he could have joined the Democrats threatening to charge Chambers with libel, or he could have withdrawn and done nothing. As to the first alternative, Chambers was not the enemy; Hiss was. Even if he had convinced himself that the meek, cooperative, pathetic-looking Chambers was the enemy, it would be—to paraphrase a remark Nixon once made about facing Governor Brown of California after facing Jack Kennedy—like swiping at a mosquito after indicating to the world that you were about to stomp on a snake. As for doing nothing, that would have been the most unbearable choice of all—the moral equivalent, Nixon lets us understand, of a rout. Therefore, though the danger to him was extreme, Richard Nixon decided to risk it: He would oppose the press, his fellow Committee members, President Truman and, if need be, the majority of the nation, because he could not oppose his own "conscience" which told him at the moment of decision that "the rather unsavory-looking Chambers was telling the truth and the honest-looking Hiss was lying." Nixon's justification goes through a series of muted but fundamental and heartfelt transformations: a sense of personal insult at the hands of a liar becomes hostility; hostility couples with insight; and insight grows morally into an act of conscience. For without conscience as his guide, a man raised in the Christian ethic cannot justify his aggression. Nixon's hypocrisy seemed to have become unconscious.

As hard as Nixon tries in *Six Crises* to baffle his feelings, he proves that he is no better at keeping up his guard, or feelings to himself, than his vanquished enemy. In his memoirs he cannot shake the memory of the "almost unbearable tensions" building up in *a man* during the decision-making process. A man must take action one way or the other, he must decide whether to fight or fly. There seems to be no third choice except to *burst*; the man, he says, who cannot decide or, having decided, cannot act decisively, will "crack under the strain," as Hiss supposedly did. After bringing this "untruthful man to justice," Nixon reflects on how "Hiss could have fallen so low." Nixon implies he won because he was moral and Hiss lost because he was immoral, with immoral men always cracking first. He claims he knew from the start "the Committee would be vindicated and I personally would receive credit for the part I had played."

Although Nixon has not forgotten the unbearable tensions of preparing for battle, he informs us that he, personally, doesn't worry once the battle is joined, instead evoking the image of "confidence, calmness and toughness." He inadvertently destroys this image not two dozen pages later, however, when he notes that throughout the long hours he worked during the Hiss matter, he suffered the "inevitable symptoms of tension." Yes, he grew "mean" to his family and friends as his temper got quicker, his appetite disappeared, along with his ability to sleep nights. No, that did not mean Nixon was cracking. "I suppose some might say I was 'nervous,' " he writes disingenuously, "but I knew these were simply the evidences of preparing for battle." Nixon was speaking of a period when the battle with Hiss had been joined for three weeks and two days.

Apparently, Nixon felt some degree of frenzy, turmoil, pain and exhaustion nearly every day of the Hiss crisis. No one does a better job of illustrating this than Nixon himself, laying it out like disorganized pieces of a jigsaw puzzle. Anticipating resolution of the puzzle eventually, however, he tries in advance to disarm the reader with an explanation of his nervousness. Offered up as advice on achieving mental health, his point is that no man can afford the luxury of being "jittery." The jitters only occur, Nixon observes, if a man permits himself to fret over the "natural symptoms of stress." On the other hand, a man is not jittery, but simply "keyed-up," when he places his nervous symptoms in perspective. They are, he repeats, one way or another, a number of times

22

the "physical evidences that the mind, emotions and body are ready for action."

During the Hiss crisis—and later in re-living it—every important step Nixon took seemed directed at shoring up his own vulnerability. In *Six Crises*, written thirteen years after imprisoning Hiss, he refuses to slow the attack and calls Hiss a caged animal, leaving our collective education to remind us that what separates man (Nixon) from beast (Hiss) is a soul. But in remembering the Hiss crisis, the climactic moment for Nixon seems to have been how he was treated in the market place. Although he made enemies among several segments of American society, the group Nixon attacks is the "liberalists": the "patsies" for Communism who "stand self-accused in all their vulnerability." He vilifies them for making up their minds (without evidence) that Hiss was innocent—even as Nixon made up his mind (without evidence) that Hiss was guilty, as well as for having "counterattacked" Hiss's accusers (i.e. Chambers but mainly Nixon) with "unparalleled venom and irrational fury." On one page, it is entirely proper for him to judge Hiss guilty on instinct; on another page not very far away, it is entirely improper—indeed irrational—for his enemies to be furious because they happen to share his opinion of the evidence against Hiss.

He called this liberal reaction a "counterattack." There can be no counterattack, however, until there has been an attack. There is no longer anything particularly elusive about his reasons for attacking Hiss in the first place. Yes, he may eventually have played politics but first he despised the man, almost from the moment they met. Whether Richard Nixon despised Alger Hiss because his essential character was, in Nixon's mind, all too like his own remains, for the moment, a question for *our intuition* to answer.

CHAPTER THREE

Nixon's fame as a ruthless politician began in 1946 when he waged an anti-Communist campaign for Congress against Jerry Voorhis, who was not a Communist. It spread following the publicity over the Hiss case in 1948, and was compounded in 1950 when he defeated Helen Gahagan Douglas for the Senate in much the same way he had defeated Voorhis for the House. His political technique of seeking patsies became the issue again as the result of the bellicose off-year campaign he led on behalf of Congressional Republicans in 1954. His themes that year were chosen for their pugnaciousness: Korea, Communism, and Corruption, and he blamed all three on the former Democratic Administration, which by then had been out of office nearly two years. He laid his groundwork with such remarks as "To sum it up bluntly, the Acheson policy was directly responsible for the loss of China. And if China had not been lost, there would have been no war in Korea and no [French-Vietminh] war in Indochina today." As the campaign came down to the wire, his language grew stronger; on November 1 he claimed that Eisenhower had fired "ninety-six percent of the six thousand nine hundred twenty-six Communists, fellow travelers, sex perverts, people with criminal records, dope addicts, drunks and other security risks . . . hired by the Truman Administration." But Philip Young, chairman of the Civil Service Commission and an Eisenhower appointee, had testified by then that not one federal employee had been dismissed by the Republicans as a security risk.

Nixon was waving a nonexistent list in the air in the same way that Senator Joseph McCarthy had done for the previous three years. Supporters of McCarthy later argued that he had been condemned merely for having led America's anti-Communist crusade. His enemies argued that his fellow Senators had censored McCarthy for his cruel lies. The second argument relies almost as heavily on mythology as the first; it isn't characteristic of the United States Congress to censure a fellow-politician for cruelty or lying, particularly if they think his lies were told to preserve the political system by punishing "enemies" who could not be punished by any other means. That's known as lying for the common good. Lying for the good of the party may be less noble but it is almost as acceptable. No, McCarthy's first crime was to be *caught* lying; his second, to be caught lying repeatedly before twenty million Americans who watched him during the "Army-McCarthy Hearings" in the spring of 1954. The third and greatest crime to the practical men of the United States Senate was that McCarthy's lies were blatant, shrill, and even insane; he hinted the Army was in Communist hands. They began to suspect that as a defender of the system he was ineffectual and as a party politician he was self-defeating, which are unnerving things for other politicians to think. McCarthy's major crime, then, was that he had not mastered the art of making it look good. Much of this cynical thesis can be attributed to Nixon himself: "McCarthy's intentions were right," he said later, but his "tactics were, frankly, so inept at times that he probably did our cause more harm than good."

Yet knowing this, Nixon repeated many of the tactics that had ruined the Wisconsinite, and therefore in 1954 did his party more harm than good. The Republicans took a bad beating; so did he. The Vice-President's "meretricious platform gimmicks" and "barefaced" *ad hominems*—descriptions used by William Costello in *The Facts About Nixon*—would be used again after 1954 and would hurt him and his party again. The traditional explanation given by historians for such failures is that Communism had worn itself out as an issue by 1954 and, moreover, the average American voter has little tolerance for hate campaigns, a sentimental theory for which there is little supporting evidence. Several hate campaigns have led to victory (or, at the very least, they did not ruin the chances for victory) in recent American history: George Smathers' campaign of sly vilification against Claude Pepper or George Wallace's open appeals to white bigots. The North is not without such illustrations either: even allowing that many other factors played a part in his victory, James Buckley's campaign in New York State in 1970 was read by a great number of ethnic voters as a coded attack on minorities. (It was a common hope among New York's law-and-order faction to trample under Republican Senator Goodell and the Democratic slate of "Four Jews and a Jig.") But none of these campaigns, including Wallace's at its worst, had the patently undisciplined character of McCarthy's attacks. Nixon's campaigns made enemies too—he acknowledged many times over that this was the price one paid for "slugging it out"[1]—but if he made enemies for being a tough campaigner, he seemed perennially to compound his enemies in both number and intensity by reminding everyone in earshot of the voting public's gullibility.

Nixon's trickiness had largely been taken at face value—as a politician's device—and it overshadowed any questions of recklessness or compulsiveness or neurosis that journalists usually feel uncomfortable discussing in public. After the 1954 election, however, a number of them did attempt to challenge "Tricky Dick" by using his own words. The most obvious opening was to take the famous "Checkers" speech of 1952, in which the then-Senator from California had defended himself against charges (planted, incidentally, by California Republicans who disliked him) of diverting campaign contributions for his private use. The consensus among Nixon watchers was that "Checkers," now that time had passed, would be less notable for its substantive arguments than for its extremely weepy style; everyone remembered "Checkers" as a "soap opera" and seeing the film again would prove it. The speech was carried September 23, 1952, on radio by eight hundred-odd stations and, more important, on television by sixty-four NBC-affiliated stations in a half-hour immediately after the Milton Berle Show, the best rated time of the week, when possibly twenty-seven-or-eight million families were glued to their receivers. Various network newsmen went after film copies of the "Checkers" speech, but all of them got the runaround, apparently even from their own

[1] His wife sensed that the tension, anxiety and humiliation of politics were destroying him, and after the election, Mrs. Nixon argued with him openly to cut out of politics, and stay out. At her insistence he signed the famous pledge to quit and carried it around in his pocket as a reminder until it was time to repeat the painful process.

networks. They were told that copies from network libraries were either "lost" or the exclusive property of the Republican National Committee and a group called the "Senatorial Congressional Campaign Committee," which supposedly co-sponsored the broadcast. The Republicans usually told anyone who asked that the film was "destroyed" or to check with Nixon. Over the next fifteen years, there were enough awkward and unlikely excuses to radio and television newsmen from all quarters to suggest that "Checkers" had been taken out of circulation deliberately and for keeps. Though "Checkers" had been a political triumph—Earl Mazo says that at least one million Americans, moved by Nixon's appeal on the air, sent letters, telegrams and petitions, mostly to the National Committee, demanding that the California Senator be kept as Ike's running mate—the program was a potential embarrassment. If it was, as they said, a "soap opera," a genre that depends on exaggeration, tears and hollow theatricality, such things could come back to haunt any rational man who had used these devices only out of expediency. Obviously, the next expedient thing to do would be to suppress the evidence.

By 1955, journalists were left only with the printed word. It conveyed enough but not the totality of the deception they remembered Nixon had played in springing "Checkers" on the public: "Not one cent of the $18,000 or any other money of that type ever went to me for my personal use . . . Stevenson had a fund too . . . and I believe that it's fine that a man like [him] who inherited a fortune from his father can run for President . . ." while Mrs. Nixon wore a plain "respectable Republican cloth coat." If he wanted to make money, he noted, he could have put Pat on the Congressional payroll but he didn't because there are "so many deserving stenographers and secretaries in Washington that needed the work." His service record was "not a particularly unusual one . . . I got a couple of letters of commendation but I was just there when the bombs were falling[1] . . . And the kids love that dog and I just want to say this right now, that

[1] He was there, mainly when the bombs were falling somewhere else. As a naval operations officer he was reportedly on Bougainville during air attacks by the Japanese, but he was apparently not in

27

regardless of what they say about it [Nixon was the first to say anything about it], we're gonna keep it . . . Let me say this: I don't believe that I ought to quit, because I'm not a quitter, and, incidentally, Pat's not a quitter. After all, her name was Patricia Ryan and she was born on St. Patrick's Day . . ." Strangely, the statement in the "Checkers" speech that caused the sharpest reaction was the reference to Pat Nixon's birthday. St. Patrick's Day falls on March 17; she was born on March 16. A little lie of no consequence, but so gratuitous and easily disproved that this lie upset observers greatly; they were bothered, it seems now, that a man of such high political cunning could be so stupid.

No matter how much his enemies defamed him, it was because he was against Alger Hiss and Communism: "Some of the same radio commentators who are attacking me now and misrepresenting my position were violently opposing me at the time I was after Alger Hiss . . . I'm going to campaign up and down America until we drove [sic] the crooks and the Communists and those that defend them out of Washington . . ." These words were the most hyper-dramatic Nixon had ever spoken, but alone they still don't convey the gulping and throbbing voice or the tears of the other palpable characteristics of "soap opera," nor do they show the uncontrolled agitation that crept over him once the performance began to grip the performer. Journalists criticized "Checkers" almost entirely (except for that one little slip about a birthday) over the debatable question of whether this was cheap drama. They had to admit, however reluctantly, that the most adroit thing Nixon could have done, he did: He got rid of the evidence.[1]

Nixon's nemeses—some of those radio commentators and columnists whom he had broadly identified as his enemies in

---

serious danger—if any danger at all—since Japanese air power had become largely ineffectual prior to May, 1943, when Nixon arrived in the South Pacific. If there were any air attacks on Guadalcanal, Vella Lavella or Green Island when he reached them, they were infrequent and casual—very infrequent and very casual.

[1] "Checkers" remained buried until 1968. Emile de Antonio, a writer and producer of documentaries (one of them about Joe McCarthy), repeated the familiar quest. He went to NBC where, in an article for the *New York Free Press*, he says a Mr. Richard Swicker of the network approved release of a "Checkers" kinescope

1952—were among an unusually large group of news executives in broadcasting gathered at a luncheon given by the Radio and Television Executives Society on September 14, 1955. Luncheons like these were normally not newsworthy and so the working press usually avoided them. But when word got around that the Vice-President of the United States was speaking, the ranks were quickly swelled by both news executives and reports from networks, daily papers and wire services. Nixon had not been seen in town for some time but they hadn't been able to get him out of their minds.

Nixon may not have forgotten them either, but he addressed himself to the majority of his audience, "the bread-and-butter boys," as they were known in the trade. He dealt with them in their own language about time buying and selling, about advertising, about promotion, self or otherwise. He showed them, man to man or, as he put it, "one Vice-President to another," that he knew their business better in some respects than they did. Fancying himself an expert in the techniques of buying time and selling candidates, he was both cynical and candid. He instructed these radio and television executives to counsel in turn any political clients coming their way that "what a candidate should do to use this medium [tv] effectively" is sell himself "like a bar of soap." No long speeches, he said with a wink; people don't have the stomach for a lot of attenuated ideas. They "buy" faces, not platforms. "People will say a spot announcement does not give an audience a chance to know the candidate. Sometimes that is a good thing for the candidate." Five minutes, therefore, should be the longest a smart politician dare stretch the message, but one minute was smarter. Saturate those airwaves with "spot" announcements and make

on August 23; then on August 26, told de Antonio it had been a mistake, that there was no print. Next, he was turned away by a Gus Miller of the Republican National Committee. Later, Miss Barbara Baiter, of Nixon's law office, said she'd check into it but, according to de Antonio, never called him back. De Antonio finally found a copy; he will not divulge the source. He has incorporated portions of the speech into a full-length documentary about Nixon titled "Millhouse, A White Comedy," and has also released the full half-hour as a theatrical short subject which has appeared in several "art houses."

sure you put them into the best time periods money can buy. (Richard Nixon would, as a result of this lecture, become the first major politician to articulate these principles in public. But it was not a matter of telling the experts something they did not already know so much as one of endorsing political shallowness—of giving us Vice-Presidential dispensation so they could shortchange the voting public with a clear conscience.) Nixon leaned across the lectern and grinned. "You all remember the 'Checkers' speech, I suppose?" Some of them chuckled at his conspiratorial tone. "Well, I want you to be the first to know"—he paused so the executives could savor the moment too, the pause also serving to illustrate that he could back up his next three words with talent:[1] "I staged it."

After a split second, the gasps were followed by laughter. Their confusion clearly meant more to him than their laughter, because although he had not stopped grinning, his grin vacillated: torn between mock and real alarm. "Now don't get me wrong," he said hastily, "I meant *every word* of that speech. I loved that dog." Because they did not know how else to react to such a corny presentation, his audience laughed heartily, and his grin broadened, then disappeared. For the next several moments the Vice-President's tone skidded between cynical boasting and nervous humor. "But let's be realistic: a dog is a natural," he reasoned—as was the cloth coat. They were "props," he said, not laughing. He corrected himself: But of course they were *more* than props. People had called "Checkers" a "soap opera." Well, it was not. While he kept looking for a way out of his predicament, something kept drawing him in deeper. Any drama to be successful had to evoke sympathy, he said; he had taken two

[1] Describing in *Six Crises* how he informed the press that he would in two days broadcast his answer to the charges of malfeasance, Nixon remembered walking into the pressroom and feeling the tension (theirs, it seems, not his); they wanted to know whether Nixon was going to quit the race or stay and fight: " 'I have come down to announce that I am breaking off—' I paused deliberately. There was an audible gasp in the room. I laughed for perhaps the first time that day and began again." He explains that he thought he "might as well have a little fun on such a deadly serious occasion" and found it especially funny when Clint Mosher of *The San Francisco Examiner* "almost jumped out of his skin."

days to prepare the speech. (Years later he would admit that before the speech, he had been worried more about its style than about its content.) "I'm a firm believer," he laughed, "in off-the-cuff speeches that take a lot of time to prepare." He had finally eased out on a cliché, stressing as an after-thought, the importance "sincerity" played in "Checkers's" success. The rest of the speech to the RTES became history. This part did not.

At the dining room door, I collided with a veteran from one of the New York dailies and told him, as nonchalantly as I could, my suspicion that Nixon had been begging for trouble. Also nonchalant, he shrugged: Nixon wasn't the first prominent politician to act the fool in public and wouldn't, he added philosophically, be the last. Since a reporter is usually willing to talk when he has no reason to fear recrimi-nations from his public or his editor, he let me in on his true feelings: He'd be goddamned, he said, if he was going to waste his time and his paper's valuable column inches to publicize Nixon's "witless" stories. He was a cynic who dis-liked Nixon but would protect him against his foibles, a para-dox that can only be explained if you understand that the less reporters comprehend, the more hardnosed they often grow.

The next day, out of curiosity I scanned the *Post*, the *Herald-Tribune* and the *Times*, and the other New York newspapers. Not much of anything was reported—a sketchy item or two about the speech having been made; where; before whom; but few other details—no stories, open or sly, about his effort to enliven the day with personal anecdotes; no allegations or editorials about shallowness or his cynicism in putting the illusion of feeling above feeling; and—of course —no description of his behavior as behavior. Evidently others had seen Nixon behave strangely before, and old habits have a way of becoming both comfortable friends and stale news, even if the news was never printed. Though Nixon had risked much, it seems, he had lost nothing.

One news item on September 15, however, is worth re-membering for its thrust, which summed up, went like this: Vice-President Nixon made a speech in New York stressing, for the benefit of politicians who planned to campaign on television, "the need for sincerity."

CHAPTER FOUR

Nixon describes his first major crisis as the Hiss case in 1948 and the second as the events surrounding the "Checkers" speech in 1952. The third, he says, was Eisenhower's heart attack in 1955. But Nixon relegated the next important one to a mere postscript in *Six Crises* because the enemy had to be disguised as a friend and the battle had to be reduced in the retelling to a temporary failure of communication. With no ranting Khrushchev in the kitchen, no murderous mob in Caracas, not even a handy subversive to appease the popular taste in villains, there could be no "major" crisis and no climactic victory. Such victory as he had would dribble Nixon's way slowly, accidentally, inconclusively, less the result of his determination than of his enemy's apathy. Though he would describe his anguish as brief, Nixon for a long time suffered bitterly at the hands of Dwight D. Eisenhower.

Nixon met Eisenhower for the first time at a luncheon in California in 1950. He was introduced as the Republican candidate in California for the U.S. Senate. Yet when they met again a year later in Paris, Nixon (who had asked in advance for the meeting and no doubt got it because he was now a Senator) was afraid that Eisenhower would not remember him. But that was not what worried Nixon most: Eisenhower "had a quality of reserve which, *at least sub-consciously* [emphasis added], tended to make a visitor feel like a junior officer coming in to see the commanding general." As long as their relationship lasted, Eisenhower rarely ever gave him reason to feel otherwise. At the first sign of scandal, the General decided to drop Nixon as his running mate without giving his guilt a second thought. Even when Nixon managed to hold onto his candidacy through "Checkers," the General was not satisfied until Nixon came to see him personally. He forced the Vice-Presidential candidate to come from

California to Wheeling, West Virginia. Nixon arrived, looking "haggard and almost hysterical," according to Garry Wills, author of *Nixon Agonistes*. As Eisenhower strode heartily up the plane ramp to greet Nixon, Nixon said, "You didn't have to do this." The remark, heard clearly by witnesses, seemed resentful and ambiguous, but it might have remained relatively unnoticed if, later, Nixon hadn't gone to such pains to alter history, to remove the touchiness, to make everything between the two men seem ideal and congenial. It made observers more deeply conscious of his true reaction. In *Six Crises* it comes out. " 'You didn't have to come to the airport,' was all I could think of to say," so that now it translates: Gee, sir, you didn't have to go to all this trouble for me. Anger and confusion suddenly become boyish amazement. In any case, Eisenhower did grin and say, "You're my boy," a backslapper, more patronizing than fatherly, which did nothing to reduce Nixon's humiliation or his sense of inadequacy.

But this father evidently wanted a son who was mature enough to succeed him as head of the old firm. Modestly Nixon claims that he had matured because of all those trips he made to foreign lands (Travel seasons a statesman.) and because of the terrible responsibilities thrust upon him by Ike's heart attack in 1955, yet at the Republican Convention in 1956, Eisenhower told Emmet John Hughes, his speech-writer, "I've been watching Dick for a long time, and he just hasn't grown. So I just haven't honestly been able to believe that he is Presidential timber." Fully recovered, the President told other friends that Nixon was a young man who managed at the same time to be "too political" without holding a genuine point of view. Nixon had believed that the way to rise politically and to ingratiate himself with Eisenhower was by doing the President's political dirty work. "All this did," says Wills, "was convince Ike that he was not made for higher things." Just about the only thing that kept Nixon alive politically was the fact that the President did not express his distaste for his Vice-President to the delegates at the convention. As General of the Armies and "chairman of the board," he avoided official arguments; and as for the Vice-Presidency, he evidently felt there was no need for serious

33

friction within the Republican Party over an inconsequential post.[1] Still, Ike had already undercut Nixon by thinking in terms of a replacement and, worse, by encouraging speculation about it. When asked on April 26 if Nixon would be back for a second go-around, Eisenhower told the press that Nixon *had not authorized him* to give "any answer that I would consider final and definite." Eisenhower was acting as if he had no right to say he wanted Nixon, and Nixon was embarrassed.

Leonard Hall, the Republican National Chairman, advised Nixon soon afterwards that he would have to make the first move if he hoped to run again. Even Ralph de Toledano, Nixon's most flattering biographer, recognizes that "the President, after all, could not be expected to bend." And although Hall insisted to Nixon that he was a welcome traveler, Nixon says, "The impression I got was that [Eisenhower] was really trying to tell me he wanted me off the ticket when . . . he said Nixon should 'chart his own course.' " In response to questioning by the press, Eisenhower had indeed recently used that phrase, and, as Nixon suggests, what better means to show he didn't want Nixon around than by "neutrality"?

(Nixon reports that Eisenhower was more "complex" and "devious" than most people realized, an astounding statement

---

[1] "Between 1956 and 1960," said Hughes, "the whole matter of political succession seemed almost to haunt Eisenhower, without impelling him, however, to take positive action to solve the riddle and to conquer his own doubts." In his confusion Eisenhower gave in to what seems incredible shortsightedness, telling Hughes after the 1956 convention that "The thing Dick may have figured was that 1960 didn't matter too much, and in the event of my disablement, he'd take over and at least have the Presidency for that long." He told Arthur Larson, a friend, that Nixon was unoriginal and uninteresting. In fact, he was hoping Larson might succeed him in 1960. The President, having survived one major heart attack, was confident he'd make it through till then, but in case he fell ill and died, did he actually think that Nixon would give up the Presidency in 1960 just because he was inconsequential and had reached the top accidentally? Ike once explained that when he disliked a man, he'd write the man's name on a piece of paper, stick it in a drawer, and forget it. Extraordinarily, he was sticking Nixon in a drawer as the Vice-President, from which Nixon slipped automatically into the Republican Presidential nomination in 1960.

about the man he claims to idolize and one which is not softened by his adding: complex and devious "in the best sense of those words.")

"When Hall left," de Toledano continues in his peculiar epic style, "Nixon—as in every crisis the man alone—shut himself off from phone calls, visitors, his staff. When he emerged his decision had been made." Nixon's supporters have always tried, particularly since he became President of the United States, to dress up their leader's habit of isolating himself; they say it's in order to reach complex and momentous decisions. But in 1956, alone, without the counsel of his wife (whose supplications to quit he finally ignored), or his political advisers (who had on previous occasions warned him against actions that would endanger his dignity), Nixon did reach a decision that was momentous in a very personal sense: He would wait no longer to be asked; he *decided to beg*. He picked up the phone and asked for an audience with the President. When they met, Nixon fumbled for a dignified gambit, telling Eisenhower that he had carefully "refrained from declaring his intentions because he did not wish to be on the ticket if Eisenhower did not want him," as de Toledano describes it.

Eisenhower, having already refrained from publicly supporting the candidacy of his own Vice-President, now told Nixon it would be okay if he went outside and announced his own candidacy to the press. If he would do that, Ike would authorize his press secretary, Jim Hagerty,[1] to say that since Nixon wanted to run, Ike would be glad to have him. Clinging to his career, Nixon did just that—treating Americans for the first time in history to the spectacle of a Vice-President forced to announce his own willingness to run for re-nomination months before the convention. The result was a personal disaster, increasing Nixon's humiliation at Eisenhower's hands without markedly reducing the speculation in the

[1] Hagerty says Eisenhower called him in and said, "Jim, Dick just told me *he would be happy to be on the ticket*, and he has made up his mind that he would like to run with me . . . Jim, you go with him and after he finishes his announcement, you say to the press I was *delighted* to hear the news from the *Vice-President*." Eisenhower's facetiousness could not have escaped Nixon, who sat next to Ike, a fixed smile on his face.

subsequent three months that the Republican Party in 1956 would find a replacement anyway.

At a press conference on July 23, Harold Stassen openly supported Governor Christian Herter of Massachusetts for Vice-President, alleging that while an Eisenhower-Nixon ticket would receive only 45.7 percent of the vote, an Eisenhower married to a Herter would receive close to 55 percent of the vote. Stassen, who had just met with Eisenhower and other party leaders, also announced that Ike "would be pleased to have Chris Herter on the ticket." "To the uninformed," de Toledano says, "this gave the Presidential imprimatur to the push." Evidently Nixon was one of the most uninformed of all, because as de Toledano then explains, "Nixon, not knowing what had transpired between Eisenhower and Stassen, was plunged into gloom and doubt."

On July 30, Stassen again visited Eisenhower at his Gettysburg farm and a day later predicted Nixon would cost Ike "millions of votes." According to Patrick Hillings, a Congressman and close Nixon associate, many Congressional Republicans decided they'd better send Nixon a petition of endorsement to bolster his ebbing morale. "He is a pessimist and was running scared," Hillings explained.

Stassen's bid to overturn Nixon was put down because he was unable to deliver the convention votes needed to get behind a replacement when, four days before the convention started, Herter withdrew his name from contention. Meanwhile, Nixon, in San Francisco trying to ward off Stassen's attack by buttonholing delegates to the convention, and with his candidacy still in the balance, received word that his seventy-seven-year-old father, Frank, was dying. He left immediately and spent over a week at his father's bedside, returning in time to make his acceptance speech. His father died shortly afterwards, on September 4.

Although the impact of Frank Nixon's death on his eldest son's behavior (particularly during the two months which followed) can hardly be assessed with accuracy because of the many other traumatic factors also at work on him at the time, the man's life must have had considerable effect. Frank Nixon had missed by a hair becoming oil-rich in California, ending instead as a small-time storekeeper, apparently without

36

friends. During the Teapot Dome scandals of 1929, Frank Nixon ranted for weeks about the crooks who corrupted freedom, possibly correlating the scandal to his own failure. It appears he didn't limit his hostility to corruption that started three thousand miles away in Washington, either. In a small, neighborly town like Whittier, he remained a harsh-tempered, combative loner, ready to argue at the drop of a phrase. One surmises that the townsfolk could not stand him, because when they had to do business with the Nixon family, they would go to his wife Hannah, leaving Frank to brood alone about injustices large and small.

Richard Nixon never crossed his father and did his best to shield his younger brothers from Frank's wrath. "He had a hot temper," Richard Nixon remembers, "and I learned early that the only way to deal with him was to abide by the rules he laid down," or be punished, as his brothers were with ruler and strap. Dick Nixon's way of staying out of trouble with his father was by bottling up his own resentments.

It is not certain that death had altered Nixon's relationship with his father or the world (There was no perceptible increase in hostility.), but it is certain that his relationship with Eisenhower did not change. On September 13, nine days after Frank's passing, Nixon attended a picnic for six hundred ranking Republican party workers at Eisenhower's farm. Standing by a fence, well apart from the crowd, Nixon said wistfully, "You know, I've never been inside his house." This quickly reached Eisenhower, who laughed, "Did you hear that? Dick says he's never seen the inside of the house here."

Speaking later for the record to the workers at large (this, after all, was a political rally), Ike was placative: If anything were to happen to the President, he said, "there is no man in the history of America who has such a careful preparation" to take over. However, the President made sure everyone understood that despite his first heart attack and a recent bout with ileitis, there was no cause for alarm (i.e., he would not die and Nixon would not succeed him): "I feel fine."

Left to decide which was more to his taste, Ike's casual ridicule or a vaguely equivocal, for-the-good-of-the-party pat on the back, Nixon returned to Washington that night and locked himself into a room at the Mayflower Hotel for five days. The public was told by his press aides that Nixon was working on his basic campaign speech which, with slight variations, was designed to cover all stops in thirty-two states. The public was also told that Nixon was working in his pajamas, insinuating that he was a man both single-minded and casual about his work. That is equally the image of a dishevelled human being. Whether he worked successfully on his speech or not, he failed during the five days alone to work off his humiliation and anger.

On September 18, over breakfast at the Washington National Airport, Eisenhower gave Nixon a strange send-off in the form of a public warning: "No need to indulge in the exaggerations of partisan political talk." Nixon would do the campaigning for both of them, but without ugly partisanship, without hostility. Exorcized of controversy and grossness, the campaign was to be waged by a "new Nixon" on the themes of "Eisenhower, peace, prosperity, progress."

This constraint had a nettling impact on Nixon. At his first appearance (Indianapolis) after Eisenhower's send-off, he became combative: "Let's get one thing straight right now," he said as if the world had already begun to challenge him. "Where our opponents misrepresent and distort the record and where they vilify the President of the United States, I shall consider it a duty and a privilege to set the record straight."

But Nixon was more concerned about setting his own record straight. In a moment of bitterness, he said he thought people were afraid to fight with Eisenhower because the President was sacrosanct so, instead, "they throw the custard pies at me." Custard pies may be thrown at clowns, but then, Nixon always seems to feel that his enemies, especially the press, are out to make him appear clownish.[1]

[1] He may even have believed, for example, that Philip Potter of the *Baltimore Sun* was out to make him look foolish. De Toledano, the friendly biographer seen frequently in Nixon's company, reported that Potter had sworn to make Nixon lose his temper before the campaign was over. Potter, who is today the Washington bureau chief of the *Sun*, is disinclined to discuss de Toledano's allegation. But in the 1950's Potter could hardly be counted as a staunch Nixon ally. In 1959 he wrote a mini-biography of Nixon

Nixon's desire to be taken seriously fed his aggressions, and the "old Nixon" in the background emerged fitfully. Campaigning in the southwest, Nixon made a radio appearance and out bubbled the charge that Sam Rayburn was a "traitor." Nixon had attacked the Speaker of the House of Representatives, the senior Democrat in Texas and the United States, on his home ground, further magnifying the enormity of the act. Rayburn was disturbed by the slander, but the strange thing is that it disturbed Nixon even more. In fact, whenever the subject was brought up again in the Vice-President's presence—generally by the press—he became, according to one of its number, "visibly upset." At one stop Nixon got so angry over being reminded about it a number of sources allege he punched one of his tormentors on the nose.

Before his campaign was a week old, it was obvious to everyone on the tour that the Vice-President was disoriented. It was, in print, attributed to "weariness" but if so, it hardly should have overwhelmed him so soon. Stopping in Louisville, he had made a mistake. He said, "And so I have a theme tonight . . ." His audience laughed, assuming it a joke. Three sentences later, the morning sun still rising, Nixon went back to "tonight." The second time, the laughter was somewhat less wholehearted.

He went on to Springfield, Illinois, where he told his audience how he had started out that morning from Houston. Actually, he had left Houston the day before. From behind him on the platform, his wife coached,[1] "No, no. Louisville, Kentucky," and Nixon, trying to smile, asked, "Where am I?" Perhaps he was simply trying to forget having looked foolish in Louisville.

Reporters noted (rarely) a number of Nixon's so-called "Freudian slips"—"bobbles," one paper called them, coup-

---

for a book called *Candidates 1960*. Nixon became the only one of several candidates to receive two biographies: Potter's writing was deemed so unfavorable (though perfectly factual) that the editors commissioned an opposing piece by Frank Holeman, former President of the National Press Club.

[1] Pat Nixon's coaching, at this time, became sharp and, all too often, public. Once, after he delivered a speech half-heartedly, according to Father John Cronin, a priest who wrote his speeches, "Pat chewed the hell out of him in front of the staff."

ling them with spoonerisms. They made good copy, and while there was also a little malice in the reporting, nobody intimated to the average reader, or televiewer, that the generally unstable level of Nixon's behavior over several days might indicate something other than normal physical exhaustion.

By mid-October, Nixon's gaffes were of less interest than his compulsion, despite Ike's warning, to exaggerate. In Buffalo on October 17, Nixon made a speech before a partisan audience, in which he accused Democratic Presidential candidate Adlai Stevenson of "playing dangerous politics with American security" because he had called for a suspension of nuclear bomb tests. He called Stevenson's proposal "ridiculous" and suggested that he was a stupid politician who had made a "major political error." If the accusations seemed ersatz, the anger seemed real.

How deep the disorientation went was only hinted at on one occasion by Reston of the *Times*. Reporters, he divulged, "have been psychoanalyzing him ever since the San Francisco Convention," and apologetically added, "and still can't make him out." Reston, who speculates confidently about the significance of entire social, cultural and political movements in his column, admitted that he was unable to make out Nixon's psyche and carefully omitted the details which inspired him and his cohorts to psychoanalyze Nixon in the first place. It was obvious, nevertheless, that Reston was determined (perhaps spurred onward by the awesome thought of a second Eisenhower heart attack) to cover all significant aspects of the Nixon campaign in 1956, even if he had to cover possibly the most significant aspects between the lines.

During this period, the Vice-President got a sore throat and could not speak without pain. Suddenly he sat up in his seat on the chartered DC-6B which flew him between campaign stops and, nodding in the general direction of the twenty-five reporters traveling with him, croaked, "I know those guys up front will say this is a phony." He pondered that prospective insult for a moment. *"They're all sons of bitches."*

An exhausted, ailing (with a cold) politician gives in to momentary anger and thoughtlessness—big deal, say his friends; they don't have to be told that Richard Nixon is human, and instead urge others to listen to him without prejudice, which means to take him at his word. According to Nixon's word, the reporters on the airplane had not said his sore throat was a fake but the Vice-President *knew* they would.

Would a reasonably intelligent man like Nixon encourage such an attack? The fact that a reporter was coming up the plane aisle and was inches away when Nixon decided to let off "a little healthy steam" (the traditional expression for such moments) was no accident. Nixon *was looking* at the reporter, which makes it harder to rationalize his behavior.

In the background were Nixon's fear of psychoanalysts and his rigid denial (through a battery of spokesmen) that he had consulted a physician who had published a book on psychosomatic medicine about the possibility of a psychic explanation for his physical pains. The absurdity of Nixon's anger mounts: Did the Vice-President—the man who feared psychoanalysts—fear that his enemies would *think* that he had *unconsciously* faked his sore throat?

Why should Nixon become incensed if a few reporters ponder the meaning of the clues Nixon voluntarily spread before them? Since they never wrote about the clues, why should he feel humiliated if they think to themselves what he says aloud?

The rare hints dropped during those early years were so oblique that by comparison the remark about psychoanalysis that Reston slipped past his censorship apparatus seems blunt. Revelations that might have rendered the Nixon personality less elusive, or more ominous, were locked up in plane aisles, hotel corridors and barrooms, rarely escaping on the lips of the more tipsy or self-confident journalists into home offices where editors and owners received them as undigested bits and pieces, and there they stopped. The press has always proved better at self-censorship than Nixon. But, above all, by what process of magical thinking—what delusional pattern where cause has nothing to do with effect—can a national leader transform journalists into mean sons of bitches for practising again and again, in newspapers, magazines and over the air a kind of self-therapy against contrary thoughts about Richard Nixon? A day or two after his outburst, for example, *The New York Times*, perhaps the least timorous of all outlets, recapitulated recent events in the Vice-President's campaign for re-election in a story dominated by the following headline:

NIXON LAUGHS OFF VOCAL TROUBLE

Other "odd" things kept happening during the campaign, but the more notorious the behavior, the less printable they became. One afternoon Nixon walked rigidly to the edge of a pool, neither looking left nor right, dove in, swam across, back, across again, got out and without so much as a smile, word or gesture to his staff around the pool, strode rigidly out of sight. A reporter suffered the eerie sensation that the Vice-President was in an ambulatory "stupor." One Sunday in Colorado, he emerged from a long Quaker service and launched into an ill-tempered attack on his family's religion. Another day, he made a televised appearance with college editors before a national viewing audience. Their questions made him mad, and they kept after him once the cameras had stopped. Suddenly he turned away and whispered loudly to an aide, "Get me away from these . . ." (Potter in his controversial biography quoted the last word as "monsters," since in 1959 stronger language would have offended the public ear.) He escaped, but into an incomplete seclusion where people with uncensored hearing remember that he "*really* blew his stack."

In Buffalo a grotesque sentiment began creeping into his speeches, unsettling the confidence of some observers who until then were willing to grant him the benefit of any doubt. So far during the campaign, Nixon had not mentioned his father's death. According to a thumbnail biography by Frank Holeman, Nixon would not even permit the press to take a picture of "his grieving family." Holeman and other admirers say his diffidence came from a refusal to capitalize on a "strictly personal sorrow." In any event, there was no need to mention it, because everyone in his audiences seemed to be aware of the fact, which reinforced any existing sympathy for the man. His opening words in Buffalo were, "My father," then a pause as if to get a grip on his emotions, "—I remember my father telling me a long time ago: 'Dick, Dick,' he said, 'Buffalo is a beautiful town.' It may have been his *favorite*

42

town." It was touching. From there, Nixon flew with the press to Rochester and then to Ithaca, home of Cornell, and in each place he made essentially the same speech (the basic campaign speech he'd written in that hotel room?), changing only the one word in this, the most critical passage—the name of the town where he was speaking.

CHAPTER FIVE

Explaining in *Six Crises* the formula which led to his putative triumph in South America over howling Latin mobs, Nixon said, "Take the offensive, show no fear, do the unexpected but do nothing rash."[1]

In May, 1958, Nixon had been advised by experts on South America, including the American Ambassador to Peru, the Chief of Police in Lima, the Rector of the university he planned to visit there, by *everyone*, without exception, not to go. He even admitted that in the probable event of mass violence, he would be blamed. Yet he could not permit the Communists to win a propaganda victory, and they *would* if he didn't go to the university; his intuition told him Latins had a contempt for fear. So Nixon rode toward his destiny. Near the gate of the university he left his limousine and, followed by his two aides, took the offensive—walking directly toward the waiting mob of—as he describes them—some two thousand frenzied, howling, Communist-led Latins. Presumably showing no fear, he began to taunt them, beckoning, then pointing at them with his outstretched finger: "Come on over. What's the matter? You afraid of the truth?" His words, shouted over the noise, were rapidly translated. It was them, as he remembered it, "against the three of us, yet [they] backed away," until a rock glanced off Nixon's shoulder. "Mr. Vice-President," whispered one of his frightened aides, "they are throwing stones."

Though they were still short of the gate, Nixon responded, "OK, all right, let's get out of here. But move back slowly, keep facing them." Nixon kept moving slowly backwards, never once taking his eye off the mob (Mobs are made up essentially, he explains, of cowards). It was essential that the enemy understand that he and his brave band were "taking our leave but not retreating."

The rocks were still flying when the three-man army reached the automobile. Then, Nixon adds triumphantly, "I could not resist the temptation to get in *one other* [emphasis added] good lick." He stood on top of the moving vehicle and,

[1] This was the fourth "major" crisis he admits to living through.

44

with an aide bracing his legs, yelled: "You are cowards, you are afraid of the truth. You are the worst kind of cowards." As the Vice-President shouted his taunts, treating the world to an extraordinary spectacle, he felt the thrill of battle, "but I had full control of my temper as I lashed out at the mob." Unsure about the impression his behavior made on that occasion, Nixon could not seem to make the point often enough. *"I intentionally don't lose my temper when other people are angry,"* he told observers.

Having escaped to his hotel without suffering any physical harm, the Vice-President was confronted there by a man who spat at him. Being spit on, he says in *Six Crises,* is "the most infuriating insult ever conceived by man." Nixon remembers that the man, who turned out to be a "notorious" Communist provocateur, was "weird," with "bulging eyes [that] seemed to merge with his mouth and nose in one distorted blob." But Nixon was not in good shape either, for he confesses feeling an "almost uncontrollable urge to tear the face in front of me to pieces." He would have, too, he says, but Sherwood, his aide, grabbed the intruder by the arm in time and whirled him "out of my path," preventing Nixon from "handling the man personally." "But as I saw his legs go by," writes Nixon, "I at least had the satisfaction of planting a healthy kick on his shins." The violence, he says, made him feel good.

In retelling the events of the day, Nixon reveals, largely unwittingly, a few significant things about his own knack for distorting reality and then acting in part on those distortions: First, none of these South Americans knew Nixon, the man; they were attacking him as a symbol of the "gringo" government they despised, yet he felt personally insulted. Also, by his own admission, he had to be prevented from mutilating the bulgy-eyed provocateur whom he later accused of "spitting on the good name of Peru," but whom he did hit just the same—once the man had in effect been prevented from hitting back. The day revealed something, too, about Nixon's self-proclaimed coolness. His hindsight description of backing away with his eye on the mob had the fantasy quality of a mythic movie cowboy showdown. And last, the man who was to become the President of the United States admits that he found his own violence therapeutic.

"I was hailed as a hero in Peru," he says later.[1]

The CIA had advised him in Caracas, Venezuela, of the peril of continuing his trip through South America, and the report was backed up by the Secret Service, which was charged with the Vice-President's safety. His decision to continue, Nixon protests, was *not* an act of bravery; it was merely that Venezuela was the most important stop on the trip. He radioed his brother Donald that he and Pat would continue "despite any danger that may be involved." Later, he told the National Press Club that he hadn't taken a trip yet "in which I have not been warned that there would be demonstrations."

Brave words, but, as he himself has admitted, he was warned of more than mere demonstrations. He and Pat were spat upon shortly after they landed, and a rubber noisemaker struck Nixon in the face. To illustrate how quickly and coolly he functions in the face of extreme danger, he tells us in his book, he considered picking up the object and throwing it back, but at once realized "I might lay myself open to charges that I was throwing things at the people of Venezuela." It almost seems from this account that Nixon's only concern was the propaganda impact of the Vice-President of the United States caught in the act of throwing a rubber whistle. But he has confessed more truthfully to Earl Mazo he, instead, was worried about his own dignity.

The next incident of violence occurred as he, in one limousine with his wife in another directly behind, moved up the highway leading to the tomb of Simon Bolivar, the liberator. Suddenly the caravan was mired in a swamp of hostile flesh, and for twelve minutes they sat there while people battered at the cars with pipes, feet, sticks, shouting "Muera Nixon [Death to Nixon]." Nixon and an aide were nicked by flying glass; the crowd, he realized, "was out for blood." While the Venezuelan Foreign Minister, sitting beside Nixon, was on the threshold of hysteria, Nixon says, "I sat there as stoically as possible." Then a thought flashed through his head that made him sick, though it was unrelated to the immediate danger: The boys and girls surrounding his car, "fanatical frenzy" in their eyes, were no older than his daughter Trica, who was then twelve. "My reaction was a

[1] Walter Lippmann called the South American trip a "diplomatic Pearl Harbor."

46

feeling of absolute hatred for the tough Communist agitators who were driving children to this irrational state." Then Sherwood, the aide who had propped him up on the top of the car in Lima had had violently restrained the spitter, pulled his revolver in order to "get" some of those "sons of bitches." Nixon stopped him, knowing "intuitively" that Sherwood (whom he does not call irrational) should not fire his gun. From Nixon's account in *Six Crises*, he was not deeply concerned that Sherwood might accidentally kill someone, although he was concerned about the mob "getting completely out of hand." His main fear was that the Communists would blame the *Americans* for starting the whole affair, a dangerous position that the Vice-President of the United States was determined not to "get caught in."

So cool-headed was Nixon, by *his* account, that he "suppressed" asking the Foreign Minister "who was close to hysterics" if he still believed the "Latin American Communists" were "harmless radicals." Once Nixon's car escaped into oncoming traffic, however, the Vice-President gave vent to his feelings by overriding an American official's suggestion to hide the badly battered limousine, instead ordering it to be left in front of the American Embassy so Venezuelan officials could "see some graphic evidence of what Communism really is."

Reflecting on the situation, Nixon explained that he had a "real letdown after one of these issues." But he knew how to bolster his morale: "Then I begin to think of what *bums* they are . . . and that you licked them." (He admitted he ought to stop thinking things like that because it's nice "to be a generous winner, if you have won.")

During his violence-filled South American tour, Nixon was on the verge of endangering more than himself. Nixon had intimated how far he was willing to go to defeat his enemies in a remark he did not repeat in *Six Crises*. "If we allowed what I would call a bunch of blackmailing bullies to keep the officials of the government of the United States from doing what we thinks needs to be done to carry out our foreign policy," he told reporters, "*then we better get off the face of the earth.*" More than one person wondered if Nixon, because several thousand South Americans did not want him in their land, was threatening the apocalypse.

CHAPTER SIX

Election years are perhaps the worst for Nixon. He feels he must emerge into the light and rub shoulders with the dreaded newsmen, revealing himself as well, sometimes at his ugliest, to the rest of the people. Senator Robert Taft sensed, as early as 1952, that it was in Nixon's character to "radiate tension and conflict"; the conservative Republican from Ohio told his friend Joseph Polowsky that Eisenhower's young running-mate had a "mean and vindictive streak." Although Taft was irritated because Nixon had opposed his becoming Presidential nominee that year, his criticism of a fellow Republican seemed unusually harsh, since it emphasized character flaws rather than political or philosophical differences. By the late 1950's, the editors of the magazine *Commonweal* feared that Nixon's campaign "tactics"—although they seemed more compulsive than tactically conceived—"would make American political life impossible because they would transform politics into a war of extermination."

Perhaps because he does himself as much damage as he does to anyone else or, maybe because of an early moral code, Nixon shows the ambivalence of a man who wants to avoid conflict yet, because of his character, cannot resist the temptation to seek it out. For instance, he had come into the 1958 campaign once again as the chief spokesman for the Republican Party, although his political instinct (and the somewhat more trustworthy indicators, the political polls) had from the first declared the campaign irretrievably lost. Even if he, as spokesman for the underdog, had pulled the classic all-American upset, he probably still wouldn't have gotten the proper credit. As a close political adviser, Murray Chotiner, said of him in a similar situation, "Dick was about the only man to stick his neck out . . . though he knew that if the party won, they would say it was because of the Administration, and if it lost, they would say it was his fault." The simple truth may be that Nixon cannot emotionally resist getting into gratuitous arguments.

"We would just be kidding ourselves if we did not recognize *right now*," Nixon declared with excessive urgency on the opening day of the campaign, "that we Republicans have the fight of our lives on our hands this November . . . Some of my Republican friends have even urged me to do as little as possible in this campaign so as to avoid being associated with a losing cause. My answer to that kind of talk is *poppycock*. We can win if we start slugging."[1] *Fight of our lives* makes a resounding rallying cry if the politician who issues it offers the least reason, even a specious one, to believe in its ominous portent. Why should the Republicans—who had two more years to go in the White House and who had won *and* lost elections for over one hundred years in spite of their constant minority status—suddenly be in a fight for their very existence as a political entity?

The answer may be that Nixon was projecting his personal predicament. In 1958, he was fighting not simply Democrats but the Republicans who did not want him and the Republicans who liked his politics but not his style or his compulsion to fight. And more than any other politician in contemporary history, even Lyndon Johnson, Nixon confuses his personal plight with groups like the party or, more often still, with large ideals. He has frequently said things like: "Win or lose, it is unforgiveable to lack the courage to fight for the principles we believe in." Significantly, Nixon repeats this philosophy after practically every losing battle, as if he were reassuring himself with the thought: It's not me they defeated, it's my principles.

Nixon's often vague principles have enabled him, again and again, to react zealously to the slightest hint of insult to others.

[1] The one time in the campaign his fellow Republicans urged him to slug even harder, Nixon refused. Conservative Senators Goldwater of Arizona and Knowland of California belittled the Vice-President for not attacking American labor. Nixon has less difficulty recognizing the silly arguments of others than he does his own: one of the reasons that the GOP was destined to lose that year, he theorized, was that five million workers had been laid off during the recession of 1957, and Nixon was unwilling to further jeopardize his party in the industrial districts.

49

In 1958, when the Democrats charged that the Administration's inept defense program had given the Communists the edge in the cold war, very quickly Nixon accused the Democrats of "rotgut thinking." The tone of the phrase—abnormally intense, a bit wild—immediately separated the comment from the standard brand of accusatory political rhetoric; the counterattack was much more savage than the attack. Everyone recoiled—Democrats, reporters, soon Republicans and even Nixon, who immediately dropped the term from his speeches and soon dropped the aide (by ignoring him until he quit) who allegedly encouraged him to use it. William Costello thinks Nixon's "basic sense of security was profoundly shaken" by his own zeal.

Less than two weeks later, nonetheless, he was at it again, this time lambasting the Democrats' "record of retreat and appeasement" which, he said, had handed China to the Communist world and started the Korean War. The next day John Foster Dulles told reporters that Nixon's habit of debating foreign policy in election campaigns was "highly undesirable," adding as diplomatically as possible under the circumstances (one Republican criticizing another) that *both* sides ought to "*calm down* on this aspect of the debate." To Nixon people this was the ultimate in ingratitude since during the same speech Nixon had said "in a nutshell [that] the Acheson [i.e. Democratic] foreign policy resulted in war and the Eisenhower-Dulles policy resulted in peace." Nixon's aides brought this to Dulles's attention, and in a subsequent statement the Secretary of State was less pointed.

But instead of the situation getting better for Nixon, it got worse; on the same day Dulles started to hedge (though without apologizing), Eisenhower began to complain. During a press conference, the President rebuked his party's principal campaign spokesman. "Foreign policy ought to be kept out of partisan debate [because] when someone makes a charge, another individual is going to reply," Eisenhower said, reminding Nixon of the ineluctable nature of action and reaction. "*I deplore that.*"

"I intend to continue to answer the attacks," Nixon promised, replying to the President who, he added, did not have the same political "responsibilities" as a Vice-President.

Though few Americans had yet fathomed their mutual dislike, Nixon seemed to feel the necessity of stressing that their argument was *not* due to "difference/s/ we have as individuals." Within hours, Eisenhower sent him a telegram, bluntly reminding Nixon that the Democrats had joined Republicans "in a common stand for a number of years on the essential foundations of foreign policy," a fact which should not, and did not, lend itself "to political argument." Nixon's pride was stung.

It is when his own pride is injured that Nixon usually becomes more dangerous to himself than anyone else. As a case in point, during a press conference in 1958, Nixon was asked a few difficult questions intended to make him comment on himself. One reporter asked Nixon to comment on a recent Herblock cartoon of a mudslinging Nixon captioned, "I would act differently if I were in the top job." Where another politician, no matter how angry he got, might have laughed off the query, Nixon—though he dismissed it—was on edge. (Frank Holeman says one nasty Herblock cartoon "is enough to ruin an average day" for Nixon.) Another question was asked concerning a published report that Eisenhower had refused to see a civil rights group seeking the President's support for some proposed legislation. Would Nixon comment? Apparently calm, Nixon began by saying that a press conference was not the appropriate place for him to discuss *his own* views on civil rights. Suddenly indignation flared. "I won't stand here in front of this fine group of newspapermen and take an insinuation that *I* have not discussed civil rights," Nixon shouted, his lips trembling, his face livid. Rigidly he stalked from the room, summarily ending the press conference, leaving reporters behind in uncomfortable silence.

Every time Nixon's anger erupts, it causes some observers to feel guilty, others confused, especially when he tries to temper these episodes with cringing salutations such as "this fine group of newspapermen." A public figure does not behave this way, they tell themselves and each other, so they try to fit the behavior into the accepted image of a public figure. Philip Potter (the reporter who de Toledano said hated Nixon), for example, observes, "It was obvious that the civil rights question, one he normally would have fielded with ease, was not responsible for the explosion. It was the way things were going and the political implications for his future." The *Baltimore Sun* reporter thinks Nixon had a mental image of his main goal, the White House, slipping forever out of reach. Potter's interpretation has the grandiose quality of political melodrama. Nixon had always yearned to reach the White House. But the collapse of a distant (and thus probably salvageable) dream was beside the point. As Nixon made clear, the point was that he believed the reporters were trying to ridicule and insult him.

He had undeniably been asked some teasing questions, but the magnitude of this injury slowly grew in his head. Perhaps it took so long because he tried to prevent it happening, but at last the fuse on his ego burned out and Nixon exploded. The question had been mild, easily deflected because it had not been about him. In his irrational state he had amplified, distorted and finally re-directed its not very important intent.

It has been argued that on that occasion Nixon deliberately lost his temper because he realized that the press conference was going badly for him and he decided to end it. However, if ending the press conference were his intention, another method would have been easier on everyone, most of all Nixon. But Nixon was at that moment in no condition to help the Republican Party or be easy on himself; he was too anxious to become a martyr.

In all it was a vintage year for him; he lost the election, the support of his hierarchy and control of himself.

CHAPTER SEVEN

The way Nixon speaks of it, his pointing finger is an important weapon in his arsenal. His first publicized use of it came during the fund crisis in 1952. As his campaign train was leaving Sacramento, California, a heckler yelled at him, "Tell 'em about the sixteen thousand dollars." Nixon shouted, "Hold the train!" but his thoughts, he later admitted, were in some disarray. Quickly Nixon opted for the device he often relies on when he's angry and says he's not: he pointed that finger, because "Instinctively, I knew I had to counterattack." In his recapitulation of the moment Nixon used an expression every movie-hungry American boy recognizes: "Then I let him have it," telling the crowd, "You folks know the work that I did investigating Communists . . . Ever since . . . the Communists and left-wingers have been fighting me with every possible smear. When I received the nomination for the Vice-Presidency, *I was warned* that if I continued to attack the Communists in government, they would continue to smear me. *They* have tried to say that I had taken sixteen thousand dollars for my personal use." Was the heckler, then, a Communist? Nixon admits he did not know at the time who the heckler was, although he claims that he later discovered that the man was a Democratic plant. In retrospect, Nixon offered what he obviously felt was a rational reason for counterattacking with his finger: he wanted to single the man out so that the partisan Nixon crowd could single him out too.

By 1959 Nixon was in Russia and pointing his finger at Premier Khrushchev. He had been informed in advance of his trip to expect a "belligerent, bullying" Russian leader who, said Nixon, relying on baseball terminology, had a dazzling assortment of curves, fastballs and wicked "spitters." But that should not have worried him since the Vice-President was not to engage in any substantive diplomatic discussions with any Russian, much less the Premier. Nixon was being sent to Russia on the strictest ceremonial basis by President

Eisenhower—to open the first American exhibition in Russia. In fact, the President and Secretary of State Dulles withheld diplomatic information from the Vice-President because they did not want him to exceed his authority. But months ahead of his departure, Nixon began "intensive planning," studying Communism, Russia and Khrushchev so that he would not be knocked off balance while "walking on eggs diplomatically." It's a tribute to Nixon's conscientiousness that he should have treated his assignments as handshaker and ribbon cutter as occasions of international importance and extreme sensitivity, but his real concern was himself: His overactive intuition told him the visit "might" turn out to be a "personal crisis for me."

It became his fifth crisis, if only because he sought to make it so—another *mano a mano* like the Hiss affair. Before his plane landed, he was "keyed up and ready for battle"; when it did land, he couldn't sleep. Nixon protests that the next day he entered the Kremlin to present his credentials in what he imagined would be a protocol visit, prepared to do more listening than talking. But Khrushchev (who, says Nixon, liked doing the *unexpected*) lit into him in a vicious, high-pitched voice over the Captive Nations Resolution passed by Congress five days before Nixon arrived in Moscow. Sponsored by two of Nixon's closer political allies, Karl Mundt and Everett Dirksen, and endorsed at least technically by Eisenhower, the Resolution officially called for the rededication and prayers of "free" people in behalf of "enslaved peoples" behind the Iron Curtain. "Any action by an authoritative body like Congress must have a purpose," said the Premier, insisting that the purpose was "provocative" as well as gratuitous, since it would change nothing. Nixon's reaction was personal; he feared that it was another of those acts his enemies stage for his benefit and that Khrushchev's anger was a spurious effort "to goad me into some rash and impulsive statements.[1] I had to make a quick decision on how to react to

[1] Edward P. Morgan, the broadcasting commentator, looked back on that meeting quite differently and perhaps with more objectivity: "Nixon came to present his credentials to the Kremlin . . . and was given hell for over forty minutes. The Communist's own paranoia revolved on the fearful theory that Nixon's appear-

his attack." On the defensive, Nixon responded that it was not provocation, merely the expression of wide-held American feeling.

The next confrontation took place at the American Exhibition in a television studio to which the two men were invited by an executive of Ampex, a manufacturer of electronic tapes for television. Khrushchev reiterated his argument against the Captive Nations Resolution and then wrapped his arms around a Soviet worker who was nearby, declaring, "Does this man look like a slave laborer? With men of such spirit how can we *lose?*" Nixon's reaction was again "to do some quick thinking," possibly stimulated less by the first question than the second, which reminded him that this was a contest in which someone won and someone lost. Nixon says he debated whether to answer Khrushchev's "outlandish and sometimes even insulting" charges then and there or be conciliatory; he ended up advising the Russian not to be "afraid of ideas." He told Khrushchev, "*You* don't know everything." The performances of both men, according to a professional tv critic, were "childish" and "boastful," but Nixon thought his own performance was the poorer of the two. Watching the tape played back on television, he saw that the Russian had been rude and mean and had cornered his guest "no holds barred," like some street hoodlum. Nixon said he himself felt like a fighter with one hand tied behind his back, like Dempsey in the first round of his Firpo fight. Peter Kumpa, a reporter on the scene, remembers that standing there in the studio, Nixon "seemed kind of paralyzed." Actually, Nixon stood there looking into the American-made camera as if praying for an ally to come popping out and rescue him, a somewhat foolish grin frozen on his face, virtually the whole time. His own performance was so disturbing to Nixon that Herb Klein, his press aide, responded

---

ance was a deliberate insult on top of the Resolution which Mundt and Dirksen had just passed back home." (Even some Americans felt that the Resolution was a high-and-mighty, gratuitous message to the Russians which said, in effect, that "We are better than you are.") When, a few months later, Khrushchev came to the United States, he told Ernie Barcella of UPI that he believed Nixon had come to Russia with "preconceived ideas."

to Nixon's anguish by attempting to stop shipment of the tape back to the United States. That failing, the State Department attempted to interfere, but the Ampex executive, aware he had a scoop, rushed it by plane to New York. (Virtually ever since, Nixon has been afraid to watch himself on television. He says it's because he worries about the way he looks; he says nothing about the way he acts.)

"I knew that he had scored heavily," Nixon recalls, "and it was imperative that I find an opportunity to *strike back* [emphasis added] so the record could be set straight publicly." Nixon was manifestly counting up the score; he felt hurt that the first and second rounds had both gone to the other guy.

The third round took place in a model kitchen at the Exhibition, where, Nixon says, he kept looking for an opening in the rotund Russian's shifty, savage offense: "We are strong, we can beat you . . ." Khrushchev said, growling and grinning at the same time. That did it. "This time," Nixon explains in *Six Crises*, "I was determined not to let him get off the hook," because he did not care for the idea that the world might think that he or his government would deal with this Communist "from a position of weakness." So drawing his finger and pointing, Nixon bravely retorted, "You are strong and we are strong. You are playing with the most destructive thing in the world," he accused Khrushchev. "It is very dangerous . . . One side cannot put an ultimatum to another." Khrushchev replied, "We will answer threats with threats." Nixon was adamant: "We will never engage in threats." But with the help of a diligent translator, Khrushchev was able to penetrate the language barrier and make a fine psychological distinction, telling Nixon, "You wanted indirectly to threaten me."

In his memoirs, Nixon remembers that the Russian Premier had argued with him "vehemently"—as his own pudgy finger, aiming at Nixon's chest, returned fire. "To some," Nixon wrote, "it may have looked as though we had both lost our tempers. But exactly the opposite was true. I had full and complete control of my temper and was aware of it. I knew the value of keeping cool in crisis."

Assuming that Nixon won this round, as Walter Lippmann said afterwards, "What were the results of winning this argument . . .? Has the frontier of freedom advanced one inch? Has the empire of tyranny receded at all?" The argument, however, did serve its basic purpose, although not necessarily well: it enabled the exercise of Nixon's ego. After each phase of the debate he hurried about asking American observers, "How did I do? How did I do?" An AP man had no trouble remembering twelve years afterwards that "he was really worried."

A few days later, still determined to maintain his composure despite the tension growing in him, Nixon walked out of a factory in the company of Georgi Zhukov, the Soviet Minister of Education, and was greeted by a large group of Russian workers who gave him the kind of friendly reception that, he says, "increasingly irritated" his hosts. He had observed the police discouraging other crowds from expressing their enthusiasm for him. On one occasion, Nixon noticed a burly character rough up a woman because she was applauding him. Striding away from Zhukov without an explanation, the guest of Russia grabbed the roughneck by the shoulders and shook him "as hard as I could." "Don't do that again," Nixon threatened at the top of his voice. "Don't ever do that again." The man he threatened was a policeman. Zhukov tried to intercede, but Nixon said, "Let's get in the car and we'll discuss this later." The moment they were alone, Nixon declared, "Mr. Zhukov, this little game you've been playing with me through your planted hecklers for the past few days has not been going well with the press, and in my opinion it is backfiring even among your own people. You underestimate their intelligence . . . They know when somebody is acting and when it is the real thing—particularly when the acts have been so amateurish.

"Now I just want to put you on notice . . . the next time I see one of your policemen trying to keep a crowd from indicating its friendship for the United States, I am going to *blast* [emphasis added] the whole bunch of you publicly," warned the cool statesman out of the West, "in a way you'll never forget . . . We don't have to make a joke out of the whole business," Nixon said, although no one had been laughing.

The Vice-President stopped in Warsaw after he left Russia and Nikita Khrushchev behind. He was still tense from that confrontation when he visited the Warsaw Ghetto and planted gladioli at the foot of the monument dedicated to the dozens of thousands of Jews who had been murdered there. At some point in the visit he made a profound remark: "We see here again what can happen when passions, *which are allowed to be nurtured beneath the surface*, are released." He looked around at the rubble, his eyes narrowed in pain, suggesting the deep sadness he felt in the presence of the dead. It seemed a touching, genuine moment, and to this day most of the people who were with him remember it just that way. But when his sadness had been filmed and the cameras were off, Nixon strode briskly back toward the newsmen who clustered around him. Jabbing a young network reporter in the ribs with his elbow (a fairly characteristic hail-fellow gesture he used), he said heartily, "Well, kid, how'd I do?" He had asked the same question after each critical stage of the trip, several times after he had spoken to Khrushchev, but Nixon had never been more chipper about it than when he stepped back from death's door.

CHAPTER EIGHT

Richard Nixon was the Vice-President of the United States, a famous figure, a potential inspiration. John F. Kennedy was an obscure Senator from New England, not especially well-liked by liberal Democrats. But Kennedy, who had an Irish temper, never lost it during the campaign of 1960 where anyone could see him lose it, while the same could not be said of Nixon. It took only a little heckling to push him over the edge and make him point that finger. "Listen," he'd demand, in what Theodore H. White called the rhetoric of kitchen argument. "Listen," or, sometimes he'd say, "I'm sick and tired . . ."—and he'd be telling the truth—"of hearing our opponents run down the United States of America." White too thought Nixon's resentments real "but he expressed them too easily." One day when he was stumping the boondocks, the finger pointed at another heckler: "I would also suggest, while I am talking about manners, incidentally, that I have been heckled by experts." Nixon's hecklers must be experts; it is essential that the good people out there understand that none but an expert could make a cold-blooded professional like Richard Nixon lose his self-control. *"So don't try anything on me, or we'll take care of you . . ."*

The Democrats and other Communists he saw planted subversively in his audience did not have to heckle him aloud to make him tremble and point; *he* could hear them: ". . . And now I want to speak to you of another kind of aggression—aggression without war, for the aggressor comes not as a conqueror, but as a champion of peace, of freedom, offering progress and plenty of hope to the unfortunates of the earth . . . The biggest problem is to arouse people to the *mortal* danger it presents and inspire the people to meet the danger."

Nixon began to campaign in 1960 well ahead, and ended in the rear, as usual. "Dick didn't lose this election," someone close to him said, "Dick blew this election." Nixon was tired, disrupted, isolated from his own advisers (He didn't trust them, and before the campaign was over many of them couldn't get into his office.). He spoke too quickly; he telescoped wholly unrelated thoughts into a shorthand gibberish; he turned things completely around for the most irrational reasons, seethed at the ridicule levelled at him by the urbane Kennedy, who, said White, exerted the same charm over Nixon "that a snake charmer exerts over a snake," the effect being "doubly harmful to Nixon's ego."

Nearing the very pinnacle of ambition, he made the obstacles in his path tangible. Early in the campaign, touring the south ("The question is not what effect this kind of trip has on the south," said one of White's sources, "it's what effect the trip is going to have on Nixon."), he cracked his kneecap against the door of his car so hard that he landed in the hospital where he fumed impatiently for days. For the next two weeks, he was reportedly angry most of the time. As Nixon himself says, the mental anguish (of not being able to campaign) was "infinitely worse" than the pain in his leg. When he cracked the same knee again, in exactly the same way, and turned ashen, one of the reporters could no longer hold back. "My God, he's trying to kill himself," he said. Nixon cracked it on the day of the first "Great Debate" with Kennedy.

Nixon did not kill himself but he did kill his chances for the Presidency as a result of the debates over television. He did not have to debate Kennedy. It's entirely possible—the flip side of self-destructiveness often being arrogance—that consciously Nixon was convinced that he could beat Kennedy at debate the way he had beaten Jerry Voorhis in the Congressional race of 1946. The earlier debates, the first high mark of Nixon's political career, had left Jerry Voorhis, who was rich, cultured and expensively educated like Kennedy, literally fumbling for words. Nixon gave a strange motive for debating Kennedy: He was *afraid* that he would open himself, he said, "to the charge that I was afraid . . ." After ego came noble principles: He did not feel, he added, that he had the right to refuse engaging in a television program that the majority of Americans wanted to see.

White considered the four debates a "disaster" for Nixon; they destroyed the carefully manufactured theme that the

Vice-President was politically mature while the Senator from Massachusetts was a kid. "If Nixon could match Khrushchev in debate," White said dryly, "then Kennedy had proved he could match Nixon." White says that the debates ruined the neat "psychological distinction" between Nixon's "experience" and Kennedy's inexperience.

After a time, in the redundancy of watching the man write his own death sentence, boredom almost chases out fascination. Nonetheless, before the debates even began, Nixon made it relatively easy for himself to lose. Though fabled as a student with an "iron butt" who can prepare himself (even if, as author and teacher Mark Harris says, Nixon does not entirely understand the meaning of everything he studies), the Vice-President failed to brief himself sufficiently for the breadth of his test in the first debate. In fact, on the morning of the first debate (which, because it was the first in history, had the largest viewing audience of the four), while Kennedy kept pumping away with his aides on every conceivable tack the televised argument could take, Nixon gratuitously assumed another responsibility against the advice of his television aides. Coddling him like a baby, they urged him to get the rest they felt he needed. Instead, Nixon decided to make a speech the morning of the debate to the hostile United Brotherhood of Carpenters and Joiners, "whose negative reaction," the aides knew (White reports) "would psychologically disturb their contender." The fact that his own people thought he needed protection might have disturbed Nixon too, because when one of the tv consultants advised him on the way to the Chicago studio to come out swinging, Nixon, according to White, said he suspected that his own adviser was working against him—that is, to the degree that the man was playing ventriloquist's dummy for Frank Stanton, the President of CBS, whom Nixon believed was interested only in an exciting show. (Henry Cabot Lodge, his Vice-Presidential running-mate, reputedly called Nixon before the debate urging him to erase his "assassin's image.")

During one of the debates, Nixon demanded an apology from Kennedy, in the name of the American "children who come out to see the Presidential candidates [and] mothers holding their babies," for Harry Truman's curses. Truman,

Kennedy's predecessor as head of the Democratic Party, said Nixon, had "bluntly suggested where the Vice-President and the Republican Party could go." "I can only say that I am very proud that President Eisenhower restored dignity and decency, and, frankly, good language to the conduct of the Presidency . . . And I can only hope—should I win this election—that I could approach President Eisenhower in maintaining the dignity of the office."

Nixon now became theatrically overwrought: "Whenever any mother or father talks to his child, [I hope] he can look at the man in the White House, and whatever he may think of his politics, he will say, 'Well, there is a man who maintains the kind of standards personally that I would want my child to follow.' " Kennedy's response was laughter. It seemed he laughed for a very long time.

A few minutes later, the debate over, Nixon retired to his dressing room and in front of the pool reporter assigned to cover backstage events, exploded: "That fucking bastard," he is alleged to have said, "that fucking bastard . . . he—he wasn't supposed to use notes."

Two days before the last debate with Kennedy, the two appeared at the annual Alfred El Smith Memorial Dinner, presided over by Cardinal Spellman, senior prelate of the Catholic Church in New York. Kennedy was exceedingly witty that night. "Mr. Nixon, like the rest of us," the Democrat remarked when it was his turn to speak, "has had his troubles in this campaign. At one point even the *Wall Street Journal* was criticizing his tactics. This is like the *Osservatore Romano* criticizing the Pope . . . One of the inspiring notes that was struck in the last [third] debate was struck by the Vice-President in his very moving warning to the children of the nation and the candidates against the use of profanity . . . And I know after fourteen years in Congress with the Vice-President that he was very sincere . . ." Kennedy went on to tell an anecdote about the meeting he'd heard took place the day before between Nixon and a rich Republican in Florida. The rich Republican complimented Nixon, said Kennedy. " 'Mr. Vice-President, that was a damn fine speech.' And the Vice-President said 'I appreciate the compliment but not the language.' And the Republican went on, 'Yes sir, I liked it so

much that I contributed a thousand dollars to your campaign!'
And Nixon replied, 'The hell you say.' " Nixon laughed
nervously.

In *Six Crises* Nixon was still seething, saying that Kennedy's
wit "irritated *them* [the audience] with an incredible display
of bad judgment." Nixon thought the effect easily predictable.
"Kennedy had received polite applause. I received a prolonged ovation." (Contradicting Nixon, the transcript of
Kennedy's speech indicates that his jibes were received by
this conservative Catholic audience with extended laughter.)

Nixon buckled, in an instance so classic that as often as it
has been told, it's worth repeating, particularly for the way
it illuminates Nixon's suicidal candor. (The more he tries to
explain one of his amazing statements, the more bizarre and
dangerous his situation becomes.) Kennedy, just before that
fourth debate, got to Nixon again. Kennedy attacked the
Eisenhower Administration for its alleged failure to adopt a
hard line against the Castro regime in Cuba. Learning that
Kennedy had been briefed by the CIA that the United States
was secretly underwriting and training Cuban insurgents to
overthrow Castro, Nixon exploded with "rage". Explaining
in *Six Crises* what happened and why, he says that it was the
first and only time during the campaign he got mad at
Kennedy personally, which would prove to be another lie, a
second on top of the first, as there would be a third soon added
to the second. "And my rage," he says, "was greater because I
could do nothing about it." He then uses the same metaphor
used in an earlier chapter regarding his battle with Khrushchev: when Kennedy acted cynically like that, Nixon again
felt like a fighter with one hand tied behind his back. (The
term quickly wears itself out as a good excuse. As one student
of Nixon has observed, "Most one-armed men have the
sense not to go around looking for brawls with dirty fighters
who allegedly like punching cripples.")

In his agitation in 1960, he acted nonsensically, and in 1962,
in publishing his memoirs, Nixon gives the nonsensical
reason why: He felt that in order to protect the CIA's secret
plan at "all costs . . . I must go to the other extreme." Which
he did: In the fourth and final debate, Nixon went on the air
to counterattack Kennedy's proposal to aid Cuban counter-

revolutionaries as "wrong," "irresponsible" and a reckless violation of American foreign treaty commitments. Instead of making himself less ridiculous in *Six Crises*, Nixon simply compounded the ridiculousness. "Strange logic," Garry Wills writes wryly. "Prevented, say, from punishing a wife-beater, one *must* punish the wife-beater's wife." Nixon's nationally televised assault was not so much against Kennedy *as against his own precious-to-him hardline anti-Communist feelings* and *against Nixon's chances of winning the 1960 Presidential election.* This sudden and spurious liberal attitude of ignoring Communism ninety miles from Miami, Florida, drew—he notes—the applause of a few liberal newspapers and commentators (who, all the same, did not give him their endorsement for the Presidency). It also did him some little harm—and this he does *not* note—among his own conservative constituency who, in part, must have thought he was going bananas.

The only way several Republicans thought Nixon could be exciting at this point was to get Eisenhower to campaign for him. But Eisenhower didn't volunteer and Nixon was afraid to ask (He says he didn't want to tire out the President.) until the last week, when he did so in desperation.[1] The Nixon who presented himself at the White House on October 31 "couldn't think either clearly or quickly," one person present recalls, "and the conversation at the table was completely irrelevant." Ike nevertheless agreed to help for the last three days. Despite Eisenhower's popularity, his public appearances were too late; Nixon had made his own mark.

In the final chapters of *Six Crises*, Nixon remembers with some dismay that before he went to sleep on Election Night, 1960, Eric Sevareid of CBS observed that it looked as though Nixon had snatched defeat from the jaws of victory. Nixon went to sleep hoping to wake up and prove Sevareid wrong. When he didn't, he knew exactly whose fault it was—not his own, certainly. He tells us, at first using his more youthful

[1] Early in the campaign, certainly a few of those in Nixon's camp, feeling free at last of Eisenhower's paternalistic yoke and acting out their high spirits, made it evident to all that they did not need the President for anything but minding the store until they could take over the White House. Their confidence seems to have diminished well before the end.

and inexperienced staff members to dilute his bitterness, before slipping into a somewhat more relevant pronoun, that when the election started going bad, they felt that he was deserted by "people *we* had thought were close and loyal friends."

During the 1960 campaign, the only conclusion one could make was that the Republican candidate generated his own crises, a word Nixon himself savors in describing the high points of his political career. In anti-Nixon quarters, a memorandum on the subject was circulated, which ended: "Actually, through probable ineptitude, he has attempted many more crises than he has succeeded in achieving . . ."

"It is the style of Nixon," Evelyn Houston was quoted as saying by Arthur Schlesinger, Jr., who became a Kennedy supporter, "or to be more painfully exact, the lack of one—that pervasive and alchemic falsity, which is an art or show-manship, a respectable talent, but a veritable Midas touch for making ersatz of the real, that has made many of us wince . . . It is the mechanizing, the demeaning, the patronizing of our perceptions and sensibilities, the subtle corruption, which I used to think was calculated by him but have come to believe is in great part unconscious, of communication on the level where we perceive not Americans, not highbrow or lowbrow, conformist or heretic, but each other."

In analyzing the outcome of the 1960 campaign, White said almost timidly of Nixon, ". . . The mistakes he made were personal—but then you'd have to get into such areas of privacy to understand it that you just have to leave it there."

CHAPTER NINE

In announcing his candidacy for Governor of California, in 1962, Nixon explained why he was giving up a profitable career in law and returning to what he called "public service": "The most challenging, the most exciting position that I can seek, and in which I could serve, next to being President of the United States, is to be Governor . . ." The excitement, though, would be negative; Nixon would lose again, and in the process blame it on his being a national figure in a local campaign, on industrialism, on the Cuban crisis, on his opponent and on the press—on everyone but himself. His "last" press conference would receive undue attention even from Dr. Hutschnecker. Everyone saw it as a personal tragedy, the final act in an aborted career. *Time* called it his political obituary. By writing it himself, however, Nixon forced the public to notice that in addition to a certain slipperiness, a certain unpleasantness of manner, he could be petty and "unpolitical" at least once in his life.

But Nixon had, in fact, lost his self-control more than once in his life and, even more destructively, his sense of direction several times in 1962 alone—not as often as say, 1956, 1958 or 1960 but more dramatically and often enough to drive away his potential following piece by piece. His wife was so afraid of what campaigning would do to him that when he told her of his intention at a party, reported by Gerry Wills, she abused him in front of everyone. The last press conference, then, was only the last piece and, because it was so well publicized, his most indelible self-humiliation.

From the beginning, the polls in California indicated Edmund G. (Pat) Brown, the incumbent Governor, was ahead of Nixon, seven or eight percentage points ahead in some samplings. Brown's advantage could have been excused as the inevitable advantage the officeholder has at the start of any campaign, if Nixon had been a relative unknown. Instead he was California's most controversial and famous politician.

Nixon and his aides were thoroughly aware of the implications: some Californians considered him a loser, others simply did not want him. Therefore, Nixon could not afford to alienate additional voters unless the act of alienation led to positive results in some other, larger part of the electorate. Though he would assure everyone—repeatedly—that he had never lost California (although he came close to doing so in 1960), indirectly, Nixon gave other, more reliable assurances to his state of mind. He was profoundly uncertain of victory.

His book, *Six Crises*, was published in late March, after he had decided definitely to run against Brown. The writing had gone badly for him. The one chapter of the book he had been determined to write entirely on his own, without any help from Al Moscow (who had been hired to collect the information and do some editing and who had worked with him, apparently to a limited degree, on the other five chapters) was "The Campaign of 1960" which resulted in his defeat for the Presidency. He had started to write the chapter just months after that defeat, and unlike Nixon's other so-called crises, this one, in which the outcome spoke so unequivocally for itself, could not be rewritten into spurious victory, at any rate not easily. It was a delicate installment, obviously not to be entrusted in the least particle to a "ghost" who had never personally tasted the bitterness of great failure. Nixon was also confronted with the problem of making the loss of his ultimate goal, the Presidency, a triumphant object lesson in the character strengthening of Everyman.

The writing took Nixon over twice the time he had planned to give it—seven months instead of three; he had to push himself to get the project done and out of the way. In that last chapter he would state that for him the greatest period of danger in a crisis came *after* the fighting—a comment surely influenced by his present mood. At least twice Nixon forgot the key to the cottage where he was writing the manuscript, and anyone familiar with the cause of Freudian slips might wonder if Nixon hated reliving the setback so much that his mind found an unconscious excuse for him to avoid work. During that unsettled period, he even misplaced his dog Checkers and had to search for hours to find him.

Writing it out evidently did not serve as adequate therapy, because months after he had finally gotten it done, his obsession with failure persisted. Election Day was in November, but by October he would flatly predict his defeat, and attempt to lay it off on an unlucky twist of fate. Soon after announcing his decision to run, in early 1962, he gave a brief interview in Arizona to a local radio team, Robert F. and Alice Lewis, who reportedly specialized in light personality and travel stories. They interviewed Nixon in one of the public rooms of the hotel where he was vacationing, treating him with considerable tact and diffidence. (In a slip of his own, Mr. Lewis addressed Nixon as "Governor.") Halfway through the ten-minute show, Nixon calmly told them about his book, plugging it as "the story of what I think are the most significant aspects of my public life," adding that the material would appear in three installments in *Life*.

"Will the publishing date have anything to do with this election?" Lewis asked. The question apparently bothered Nixon, but if Lewis was trying to elicit the image of a clever politician who believed the art of his craft was in the timing, it was no more than the image Nixon himself had always tried to project. Nixon replied too hastily, in fact stepping on Lewis's question before he had completely gotten it out; he insisted that if the campaign and the publication date were the same, it would be "only by coincidence."

Then Mrs. Lewis remarked, rather than asked, that becoming governor might not be either "relaxing or easy." Nixon audibly tensed, assuring Mrs. Lewis that he did "like to relax—and all of us do, and all of our listeners do, but we must remember if that's all we had to do, we'd be pretty bored with life . . . so I think *we need challenges* . . ." In print, the quote seems windy, still without conveying any of the difficulty Nixon had spitting it out.

Mrs. Lewis, who had been alternating with her husband, asked the next question out of turn. Perhaps fumbling for a delicate phrase that would spare her touchy guest further embarrassment, Mrs. Lewis allowed her query to grow long and involved, but her aim nonetheless was clear: to learn if Nixon anticipated trouble winning, a question asked, in one form or another, of every candidate by every interviewer.

Could a man like you, she asked, to use some of her words, become a "prophet in his own land" where "they know you so well, and are not objective about you?"

There was a striking silence, especially in contrast to Nixon's earlier talkativeness. He spoke with infinite slowness after a fairly long interval, his voice rising in suspicion. "Now when you mean 'objective'—in what that [sic] they tend to, ah, ah, to, to, ah—" The sapper had reached the mine: "under—" Nixon took a very deep breath and was at last able to utter the one word which possessed disastrous connotations for this politician: "—underrate—or overrate a man."[1] The more accommodating word "overrate" shot out at high speed, but the Nixon machinery had almost conked out. "You mean that a man is without *profit* [sic], ahhh, except in his own country? Aaaaah, I mean, ehh, a man is without—" It was so obvious that the guest was in agony that Mr. Lewis had to save him: "Honor," he prompted and Nixon clutched at this lifesaver and cried, "Honor," managing to add, "in his own country," only to flounder again as he strained to make his difficulty seem like a giant put-on. "Maybe profit too—because the two," said Nixon, laughing nervously, "sometimes go together."

The Lewises also laughed, thereby restoring enough of Nixon's confidence so that he could finish answering the question which threw him so wildly out of whack by implying, unintentionally, that Californians knew him too intimately ever to vote for him. Though he could now talk, Nixon was not entirely coherent. "This could be," he continued in a vague reference, possibly to the strange mating of honor and profit (understandable, however, in Nixon, who believes in self-made men like Horatio Alger). "Although in the last election I carried California, which is one of the industrial states which instigates [sic]—indicates—a considerable amount of support there. But it is true that when an individual is on the national scene," he added, acknowledging now in another way what the polls and his own disaster-prone mood foretold, "there is sometimes a tendency for people on the

[1] The Lewises donated a tape recording of the program to the library at Lincoln Center, in New York City, where it was replayed repeatedly until every painful syllable and pause was confirmed.

local scene to maybe *resent that* and prefer that he be primarily and only a local personality."

He had just given one, probably two, excuses for losing. Why, one wonders, did Nixon relate his prior success in California to the fact that it was one of the industrial states? When he won California in 1960, it was *despite* the Democratic leanings of the labor vote which dominated industrial returns in California and the other industrial states. Had he inadvertently suggested that if Nixon lost California in 1962, we could blame it on instigators seeking, as they had in 1960, to undermine the considerable amount of support he had in his own state? Psychologically, the proximity of two thoughts usually means something, but the solution is relatively unimportant, for Nixon then supplied a conscious if equally irrational argument for his loss—*it would be because local voters resented national personalities.*

Having offered that excuse, he took steps during the campaign to remind local voters that he was a national, nay, international personality, by reassociating himself with the issue that had brought him his only personal victories and could now bring him his next defeat. Nixon rehabilitated the threat of Communism. In the state house? It really didn't make any difference how logical the issue was in a local election; logic is no handmaiden to politics. His aides, after conducting a private poll, found anti-Communism a viable issue in California. Although it did little more than reinforce the instinct to recreate the source of his victories over Jerry Voorhis and Helen Gahagan Douglas, the poll doubtless was accurate; the state did have a large population of displaced midwesterners, many of whom, particularly the older ones, saw godless Red agents behind every rose bush and citrus tree. If Nixon could frighten them enough to leave their geriatric beds and go out and vote, it required no mystical foreknowledge to realize they *would* pull the lever for him because, for them, all liberals courted Communism. But Nixon *knew* he had to be careful; he could use the issue but not everywhere. If California's older population had grown in the twelve years since he had overwhelmed Mrs. Douglas for California's Senate seat, so had the younger population, and considerably faster. Many war babies, voting for the first time in 1962, could be counted among those who had not yet been condemned by arteriosclerosis of the brain or by tunnel vision of the verities. The concerns of the younger and often better educated population of California ranged from improving education to better administration of welfare, taxes and the State house. In 1962, during the peaceful months before Kennedy and the Russians had their showdown over Cuba, Communist subversion did not trouble them as much as the absence of trust among civilized nations. Thus to be effective, Nixon merely had to be selective in choosing the occasions on which to evoke the Red Menace (which he situated eighth among his twelve basic campaign issues). This would have been entirely in keeping with his oft-boasted technique for successful electioneering: adapt the basic campaign speech to each audience and each occasion.[1]

Nixon seemed too near a state of collapse throughout much of the campaign to follow his own well-reasoned political rules. For example, he appealed for votes to a large group of California educators meeting in San Diego, by opening with this ringing rhetorical question: "What are our schools for— if not for indoctrination against Communism?" San Diego being heavily conservative territory, the question should have brought thunderous applause. Instead a tremor of anxiety and displeasure passed through the crowd of schoolteachers who knew, as Mark Harris says, that education never was "so simply *that*"—not even in California where odd notions occupy almost as much space in the landscape as automobiles.

Harris was present on this occasion for two reasons: as a writer, to prepare an article about the 1962 campaign for *Life*, and because he himself was a teacher in California and was, like the rest, anxious about the future of education in the

[1] In 1967, Stephen Hess and David Broder, the essentially cautious and sympathetic (to Nixon) co-authors of *The Republican Establishment*, noted that the man always "compounded his own problem," by letting reporters see "Nixon the Manipulator, the man of technique, not of substance . . . Nixon is not content to be admired. Rather than let the reporters discover for themselves how he adapts his basic speech to the situation, he goes on to say, 'Now, this is a pretty conservative district, so you'll notice I don't bear down as heavily on . . .' or, 'The Democratic incumbent here has been a very good Congressman, so I'm going to have to stay away from personalities and concentrate on . . .'"

state. Harris feels Nixon could not help but see what he himself saw in the audience: "a stiffening, a sudden upturning of heads and straightening of backs, for he began to qualify . . . having said too much and gone too far, but he had lost with a single breath the best opening attention of a considerable body of people." Actually he hadn't so much turned them away, as off. These teachers were also civil servants, subject, in one way or another, to the ravages of the upheaval that comes with a change of administrations. Instead of placating them by tuning in to their parochial interests and requirements, the speaker offended their intelligence and scared hell out of them at the same time. In the fifties, which were too recent to have been easily forgotten by educators, the Red Menace preceded the loyalty oaths, as the oaths preceded the faculty purges. Nixon had radically revised education's purpose and guaranteed that those who came to him in anxiety left him in fear. "The moment," Harris writes, "had been so poorly chosen for a sentence so dogmatic that I began to wonder, as I would often wonder afterward, whether it was not his hidden will to lose, his wish concealed even from his own eye, to end himself in politics and thereby end the tension between himself and what he had once begun . . ."

Added to other occasions like it, there can be small doubt that Nixon, ten years after Senator Taft's analysis, was still radiating tension and conflict; some deep part of the man desired to scare hell out of those teachers, most of whom, by his lights, were probably liberals; and even if they were conservatives, his question was not so much conservative as reactionary. Richard Nixon has never seemed entirely happy with the support of the many, for so long as he can conjure up even one enemy, he will concentrate on him and, in his less rational moments, provide the one act or gesture which can give even the most illusory enemy a concrete form. And only an accumulation of such occasions over the years gives substance to the possibility that Nixon might have been trying to separate himself unconsciously from victory and from people who came to listen skeptically. How dare they be skeptical—unless he personally supplied the reasons, which he often did.

Nixon is as distraught by these charged episodes as his

audiences and, seeing the reaction, begins to back off, to modify, to slur, to equivocate, but by then it's too late. In analytical psychology, there is a premise which has relevance here: the result of a person's actions generally betrays the motivation for these actions.

Harris's article for *Life* was enlarged and published two years later as the book *Mark the Glove Boy* which, because of its perception and dedication to truth rather than objectivity, was one of the best political biographies (it was also an autobiography) of the sixties. The book did not receive the attention it should have, though, because 1964 was a year when Nixon was of no particular interest to the reading public, which reckoned he was no longer a political force. After the speech on education, Harris says, he sought out Nixon to question him more closely on this matter of using the schools primarily for anti-Communist indoctrination. Nixon was not about to fall into that trap again; evading it by saying he had not been talking about "socialism," he walked away. Harris asked the same question a day later, in front of a crowd of reporters. Nixon, who becomes rather too attached to techniques that have worked once but have little chance of working twice on the same people, repeated, "Remember, I didn't say socialism, I said Communism."

Harris had never mentioned socialism. Harris exploded: "I don't care who. The point is you're telling me how to run my classroom, it's out of your jurisdiction, you haven't the facts." He went on to charge Nixon with having faked knowledge of the problems facing San Francisco State College, where Harris taught. "It's like your telling me the other night we need a bigger auditorium."

"My goodness," Nixon said, "you're not comparing Communism to auditoriums, are you?" (Harris didn't speculate, but at this point in his anecdote one begins to wonder if Nixon's evasiveness was deliberate or the result of disorientation.) Suddenly he spun out of the center of the crowd and fled as he had before, his shoulder *slamming Harris in the face*. He strode to the edge of the crowd, a considerable distance, and was astonished to find himself literally facing a stone wall. Harris had begun to chase him, still shouting: "See, see you say you'll answer questions but you walk away;

you walked away last night." Unable to flee further, Nixon spun around, his mobile features remotely suggesting the conflicting emotions that had been passing through his mind. At first it almost seemed he was happy that the wall had prevented him from carrying on "so long and so purposeless" an escape, but abruptly he pointed a finger at Harris and bellowed, "Don't point, don't point, keep your hands down."

Though Nixon, according to Earl Mazo, would resort in the later stages of the California race to every "wile" learned in his years of politics—including one on the eve of the election that Mazo, an appreciative biographer, and others label "another 'Checkers' speech"—Nixon would still lose. He expected to lose before he started, but that may not be as important as his compulsive contributions to his own defeat. At no point, however, did he seem emotionally capable of accepting any part of the blame; if he did not unconsciously blame industrial "instigators" for doing whatever things instigators do in opposing the forces of light, there were the conscious excuses.

He told the Lewises before the campaign began that being a national figure could indeed hurt his chances, yet he did not seriously take up local issues. The most interesting excuse for losing, however, was the one he gave on October 22, almost three weeks before Election Day, as he sat staring at the television screen while President Kennedy announced the blockade of Russian ships carrying missiles to Communist Cuba. *That* settled it for Nixon—he turned to his companion and declared that he had *just* lost the election. Why? It seemed that the voters in the state of California would pay no attention to a local campaign now. While Nixon could not announce he would lose publicly, according to Mazo, "he privately predicted he would."

How odd. The only candidate for governor to battle the scourge of Communism during his campaign believed he had just lost the war, because the scourge of Communism seemed, for the moment, to be so very real that the President of the United States felt he had better follow Nixon into battle.

Gifted as he was in the art of politics, only Nixon could draw such a conclusion from such a set of facts. His last excuses would come much closer to Nixon's real feelings, for they conceded that certain persons and groups took advantage because they disliked *him*.

Like so many other bad moments in his life, Nixon's ignominious press conference on November 7, 1962, was not only shocking, it was rash, catching his own aides by surprise. Nixon himself had ruled it out.

The night before, and throughout the very early morning hours, he preserved the fading hope that a miracle would happen—that somehow the late returns from conservative Orange County and San Diego would reverse the tide which, for all practical purposes, had already swept Brown into the Governor's office for another term.[1] Reporters waiting below in the Beverly Hilton Hotel had been clamoring unhappily for some word from Nixon, and Herbert Klein, his chief press assistant, came into Nixon's suite that morning to urge him again to put in an appearance in the press room. By now, Nixon's refusal was based less on faint hope than on pure pique. "Screw them," he snapped. Out of a mistaken sense of obligation to the reporters or out of blind faith in Nixon, or obtuseness created in some degree out of his own exhaustion and a single-mindedness about his job, Klein softly persisted. "Screw them," Nixon said several more times, according to Jules Witcover, who gives a detailed account of the meeting. "Screw them. You make the statement," Nixon ordered, the last remnants of his tattered self-control evidently frayed. "You make it."

A few of Nixon's aides were reportedly quite relieved by his decision. If the reasons for it were not entirely rational (a fact they were not likely to admit even to themselves), they realized that the effect at least would be. Nixon would head out the back door for home, where his wife, who could not face another defeat in public, was waiting. In this way Nixon would remain isolated, invisible, and thus safe from further

[1] Witcover says that by morning a Nixon victory in California was "beyond all rational judgment." Witcover reports that when he could no longer deny his defeat, Nixon said, "Losing California after losing the Presidency. Well, it's like being bitten by a mosquito after being bitten by a rattlesnake."

harm, while Klein carried out the obligatory and painful formalities—the reading of a concession statement coupled with a congratulatory telegram to the winner (the people have spoken . . .), the answering of a few questions from reporters about the future (Herb, now that he's . . .). Because Nixon had lost, and there was no doubt about it by morning, a handful of the reporters who, for good reasons or bad, truly disliked the man no less than he imagined they did, dropped any guise of respect. "Where's Nixon?" one immediately demanded. "The boss won't be down," Klein smiled. "He plans to go home and be with his family."

Klein would briefly operate Nixon's "protective machinery," but as Garry Wills says, Nixon did not want it to function. Neither did the more aggressive aides also in the suite watching journalists go after Nixon's surrogate on tv. Murray Chotiner, the fighter, and H. R. "Bob" Haldeman and John D. Ehrlichman, two temperamental gentlemen who later joined Nixon in the White House, were there; and someone urged Nixon to go downstairs and give 'em hell. Just about then Nixon, staring at the television set and the reporters twitting Klein, reversed his decision. They had stabbed him with ridicule (they had flung "custard pies" at him as long ago as 1956), they had ruined his career (the only career he wanted) but he was not going to let them chase him into hiding. On television, Klein kept talking, parrying the taunts in his squinting, even-tempered fashion, perhaps thinking that Nixon was already on his way home to Pat and his two daughters.

Suddenly Nixon appeared in the press room and, followed by some of his embittered aides, he swept up to the podium, interrupted Klein and let the bitterness flow. His impulse apparently was to be manly, but Nixon proved petulant. He may have been aware that only silence could restore his manhood and dignity, but he was unable to achieve silence.

The famous "last" press conference was riddled with ambiguity, anger and example upon example of the waxy flexibility that is essentially neurotic but on other occasions had been mistaken for intelligence because it made Nixon difficult to pin down, to understand when he was cornered. There were seventy or eighty reporters in that room in 1962—

the largest assemblage of professional witnesses to Nixon's behavior at any time during the California campaign. He turned jerkily from side to side and saw all his enemies or, as someone else suggested, perhaps he was seeing the grievances —all of the times he imagined that they had knifed him. But Nixon hadn't been knifed, he had barely been nicked, and, in the most important sense, they would never touch him.

They reported those fifteen emotional minutes, but they didn't put them together with all those other times the man was not at one with himself, the other times he had lost control; they didn't systematize it, show it was not something new. So when it was all over, the misconception of him as a cool customer who had lost control of himself that one time in his career still prevailed in most circles, due partly to the custom of the American press establishment to find rational excuses for irrational acts.

And, naturally, when he won the Presidency in 1968, a great many Americans took his victory as irrefutable proof that it was a solitary systems failure, Nixon's single neurotic aberration. Journalists would report the last press conference only because they were all present (No one man alone likes to be witness to a nervous breakdown.), because network television cameras were relentlessly recording the naked truth, forcing them to do the same, and because some of them figured that he had lost the power to retaliate.

Those fifteen minutes in the Beverly Hilton Hotel that November day were truth's perfect mirror image, for every time the losing candidate declared that he was not complaining, his sourness, the halts and jerks of neurotic affect made it plain that he *was* complaining. Those he said he did not resent, he plainly resented most, on a day when he resented virtually everyone, including his fellow Republicans in California.

His gibberish may not have been purposeful but it does seem to have had meaning, alone and taken as one of many occasions like it: "Good morning, gentlemen. Now that Mr. Klein has made his statement, and *now that all the members of the press are so delighted that I have lost*,[1] I'd like to make a statement of my own:

[1] Any of Nixon's words which are italicized in this section are the result of the author's judgment.

"I appreciate the press coverage in this campaign. I think each of you covered it the way you saw it. You had to write it in the way according to your belief on how it should go."

Ralph de Toledano wrote something about Nixon and the press that might give Nixon's confused syntax meaning: "His feeling . . . that he was more sinned against than sinning had an objective basis. The passions he aroused derived from a visceral reaction in those who had been proven wrong about Alger Hiss, about his 'secret fund,' about Communism, and about his foes." De Toledano is saying that reporters, himself excluded, had predicted Nixon would lose, or had favored his opponents, again and again, and because Nixon *always* proved them lousy as seers, they got mad and tried to make a fool of him. De Toledano attributes such delusory feelings to his friend, Nixon.[1]

"I don't believe publishers should tell reporters to write one way or the other." But he did, or would: by 1971, Nixon would be taking his case directly to publishers and their highest editors, who largely took him on faith, as he sensed they would. He has, in *Six Crises*, characterized the majority of reporters as Democrats and the majority of publishers as Republicans, whose "natural" biases have a "conscious or subconscious" effect on their choice of words. Elsewhere too, Nixon has shown interest in the unconscious; one senses, but cannot prove, that his interest now was in the conscious or "subconscious" significance of the fact that reporters see him considerably more, and theoretically know him considerably better, than publishers and editors. "I want them all to be free. I don't believe the FCC [Federal Communications Com-

[1] By 1971, during a rare private interview with Allen Drury, Nixon had other reasons to offer about why reporters hated him: "I have one of the most hostile and unfair presses that any President has ever had, but I've developed a philosophical attitude about it. I *developed it early* . . . I don't care. And you know?—that's what makes 'em mad. That's what infuriates them. I just don't care. I just don't raise the roof with 'em. And that gets 'em." Yet talking to Drury, who had come to him as a biographer with guaranteed friendly credentials, Nixon showed flashes of wayward anger: For example, in the midst of an unchallenged monologue about invading Cambodia, the President gave Drury "a sudden sharp direct look" and said, "I know more than they [the press] do or you do about it."

mission] or anybody else should silence . . ." He mumbled the last word, or perhaps swallowed it would be more accurate; when he became President, the FCC began making veiled threats against networks and network commentators only after the Nixon administration accused them of being unfair.

"I have no complaints about the press coverage. I think each of you was writing it as you believed it." He would say this a half dozen different ways, never with any conviction, but perhaps trying to convince himself through constant repetition that he *was* above complaint.

"I congratulate Governor Brown, as Herb Klein has already indicated, for his victory . . . I think that he will now have certainly a position of tremendous interest for America and as well as for the people of California." (If Brown plays his cards right, he can run for President.)

"I wish him well, I wish him well not only from the personal standpoint (now follow this segue) *because there were never on my part any personal considerations.*

"I believe Governor Brown has a heart," Nixon said unhappily, "even though he believes I do not.

"I believe he is a good American, even though he believes I am not . . . I am proud of the fact that I defended my opponent's patriotism.

"You gentlemen didn't report it . . .

"You gentlemen and all the other ladies and gentlemen who ruined it for me.

". . . He won and I want this state to be led with courage." He thought Brown lacked courage; during the campaign, as if challenging the villain in a western, Nixon ordered Brown "to come out and fight like a man." "I want it to be led decisively," he lectured Brown, "and I want it to be led, certainly, with the assurance that the man who lost the campaign never during the course of the campaign raised a personal consideration against his opponent—never allowed any words indicating that his opponent was motivated by a lack of heart or a lack of patriotism to pass his lips. I am proud of the fact that I defended my opponent's patriotism." Throughout the campaign, while his underlings issued "smear" pamphlets against Brown, as Brown's people did against him, Nixon busily defended Brown's courage and Americanism by raising the spectres of his opponent's cowardice and un-Americanism and then by denying them. But Nixon's protestation seems to be his single conscious equivocation in the press conference. That he was momentarily capable of deliberate cunning may have an explanation: he was, at that moment, concentrating on Brown rather than on himself; few men, even in the worst of times, are completely irrational.

"You gentlemen didn't report it, but I am proud that I did that. I am proud also that I defended the fact that he was a man of good motive, a man that I disagreed with very strongly, but a man of good motives.

"I want that—for once, gentlemen—I would appreciate if you would write what I say, in that respect. I think it's very important that you write in—in the lead—*in the lead*." If the journalists had heeded him, this would have been the headline over the story of the press conference: NIXON DEFENDS GOVERNOR'S REPUTATION, DENIES BROWN COWARD OR COMMUNIST. Although a few newspapers might have indeed run such headlines, painting Nixon as a defender of the faith, the speaker's insistent and spurious defense of Governor Brown was hardly the lead to the story, as Nixon, even in his confusion, must have realized. If, once more, the newspapers bypassed the important story, the Nixon image once more would have been spared; the important story was Nixon's antagonistic behavior.

"Now, I don't mean by that, incidentally, all of you. There's one reporter here who has religiously, when he was covering me—and, incidentally, *this is no reflection on the others, because some of you, you know, weren't bothered*. One reporter, Carl Greenberg—he's the only reporter on the [Los Angeles] *Times* that fits this thing, who wrote every word that I said. He wrote it fairly. He wrote it objectively. I don't mean that the others didn't have the right to do it differently. But, Carl, despite whatever feelings he had, felt that he had an obligation to report the facts as he saw them." *Some of you, you know, weren't bothered*—by what? The ambiguity itself radiates anger; the reporters weren't bothered about him but he was bothered by them. It's almost as if Nixon

80

were bothered by their lack of religious zeal. Only Greenberg treated his word as gospel, every bit of it worth writing down and reporting, he suggests, even as he adds that Greenberg may have hated him like all the rest. He complimented Greenberg for writing "objectively" and for writing "the facts as he saw them." What this contradiction obviously means is that by writing down every word, Greenberg was presenting the facts *as Nixon saw them*, and to Nixon, that equates with objectivity, an irrational belief that carries over even into his rational moments.

During the campaign Greenberg also covered Brown, and Mark Harris indicates his reporting technique: Brown came to Los Banos, California, to deliver a prepared text that had been released to the press hours earlier. In fact, Greenberg had already written his story, based on the release, and had wired it back to the *Times*. But Brown fooled all of the reporters by delivering instead a discursive, extemporaneous speech that didn't resemble the advance handout. Greenberg was being forced to kill the story he had written in advance, making him "disconsolate" according to Harris. Harris claims he argued with Greenberg "into the night" to persuade him to report what Brown had actually said, not merely kill what he hadn't said, since the extemporaneous speech revealed Brown's unrehearsed self: "Greenberg seemed to be saying it was the Governor's responsibility to honor the prepared address, that somehow the event was less important than the report in the press." If that was Greenberg's technique all the time, no wonder it pleased Nixon, whose prepared texts reveal less of himself than his off-the-cuff remarks, as now:

"*I am saying these things* about the press because I understand that *that was one of the things you were particularly interested in. There'll be no questions* at this point *on that score.*" Again that ambiguous hostility: he was attacking them, he explained, only because they had allegedly *asked* for the truth about themselves but now, if they asked him to justify the attack, he would refuse to. He would be petulant instead: "I'll be glad to answer *other* questions."

Nixon then applauded his volunteer workers: "It was a magnificent group . . . Our hundred thousand workers I was

81

proud of. I think they did a magnificent job." Nixon now reached what he obviously had a compulsion to say all the time: "I only wish they could have gotten out a few more votes in the key precincts, but *because they didn't, Mr. Brown has won and I have lost the election.*" The bitterness reached out and touched the people who were supposedly on his own side. The thing Nixon said proved inadvertently true: the reporters were so absorbed by his attack on them they largely ignored Nixon's attack on Brown and totally ignored his ill-will toward Republican party workers. After attempting to damage their reputation a little bit, Nixon rapidly moved on to other election results. He admitted he knew nothing about the Congressional returns at that early moment, but it was clearly safer ground. He even deferred to the reporters by asking them for the results. Nixon was only sure of one thing: victories by Rockefeller in New York, Scranton in Pennsylvania, Rhodes in Ohio and Romney in Michigan would revitalize the Republican party for the 1964 Presidential elections.

"Now it will be revitalized, of course, *provided the Republicans in California* [he couldn't stay off the backs of these others who had failed him] *also can* [sic] *under new leadership —not mine—*because I have fought the fight and now it's up to others to take this responsibility of leadership, and *I don't say this with any bitterness because I feel that's the way it should be.* [You magnificent workers didn't do it for me; maybe you'll be more willing to do it for the next guy.]

"But when you look at New York and Pennsylvania, Ohio and Michigan and the solid Republican midwest, 1964 is a horse race," he said in his third but not quite final reproach of his supporters. Then Nixon came to a fourth irksome fact —Jack Kennedy's popularity: "*I say this with no indication that I don't think that President Kennedy has immense popularity—at the moment—*popularity which came out as a result of his handling of the Cuban situation." The same situation that he claimed as far back as three weeks ago would defeat him in California, although obviously it would not defeat Rockefeller, Rhodes, Romney or Scranton.

In this oblique way, Nixon alone was running against Kennedy, again, and setting the stage, one thinks, for a defense of his loss to Kennedy in 1960. Peculiarly, "with *no* indication that I *don't* think" illustrates how two negatives in defiance of the rule end up, in impact, as nothing but a third negative. Of course, the obvious translation deserves a hearing: Kennedy's popularity was transient, built on a bit of luck that would be meaningless by the next election and, as a result, Nixon was saying, the Republicans would beat him in 1964. On that basis, the remark sounds like the typical and reasonable rallying cry of a practical politician. But, unfortunately, Nixon's mood that morning was not reasonable, so instead it may be Nixon was reassuring himself that Kennedy's popularity was insufficient to have beaten him. Kennedy couldn't have won, he implied, except by trickery. "My little daughter Tricia," Nixon had said the previous May when it seemed he had trouble wiping the Kennedy defeat from his mind, "says she doesn't blame the people who voted for him; she blames the ones who counted the votes in Chicago."

Little Tricia was sixteen, but out of the mouths of babes . . . In his book, Nixon has Julie, his younger daughter, making the accusation. He quoted her as saying that Kennedy stole not only Illinois but Texas as well and that her father should never talk to Kennedy again because he had been a nasty campaigner.

By 1964, Nixon said, Julie was only joking; but he could not have been amused; shortly after winning his second nomination for the Presidency in 1968, he took an elaborate and extraordinary precaution. In August, he enlisted Louis B. Nichols, a former high-ranking FBI man, and a one hundred thousand-member volunteer "army" to stop the Democrats from robbing Nixon of the Presidency twice.[1]

Elaborate precautions do make sense, because elections *are* stolen; perhaps even the election of 1960, as Nixon says, was stolen. The relevant question, however, is why Nixon alleged that Kennedy's popularity was transient: was Nixon, the politician, providing a rallying cry for Republicans in 1964 or was Nixon, the loser, seeking out another oblique rationalization of his defeats in 1960 and 1962? If Nixon could even half convince himself, in his sour, confused state, that Kennedy

[1] In 1969, Nichols, writing for *Reader's Digest*, explained that the effort to stop vote fraud was called "Operation Integrity."

had not beaten him honestly in 1960, then certainly Nixon could half convince himself that Brown's luck, not Nixon's lack of popularity, had beaten him in 1962. It became clearer within a paragraph that he *had* to impugn Kennedy, if merely to prove himself the better man:

"But, on the other hand, now the problems arise," he lectured. "What will happen in Cuba? *Can we allow the cancer of Communism to stay there* . . . Are we going to continue any kind of an agreement in Cuba, *which means that Khrushchev got what we said we would never agree to* . . . and that is, in effect, ringing down an Iron Curtain around Cuba. These are the things that Mr. Kennedy, of course, will have to face up to, and I just hope—and I am confident that if he has his own way he will face up to them . . . if he can just keep [the "wooly heads," was Nixon's expression] away from him and stand strong and firm with that good Irish fight of his, America will be in good shape in foreign policy."

Was Nixon hinting that Kennedy was selling out the country to Communism (which would have been a totally inexcusable charge considering Kennedy's blockade of Cuba)? Garry Wills thinks he was, but "again aware of danger," writes Wills, "he withdraws: Kennedy is all right." Instead of attacking dangerously, Nixon had found that he could express his hostility for the winner in 1960 by patronizing him: If Jack could learn to stand strong and firm and face up to things, he might turn out all right.

"Domestically—I'm answering these questions because I know that some of you will ask them—domestically, the economy needs to get going again. The Cuban thing, of course, has a tendency to obscure that." Nixon jumped suddenly from Kennedy and Cuba to government contracts and California. "A lot of defense contracts have come into California and other areas. *I'm not complaining about it. That's the way the political game is played.*"

Nixon plainly meant that the government (i.e. Jack Kennedy and the Democrats) had deliberately put defense money into California to beat the Republicans and, in his frame of mind, perhaps Nixon in particular. But what is more startling is the juxtaposition: was he saying also that the President had somehow arranged the Cuban crisis to frustrate Nixon *politically* in California? Is there another way to explain the abrupt jump from one Administration action to another? In any case, Nixon *was* complaining.

He spoke for a short time about moving forward economically and sneaked in (the press was still on his mind) a totally unrelated plug for Ed Tetlow of the London *Telegraph*, the one other reporter in the room Nixon seemed to feel had been fair to him.

"One last thing," he said the first of three times. "What are my plans? Well, my plans are to go home. I'm going to get acquainted with my family again. [Good; a good, safe traditional ploy, not without its appeal, either.] And my plans, incidentally, are from a political standpoint, of course, to take a holiday. It will be a long holiday." An enforced holiday. "*I don't say this with any sadness.* I couldn't feel, frankly, more—well, frankly . . ." When Nixon begins "frankly," or "candidly," or starts by making things "clear" as he did compulsively throughout the 1968 campaign, confusion is bound to follow. It may be, as Mark Harris says, that Nixon lacks the ability to hold two opposed ideas in his mind at the same time; it may be especially true when Nixon is groping for a second idea that can offset the humiliation and hostility of the first idea. ". . . Well, frankly, proud of my staff for the campaign they helped me put on. [Why should I be sad? *They* were the ones who lost the election.] We campaigned against great odds. We fought a good fight."

The cliches seemed to have a reassuring effect on Nixon; he was swept up momentarily by the sound of them, and became courageous: "We didn't win, *and I take the responsibility for any mistakes.*" That sounded so manly and decent, but he couldn't resist ruining that image, too: "As far as they're concerned, they're magnificent people, and I hope whoever next runs California will look at my staff and take *some* of these people—*use* them—because they are—they are great political *properties*, shall we say, putting it in the—in a very materialistic way." By demoting them from people to properties, Nixon simultaneously reduced their worth, their humanity.

"*One last thing*: people say, what about the *past*? What about losing in '60 and losing in '64? [sic]." It seems his mind couldn't stop running from one defeat to the next.

85

"I remember somebody on my last television program said, 'Mr. Nixon, isn't it a comedown, having run for President and almost made it, to run for Governor?' And the answer is I'm proud to have run for Governor. Now, I would like to have won. But not having won, the main thing was that I *battled*—battled for the things I believed in.

"*I did not win. I have no hard feelings against anybody, against any opponent and least of all the people of California.* We got our message through as well as we could. *The Cuban thing did not enable us to get it through in the two critical weeks that we wanted to,* but nevertheless we got it through and it is the people's choice."

Just as he had lectured Kennedy, he now would lecture Brown on becoming "more decisive" in order to move the state ahead, "economically, morally and spiritually, so that we can have character and self-reliance in this country. This is what we need . . ."

"*One last thing* [actually one last thing for the last time]: At the outset I said a couple of things with regard to the press that I noticed some of you looked a little irritated about. And *my philosophy* with regard to the press has really never gotten through. And I want to get it through—

"I believe a reporter has got a right to write it as he feels it. I believe if a reporter believes that one man ought to win, rather than the other, whether it's on television or radio, say so. *I will say to the reporters some times that I think well, look, I wish you'd give my opponent the same going over that you give me.*

"And as I leave the press, all I can say is this: for sixteen years, ever since the Hiss case [which was fourteen years earlier; as if he willed to turn things around, he said at another point in the campaign, fourteen when he meant sixteen], *you've had a lot of fun—a lot of fun—that you've had an opportunity to attack me and I think I've given as much as I've taken.* [I.e. I'm just as much of a man as any of you.] It was carried right up to the last day: I made a flub—*one of the few that I make,* not because I'm so good on television but because I've done it a long time. I made a flub in which I said I was running for Governor of the United States. The Los Angeles *Times* dutifully reported that." Presumably, he did not mean Carl Greenberg.

"Mr. Brown, the last day made a flub—a flub, incidentally, to the great credit of television that was reported—*I don't say this bitterly*—in which he said, 'I hope everybody wins. You vote the straight Democratic ticket, including Senator Kuchel.' I was glad to hear him say it, because I was for Kuchel all the way. [Kuchel was a liberal Republican who won.] The Los Angeles *Times* did not report it.

"I think it's time that our great newspapers have at least the same objectivity, the same fullness of coverage, that television has. And I can only thank God for television and radio for keeping the newspapers a little more honest. [By the late sixties, his administration repeatedly would attack television.]

". . . I want newspapers, if they are against a candidate, to say it. [Nixon cited several American newspapers which were against him.] I believe they should say it. *I don't mind reporters saying it.* I would hope that in the future, as a result of this campaign, that they would try at least simply to see that what both candidates say is reported, that *if they have questions to ask of one candidate, they ask the same questions of the other candidates.*" In other words, Nixon didn't think they ever teased Kennedy or Brown the way they teased—and persecuted—him; they had their fun, but it's all over because now he was dealing:

"The last play [sic]. I leave you gentlemen now and you will now write it. You will interpret it. That's your right. But as I leave you I want you to know [he would taunt them with his absence]—just think about how much you're going to be missing:

"You won't have Nixon to kick around any more, because, gentlemen, this will be my last press conference and it will be one in which I have welcomed the opportunity to test wits with you. I have always respected you. I have sometimes disagreed with you.

"But unlike some people," he laughed, "I've never cancelled my subscription to a paper and also I never will." That was yet another swipe at Kennedy, who as everyone in the room knew, had cancelled the White House subscription to the New York *Herald-Tribune* because he didn't like what they wrote about his administration. So, Nixon was admitting it: the newspapers *did* attack others besides him. As for his never having cancelled a subscription, it was technically true and absolutely meaningless because, if not then, Nixon would eventually stop reading newspapers and watching tv news; as President he prefers them predigested and capsulized by the White House staff, as much to spare himself the agony, he ultimately confessed, as to save himself the time. Yet he would argue:

"I believe in reading what my opponents say, and I hope that what I have said today will at least make television, radio [so they were not absolved after all], the press first recognize the great responsibility they have to report *all the news* and, second, recognize that they have a right and a responsibility, if they're against a candidate, *give him the shaft*." It seemed like an order to his own firing squad. "But also recognize if they give him the shaft," he smiled, "put one lonely reporter on the campaign who will report what the candidate says now and then."

The smile disappeared. "Thank you, gentlemen, and good day."

It was the fall after the fall.

While other politicians, many of them Presidents, lost their tempers—Wilson, Kennedy, Truman, Eisenhower, Lyndon Johnson, Franklin Roosevelt—and while Wilson, Roosevelt and Johnson, and Abe Lincoln too, had their own mental and emotional problems—none had ever exploded in quite this way. Nixon's performance, says Wills, "had a stingy and secretive air . . . it was not irony that made the thing oblique; it was the *unwilled* [italics added] automatic baffling of *any* move on his part. He does not know how to break down." Wills's contributions to the understanding of the last press conference are, with this exception, uneasy. Nixon did not scream or bellow or tear his hair but, for all intents and purposes, he had broken down. "When you are not at one with yourself in a given matter," as Carl Jung said in lecturing on complexes, "you are approaching a neurotic condition." Is there any doubt on that morning that Richard Nixon was not at one with himself?

More in admiration than criticism, biographers Earl Mazo and Stephen Hess imply that Richard Nixon puts one over on everybody with *Six Crises*. His very theme, they say, is "something of a gimmick." Mazo and Hess come from the faintly sniggering school which sees Nixon's crises as exaggerated post-mortems that their favourite politician holds up—like an Olympic torch—as symbols of suffering, perseverance and finally conquest.

But William Costello views Nixon's 1962 autobiography as a "stark revelation of the restless, frustrated, diffident psyche" wrapping itself in a "cloak of masochism . . . never unaware of nameless, faceless enemies waiting to pounce."

Such conflicting opinions leave the widespread impressions Nixon is either very clever, always capable of keeping his public off balance, or that his book is a litmus test, to be colored in accordance with one's prejudices. But if Nixon's public is confused, it may be because Nixon too is confused. He was as ambivalent in his motives for writing *Six Crises* as he was for involving himself in the crises, themselves. Part of Nixon was self-serving: he wanted to advertise himself; part of Nixon was self-destructive: he was unsure whether he was worth advertising. The book illustrates the point clearly.

Begun after his loss to Kennedy, *Six Crises* offers highly principled motives for each of his disputes: with Hiss and Khrushchev because they were deceitful and threatened freedom; with the Republican Party and the Republican President (The crisis was not Eisenhower's heart attack, but Nixon's struggle for Eisenhower's recognition.) because they were misled by amateurs who did not know their politics; with the mobs in South America because they were misled by professionals who knew their politics only too well; with Kennedy in the debates because the American voter willed it.

However, even as Nixon seeks to prove in print that his anxieties result *from* crisis situations, the idea emerges— though the author tries censoring it—that Nixon's anxieties result *in* crisis situations.

Nixon, as a reporter for *The London News Chronicle* once observed, always feels "on trial" and must therefore put himself to the test again and again. What emerges is courage in the attempt and cowardice in the execution: having put himself on trial, Nixon is okay until he has to face the jury, at which time he begins dodging and retreating while, at the same time, trying to appear straightforward and manly. The verdict Nixon inevitably hears is that the defendant looks guilty as hell and more than slightly foolish.

The man who later told a reporter he thinks it a waste of time psychoanalyzing one's self explains in the introduction to *Six Crises*: "What I have tried to do is distill out of my experience a few general principles on the 'crisis syndrome.'" Even on the verge of launching into a crude self-analysis, Nixon is already backing away—putting · sanitary quotes around the two words to dissociate himself from their infected definition: the aggregate symptoms of a disease at its severest moment.

Allowing himself to be guided by Northwestern University political scientists then engaged in studying "crisis behavior," Nixon poses these questions as the foundation of his autobiography:

Is it possible to be rational in crisis situations? Can he separate "empirical" and factual matters from his own "emotional reactions"? Do his crises have several elements in common? Does he feel exhilaration or enjoyment during crisis? Do crises teach him anything about his own "basic strengths" or "personal weaknesses"? Is he relieved from anxiety and tension when the crisis is over?

Significantly, he had undertaken *Six Crises*—both the book and the situations—to prove that he was a man to be taken seriously. Yet having raised the questions for "a better understanding of that intriguing and vitally important subject," Nixon could not face the answers. The more he squirmed, the stranger he seemed, until the book took on the flavor of *Alice Through the Looking Glass*: incorrigibly perverse. As the reader confronts each of Nixon's crises in retrospect, he also recognizes Nixon's inability to cope. Time and again, a basic, self-punishing vestige of honesty restrains Nixon from turning a defeat into a victory or from manufacturing majesty out of frayed nerve ends.

Nixon says in the book that he is never nervous while thinking through the foregone conclusion about how to advance on the enemy. Rather, the decision-making process generates "almost unbearable tension," which keeps building until he feels he must explode. But Nixon, says Nixon, does not explode. During the battle he remains "coldly objective": he cannot eat or sleep and he "blows his stack" instead. Then at the end, when the battle is won, *only then*, does the "most dangerous period" begin. After the "Checkers" speech, for example, he collapses into a state of self-pity and near hysteria. He cannot understand what more Eisenhower, whom he alternately characterizes as devious and straightforward, complex and simple, steely and warm, wants from him and must be restrained by the resident wise men (Murray Chotiner and Rose Mary Woods, his secretary) from quitting politics on the spot. What results is the chronic Nixon aftermath, in which exhaustion deprives him, he says, of "the necessary cushion of emotional and mental reserve." He has a rather delicate name for the period of his "greatest danger," a "letdown." His letdown dissipated rapidly after the "Checkers" business, but it seems to go on forever after the Hiss matter. Writing the Hiss chapter for *Six Crises*, he still hears the whispers of judgment and feels the "residue of hatred and hostility toward me." With the clatter of battle in the past, the real crisis begins. Now, in the silence, Nixon has altogether too much time to contemplate the overriding question he dares not ask in his foreword but which (regardless of how many different ways he phrases it) ends every chapter of his book and most chapters of his life: *Have I failed me?*

Therefore, when Nixon says that writing *Six Crises* became his seventh, it was neither the cheap literary conceit his enemies thought it to be nor the clever "gimmick" his friends saw it as. It *was* Nixon's next crisis—once more precipitated by himself. As with each of his other crises, he created for himself a new source of derision when his conscious purpose had been to create exactly the opposite. Mark Harris said: "Nobody had ever warned [Nixon] that the enunciation of a world view toward the end of private ambition was a torture of credibility which the English language would never contain. Under sufficient, prolonged exposure his reason was bound by stages to fade and vanish."

Six Crises was as much a bafflement to Nixon as any of the other crises he had authored. His problem can be articulated in language fans of *Alice* might appreciate: *Richard Nixon must proclaim his great schemes are selfless while insinuating,*

boastfully, that they are self-serving, because underneath he
suspects that they are trivial and self-destructive.

Rather than blame himself, Nixon has to find enemies to blame for the failures of his character. Arthur Schlesinger Jr. some years ago said, "One has the uneasy feeling [that Nixon] is always on the verge of pronouncing himself the victim of some clandestine plot."

There was, first, Nixon the boy. His knack for discovering illusory enemies existed long before he entered politics and even before he had reached chronological maturity. As a high school sophomore, Nixon made a speech defending the Constitution of the United States against "a great wave of indifference to [its] authority, disrespect of its law, and opposition to its basic principles [which] threatens its very foundations." Fifteen-year-old Richard asked, "Shall we of the present generation allow this instrument to be cast into disrepute? Shall we be responsible for its downfall?" Donald Jackson, of *Life*, exhumed the speech which won for Nixon a public speaking prize of thirty dollars. Jackson detected signs of the Nixon who, even in boyhood, "perceived a grave but unspecified threat . . . An invisible army of disbelievers was out there, and young Richard was at war against them."

Classmates first in high school, later in college, gave clues to more concrete enemies. The following anonymous item appeared in his high school newspaper: "Nothing is *funnier* [emphasis added] than to call Richard Nixon 'Nicky' and watch him bristle. I did it once and he was too surprised to speak, if you can imagine Nixon inarticulate." His putative high school sweetheart claimed Nixon did not know how to be "personable or sexy." People were always picking on him for his personality, and even when he got out of high school, it was the same. A college classmate told Stewart Alsop: "Dick sensed his 'unpopularity' among his friends who thought he was not entirely a 'regular guy' by going out for football. He was trying to overcome a psychological factor which he and all of us knew—he wasn't meant to be a football player."

The collective image afforded by classmates is not of a sissy but rather of an awkward, seething youngster, constantly trying to impress his peers and rarely succeeding. His habit as a boy was to strike out at enemies who were faceless, nameless and could not strike back.

But Nixon, himself, gave the clues to an earlier and more basic source of pain than even his classmates. Richard was afraid of his father Frank. "I learned early," Nixon has said, "that the only way to deal with him was to abide by the rules." His brothers had been strapped for less. At seventeen, Nixon remembered that his parents had tried to turn his infant brother Arthur into a girl: "to make him one as much as possible" by forcing him to grow long hair, thus giving the child "grief." This parental outrage against a dead baby brother had been invoked to illustrate another point, or so it was meant to appear. In a high school essay ostensibly about godless college students, Nixon asserted that despite his parents' cruel treatment of Arthur, the baby never lost his love of God: Two days before Arthur's death, Richard came upon him reciting the Lord's Prayer.

Beginning with his parents, other people have always brought Nixon "grief." He cannot get along with people and in moments of bitter self-recognition, openly admits the fact. "If the time ever comes when the Republican Party and the *others* [emphasis added] are looking for an outwardly warm, easygoing, gregarious type," he said in 1958, "then *they will not* want the sort of man I am." That remark resounds with combativeness. He is challenging his jury—both those on it he can identify and particularly those he can't. He resents them for judging his fate, even though he has put himself in their hands.

In his career, Nixon has offered many justifications for his unpopularity. As the Vice-President, he said, "In my job you can't enjoy the luxury of intimate personal friendships. You can't confide in absolutely anyone about your personal plans, or personal feelings." Alben Barkley, Lyndon Johnson, Hubert Humphrey, Harry Truman, to name a few Vice-Presidents, did not surrender the luxury of intimate personal friendships, possibly because the Vice-Presidency leaves more time for personal and private pursuits than any other job in government. A Vice-President has no real function other than what the President gives him, and, to Nixon, Eisenhower gave little—certainly little that he might have had to keep secret from the friends he didn't have.

93

Another justification for his unpopularity is his politics. Democrats hate his politics; reporters hate his politics; even "intellectuals" hate his politics. "Many," he said of intellectuals when he was running in 1968, "have a double standard. If you happen to support their point of view you can be a drunk, a stupe, fall on your face in a press conference . . ." (Nixon seemed to be referring to his own press conference of 1962.) Possibly the few times in his life when Nixon was able to identify with an intellectual was when that particular one was *also* under attack. For example, Nixon told Jules Witcover that when he had a decision to make, he liked to sit "on his rear end and dig into the books. In this respect I'm like [Adlai] Stevenson. He was criticized," Nixon observed, because as an intellectual "he needed time to contemplate."

Nixon has also said he is an introvert in an extrovert's business—which is a fact, but it raises a deep question: Why choose a career that brings with it such agony? Nixon may have entered politics to win or to develop a base of power toward which esteem automatically flows. But considering his capacity for punishing himself, he may have instinctively chosen politics because it is the career where he can constantly put himself to the test and where he can fail even when he seems to be succeeding.

Or, finally, perhaps Nixon has stuck to politics—despite his wife's wishes and his own fears—because it enables a man afraid of intimacy to reduce friendship to a business commodity and inflate a personality trait for creating enemies into a political necessity.

This is where Nixon's "principles" become important. His anti-intellectualism, obsession with lawless mobs, nationalism, espousal of wars for peace, his faith in the profit motive[1]

[1] Judd Marmor, clinical professor of psychiatry at the University of California, Los Angeles campus, sees free enterprise's competitive ethic, nationalism and wars of justice as the three "sacred cows" that will destroy us all. Together, they have become "seriously maladaptive in terms of [man's] survival." He doesn't think the pathological cases among us—the "defectives," he calls them—are as dangerous as the "normal" people who worship these cows. The fact that average citizens feel the same way, however, makes it infinitely easier for the neurotic to assert that the causes are just and therefore worth dying for.

and his sense of a Communist conspiracy are convenient pandemic principles on which he can feed his instinct for aggression. But he does not always use them for that purpose. He even seems capable of setting them aside for conscious political advantage—until they are opposed.

In his lifelong preoccupation with himself, Richard Nixon has found challenges degrading, as if the smallest doubt were somehow a jeer.

CHAPTER TEN

Pat Brown was wrong to charge that Nixon wanted the California State House in Sacramento as a launching pad for a second Presidential bid in 1964; according to Jules Witcover, "Nixon actually had hoped to use it as a four-year hiding place" so he wouldn't have to run "another losing race against Kennedy." Though Witcover's novel theory gives Nixon less credit as a politician than Brown's, it still does not take into account the quintessential Nixon, who in running from danger generally finds new and self-destructive places to run.

After his humiliation in California, a sound job and an unsound instinct pushed him toward New York City, which harbored more potential Nixon enemies than any other place in the country. It was the media and intellectual mecca of America, hardly a congenial kind of capital for Nixon. But he gave the usual reason: "New York is a very cold and very ruthless and very exciting and therefore an interesting place to live. The main thing, it is a place where you can't slow down—a fast track." It was the town where a famous out-of-work candidate could capitalize on his stature and make more money than he'd ever seen in his life as a politician, and consequently, Elmer Bobst, the chairman of Warner-Lambert and a Dutch uncle to Nixon, along with other millionaires who backed him in 1960, advised him to go east. The first thought they had, as they contemplated Nixon's future while sunning in Florida on Bobst's yacht, *Ailsa V*, was that he should join the venerable investment banking house Eastman, Dillon. Then, the story goes, Bobst was reminded that after losing in 1948, Tom Dewey went into law. Law, practised in a dignified New York firm, often leads back into politics.

After a scouting expedition, Nixon's chief career counsellor Bobst decided on Mudge, Stern, Baldwin & Todd, the distinguished middle-sized house which handled the Warner-Lambert legal business, rumored to be worth about $800,000 per annum. In 1963 Mudge, Stern, Baldwin and Todd became Nixon, Mudge, Rose, Guthrie and Alexander, Nixon automatically rising from a thirty-five-thousand-dollar-a-year Vice-President to a two-hundred-thousand-a-year lawyer with a private practice and one client, Warner-Lambert.

A few weeks after Nixon's arrival, a photographer spotted him idling on a Manhattan street corner. The next morning the papers were plastered with a picture of Richard Nixon surrounded by pedestrians, seemingly totally indifferent to his presence. The caption was: "Nixon, the Forgotten Man." Nixon got on the phone to the Associated Press. The people were not looking at him, he insisted, because they were waiting for the light to change. Here was Nixon who had barely walked out on the fast track for a few warm-up knee-bends— only to find the spectators showing more interest in the starting gun than the star runner. What hurt was that the press had humiliated him again.

In fact, they had started working him over weeks before he officially admitted he was moving to New York. In March (four months after the California election), Nixon called in the metropolitan press to show he held no grudges and they dutifully asked the question reporters ask of former Presidential candidates: What did he think of President Kennedy's policies?[1] And he said, "If I were President Nixon . . ." Answering the second question, he said, "If I were President Nixon . . ." Tom Glennon of WCBS-TV said, "You mean, sir, if *you* were President Kennedy."

There was a brief pause before Nixon rebelled: "*I know exactly what I mean.*" Mechanically, another question was asked and the victim, following a familiar path of deterioration, began to sputter, and sweat broke out on his upper lip and forehead. When some reporter asked him whether he considered New York City a new base for his political operations, Nixon, at least two reporters agree, became "all but catatonic."

[1] The following, extracted from a pitifully frail volume called *The Wit and Humor of Richard Nixon*, may have been uttered at the same conference, but no one can remember for sure: "The Kennedy Administration is brilliant from the standpoint of salesmanship, brilliant from the standpoint of public relations, but the product doesn't live up to the words."

It was moments like this which sent him back to Arnold Hutschnecker for treatment for emotional problems that may not have been quite as amusing as his old psychosomatic pains. Nixon came (reportedly at the urging of his wife) even before the Nixons took up residence in New York.

In 1964, less than two years after Harriet Van Horne witnessed Nixon entering Hutschnecker's Park Avenue office, the doctor published *The Will To Happiness*. Among other tales, the book contained the case history of a tax man who bore, perhaps by purest coincidence, a striking resemblance to Nixon. According to the doctor, there was this unhappy housewife whose husband's chronic emotionalism had destroyed his career. The patient-to-be was a former trial lawyer who had been disbarred by "the judge," according to Hutschnecker, after repeated warnings to stop losing his temper in court.[1] The lawyer had been unable to stop. Now his temper was doing the same thing to their marriage, so she insisted her husband go see the psychotherapist. But first she entered Hutschnecker's office, to warn him that her husband was so violently hypersensitive, and presumably reluctant, that the least provocation by the doctor might well be "fatal" to successful treatment.

The patient was rather "fatalistic" about his temper and in explaining himself to the psychotherapist he said, "It is the Irish in my blood." But the patient gave a less ethnic reason too: he could not tolerate "injustice," even in court. It left him raging and fuming. "There is," he philosophized, "a great deal of injustice in the world, and it will only grow stronger unless it is vigorously opposed. A man must have *principle* [emphasis added] if he wants to retain self-respect.

---

[1] Although there may be exceptions, legal experts characterize it "highly unlikely" that one judge or any group of judges, for that matter, will disbar a lawyer for even the most grievous and repetitious outbursts in a courtroom. Many lawyers have been fined, censured, suspended for that kind of behavior, but eventually they were permitted to practice once more. As a rule, only the bar association will disbar a member for some flagrant violation of the legal canons, one of which is not a bad temper. Like all doctors who publish case histories, Dr. Hutschnecker does disguise facts to protect his patients and because he's a physician and not a lawyer, he may merely have been cavalier about this detail.

Fighting for a principle may get one into a lot of trouble, but losing self-respect is the end and about the worst thing that can happen to a man."

But Hutschnecker was not impressed with his patient's glib excuses for the tragedy. Presumably after some digging, the doctor found a likelier origin: the patient had had an evil-tempered father whose voice alone "could stir his blood." As a boy, the patient repressed the urge to fight his father, simmering inwardly even as he decided never to let anyone else bully him like that. Hutschnecker analyzed that beneath all the talk of principle "there was a neurotic tendency to quarrel/*and*/he did not know that he was motivated by a militant need *to oppose* any type of rebellion." Hutschnecker further found that his patient's explosive hostility released him of terrible tensions and, in a way, that was good. But unfortunately the patient's conflicts with "external" obstacles (i.e., the judge) forced him out of the one meaningful career in his life, courtroom law, into advising people on how to save on taxes which, Hutschnecker suggests, the patient considered an ignoble commercial occupation.

Only days before being spotted going into Hutschnecker's office, Nixon, too, had become a tax man. Though underlings in the law firm would do the work, as Bobst evidently conceived it, Nixon would oversee the taxes and other commercial problems of his one client, Warner-Lambert.

In 1964, ostensibly travelling the world for Pepsi Cola, his second and only other personal client, Nixon quickly finished off some business in Finland and, on an impulse, took a twenty-hour train trip in order to make an unscheduled stop in Moscow. He arrived fairly late in the evening and, sometime after 11 p.m., he was on the street seeking out his old adversary Nikita Khrushchev, who was no longer the Premier of Russia, but nobody answered at Khrushchev's modest apartment.

Within the day, a transparently frustrated private American citizen was scouring the Russian capital for new debating partners. He argued loudly with the deputy director of Moscow State University about a wide range of topics. He also accosted a Moscow policeman and, according to *Pravda*, asked him stupid questions. Nixon then stopped strangers on the street, inviting them with somewhat forced amiability to be his guest. The Communist newspaper called it "a real clown's act."

Within months, he exposed himself to similar ridicule at home. In July, Nixon made his way to the San Francisco National Republican Convention of 1964 as a man without a campaign organization of his own and very little chance of upsetting Barry Goldwater, who controlled the conservative bloc which in turn controlled the convention. Nixon, who said he was not running but implied that he would not reject a draft, knew the only way he could possibly come out of the convention as the nominee was to act as the impartial senior statesman of the Republican Party and hope that the liberal Scranton, Romney and Rockefeller factions could wrest enough strength from Goldwater to create a deadlock and the need for a compromise candidate. It was the logical role for the nominal party leader and former Presidential candidate. The man in the middle had nothing more to lose and possibly everything to gain by keeping his cool.

Instead, he summoned the press soon after arriving in San Francisco and said that Goldwater was a "reasonable man" and not, as Nixon rather gratuitously put it, "some kind of nut, a jerk, a wild man." Goldwater men auditing the press conference blanched. Reporters, remembering bygone days, blushed with embarrassment. Witcover said this moment perfectly illustrated Nixon's talent for advancing "the opposition's work." Then Nixon went on to make the Republican governors squirm too. After a few "inane" opening remarks at their caucus, the non-candidate awkwardly announced that questions were welcome. There was silence. A governor told columnists Evans and Novak, "Nixon was waiting for us to ask him to run for President. It was unbelievable, just unbelievable." Others felt he was more pathetic than unbelievable.

Members of his own party repudiated him to his face. For example, he turned to William Scranton of Pennsylvania, a candidate with little chance of capturing the nomination (although a slightly better chance than Nixon) and began a non-stop monologue, the essence of which seemed to be that "somebody else" should be nominated instead of Goldwater.

Scranton listened until he could no longer contain himself. He turned on Nixon and said something to the effect of "Dick, if you want to run for President, why don't you just go ahead and run." Their meeting ended abruptly.

Scranton later explained, "[Nixon] went on and on, and that was what disturbed me." Then a Republican tactician from New York told Nixon that the nomination "is gone" and, according to Witcover, added that if Nixon did not stop standing around in the pathetic posture of a mendicant, "You'll make a fool of yourself." This belated advice only angered Nixon further.

But after Goldwater's defeat, Nixon almost looked like a winner. Many Republicans began comparing Goldwater's disastrous loss to Johnson with Nixon's marginal loss to Kennedy, and when Nixon came to visit, they received him as the real party leader. He also had the esteem of law partners who delighted in the prestige Nixon's name lent their firm. Perhaps equal to these circumstances in their positive effect on his ego was the fact that the press had stopped taking potshots at him.

One reason, according to David Broder of *The Washington Post*, was that there was a whole new crop of reporters who had no first-hand knowledge of the "Checkers" speech, the Hiss case or Nixon's behavior in the 1960 Presidential race. Except for a man permanently assigned by the Associated Press (which figured as early as 1966 that he was a viable candidate for 1968), the reporters passed in and out of his life like so many transients, interested in Nixon yet not devoted to the subject; like the members of the Republican Party, they were frequently flattered to be in the presence of a man who had once run for the Presidency of the United States.

By 1966, all of this, perhaps along with Nixon's visits to Hutschnecker, kept Nixon's ego at safe levels. But even though there was a total absence of anger in his observable behavior, he'd do something every now and again to hint that certain battle lines were still drawn in his mind.

For instance, his only courtroom appearance for Nixon, Mudge was in a case against a representative of the press. It was in 1966 and he defended before the U.S. Supreme Court a judgment handed down by the New York courts in favor of James J. Hill, a client who had won thirty thousand dollars from Time, Inc. in 1963.

Hill had charged *Life*, a Time, Inc. magazine, with invading his family privacy through a picture story about the play "The Desperate Hours," which was a fictionalization of the Hills' experience as hostages of three escaped convicts. When the Time, Inc. appeal reached the Supreme Court, Nixon decided he was the right man in the firm to be the magazine's adversary. In his oral argument, Nixon noted that if the Time, Inc. appeal were upheld, it would license "every scandal sheet in the country . . . to lie about individuals for the purpose of trade." But lying was not the issue; the issue was invasion of privacy, and the Supreme Court rejected Nixon's fervent appeal five to four.

One day in March, 1966, Lady Bird Johnson walked into her husband's room in the White House and discovered Nixon sitting there, "relaxed, affable and well tailored." He was telling Johnson, "You know this is a campaign year and I'll be getting out, speaking up for the Republicans." Then he eagerly volunteered, "But there won't be anything personal about you in what I say about the Democratic Administration."

That fall, however, after Johnson held a heavily-publicized meeting with South Vietnam's leaders in Manila, Nixon charged the President with grandstanding so that Democrats could win an election. Johnson, whose hypersensitivity can match Nixon's, retaliated. Dripping sarcasm, the Texan remembered that Eisenhower had asked for a week or two to figure out what Nixon had accomplished as his Vice-President. Then he accused Nixon, who was out on the hustings nearly every day of the 1966 election race, of being a "chronic campaigner."

In one sense, the President's assault was extremely helpful to Nixon's political future, because it singled him out as the leader of the Republican opposition. But just when everything was going so well, Nixon allowed himself to get upset. "By attacking me rather than responding to the points which I raised," Nixon said, "he has struck at the *very roots* of democracy. Is every public figure who rationally questions the means to achieve our goals in Vietnam to become the *victim* of a Presidential attack to silence his dissent?" (Three years later, when he was President, Nixon's question would come back to haunt and outrage him.) Nixon's tone grew more wayward. The next time he spoke to the press, he said, "The President tends to have an attitude that unless you go all the way with LBJ, you don't go any of the way. *He isn't going to get away with that with me.*"

This angry and empty threat, and Johnson's label of "chronic campaigner," may have been psychical alarm bells that Nixon for once heard and heeded, because directly after the Congressional campaign he declared a "sabbatical" from politics, a decision made easier by the ego-boasting probability that for the first time in Nixon's career, his participation in a national campaign actually helped his party win.[1] He did not constantly have to prove himself by getting into positions that might endanger him. But shortly after announcing the sabbatical—late in 1966—he found an occasion to boost his ego in a "private showing," where there was not likely to be much criticism or gossip if he blew his lines or lost control.

Nixon had definitely decided to run for the Presidency before the close of the year, and like any Presidential aspirant, he needed an "economic game plan" on which to campaign. But like many—most—politicians, Nixon was not a good economist. On the other hand, he has an excellent, even awesome memory, so he invited a dozen or so economists to meet with him at the Links Club in New York City and give him ideas he could parrot in his campaign.

About ninety minutes before the meeting, however, he called one of the economists who was to attend and announced that he had discovered that George Romney, who was also interested in the Presidency, was sending a spy. Nixon named the spy. It was an intrinsically dramatic moment. "I've got to make a quick decision whether to cancel our meeting."

[1] Part of the Republican victory was attributed to Johnson's increasingly poor image (he had opened the "credibility gap") and his widening of the war in Vietnam; another, to the natural advantage of the "outs" (it was the first national campaign for Nixon in which the Republicans did not control the White House). But the Republican gains in Congress were so substantial that some part of the victory was felt by many to belong to Nixon's more subdued and persuasive approach to political rhetoric.

Thinking his advice was being sought, the economist on the other end of the phone advised, "Cancel." "No," Nixon said quickly. "If I cancel, Romney might catch on we're on to him." There was no time to warn the other participants, Nixon said. He'd convene the meeting as if nothing was amiss. Of course, this posed a serious problem: if the other economists talked freely to Nixon, the Romney man would have an excellent idea of where Nixon's "game plan" was leading.

Nixon's solution was to do *all* the talking for nearly two hours, then without hearing a single significant idea from his advisers (who were certainly aware that they'd not been called to hear a Nixon lecture on economics) adjourn the meeting. Many months later, the man he had warned in advance remembered, "Nixon gave a game plan that was a total fake and nobody caught on."

"I thought you just told me that his knowledge of economics was 'lousy'; how could he fool the experts?" he was asked.

"He did. He called them all—all but the one man—later, and they were astonished to hear that the meeting had been a pure hoax."

"But they'd been asked to come to do the talking: weren't they suspicious?"

"I don't know how to answer that," the economist said, "except to tell you that he was brilliant in the clutch."

"Whose ideas was he spouting if he doesn't understand economics?"

"Mine," the economist said.

The story seems to illustrate Nixon's unceasing need—no matter how repressed it is for the moment—to expose himself to questionable risks. Moreover, it forcibly illustrates the willingness of many otherwise intelligent human beings to accept without question the questionable behavior of famous and powerful men, particularly if at the moment the powerful men are spouting ideas with which they agree.

Nixon limited himself in the late part of 1966 to only one irrational moment in public, accusing the W.E.B. DuBois Club of "typical" Communist trickery in choosing a name that Americans would confuse with the Boys Club of America, of which Nixon was an officer. Named after a venerable black New England radical, the DuBois Clubs could now carry out their subversive activities, Nixon argued, under a cloak of mistaken identity.

For most of 1967, Nixon wrote a syndicated column, travelled and rested, leaving the battle to his potential rivals for the nomination. Consequently, George Romney, who said he had been "brainwashed" in Vietnam and made enough other *faux pas*, talked himself right out of the picture. Nixon's abstention, feel Witcover and Broder, among many, was successful. Indeed, it may have been the most successful strategic move Nixon ever made. The Republicans he had helped toward victory in 1966 remained indebted. For his part, he merely kept from doing or saying anything ridiculous before the convention.

This was a different kind of isolation for Nixon. Previously, he had run away to hide his anger and humiliation. Now he seemed to be stepping away—not to hide his anger but to avoid occasions that would inspire anger or foolishness. Witcover believes that in the years just before Nixon wdn the Presidency, he carried out "one of the most effective exercises in self-analysis and self-rehabilitation in the history of American politics." Witcover figured that Nixon had outside help, but proof was inadequate: "It has been suggested, in fact, that Nixon underwent professional psychoanalysis in those years. The suggestion has been denied . . ."

But if the neurotic in Nixon was dormant, the neurosis was not. Because of this fact, the political sabbatical that he announced in 1966 lasted, some observers feel, until the completion of the 1968 campaign, making his victory the first in the age of mass communications to be won by political "moratorium."

H. R. (Bob) Haldeman and other campaign guides feared the worst—that Nixon would first exhaust himself and then his image, in that order, by activity and overexposure. They babied him, they made him nap during the day, every afternoon, and no more barnstorming all fifty states, no more uncontrolled environments in which the germ of dissent could be heard (by Nixon), infecting him with the impulse to accuse the opposition of treason.

"He would not debate. He would not go on the question

shows," writes Joe McGinniss in *The Selling of the President 1968.* "He wanted no part of the campus. The city slum was a foreign country . . ." His televised panels were comprised of friendly faces which asked him friendly questions.

The Nixonites avoided emergencies when they could, but if necessity demanded they put their man onto enemy turf, everybody was nervous. When Nixon made a last-minute stand on "Face the Nation" before Election Day, because he sensed he was losing, his people clustered in fright before the set. The next morning one of his media people, Al Scott, sighed: "He didn't hurt himself. That's the important thing."

"We started Nixon off in 1960 sick and under medication," says the Haldeman memorandum which guided Nixon's destiny in 1968, "and then we ran his tail off." Theodore White thinks the memo's implications "disturbing." Nixon was being hidden and vacuumized, some said, because there was so little of substance to see: a cheesecloth politician.

But, on the contrary, Nixon was being hidden and vacuumized because there was so much to see which voters might find unacceptable. Better the dull, smooth and complacent Nixon of 1968 than the "vicious, untrustworthy and unstable" Nixon of 1960, writes White. White, who seemed to think him healthier than before, still found him "choppy, allusive, almost chaotic, as the thinking outran the words" at certain times.

So the Nixonites adopted a policy with the press: Their man would see any of the big publications—*Life*, the dreaded *Times*—on request, but to make sure that they didn't get too close for too long, they'd be escorted to him just before his campaign plane landed and they were allowed to stay only until the plane taxied to a stop. They were known as "three-bump" interviews. And with other powerful people, the ones who did not transcribe interviews but brought money and votes, Nixon would be smart and listen. He told White *he* was going to listen because Lyndon Johnson did nothing but talk all the time from the minute you entered his presence.

The closer to the end, the more he wore down, fluffed, jittered. When his aides organized a press conference, they locked out the cameras and microphones so the flubs couldn't be transcribed for posterity. But you couldn't always control the environment. There always had to be some germs.

Nixon's boys had gotten together a panel in Philadelphia they thought he could live with on television, after they shed the psychiatrist whose presence they believed would give the candidate nervous prostration. But a clinker in the form of an articulate Democrat (who had his own talk show) slipped somehow into the orchestration.

His name was Jack McKinney. His questions were professional, and that alone was enough to make Nixon wary. Joe McGinniss said that with McKinney, Nixon lost the advantage of control that he had facing "the loose syntax and predictable sloppy thrusts of amateurs."

Nixon dodged McKinney's questions badly, hobbling away until even a friendly housewife could sniff the wounded animal. Suddenly she wondered if civil disobedience was ever justified. "There were philosophic implications there he didn't like," McGinniss says. "He knew he would have to watch her too. The first line of sweat broke across his upper lip." His jowls began to shake. McKinney started in again, preventing Nixon from moving along with the automatic smile to the next easy question. This exchange ended with McKinney's charging—on a show paid for with Nixon's campaign money—that on the basic issue of the war in Vietnam, America was being asked to vote for him "on a wink and a smile."

Nixon got back on the right track, looking good, people thought, but the jitters had started, leading the same day to bigger mistakes in Philadelphia. The candidate decided on an unprecedented visit to a black neighborhood. A black clergyman showed him around a shopping center built with black capital and run by black management. Nixon said, "I see, isn't that interesting" and rubbed his hands together.

"The candidate was clearly eager to say something," says Gloria Steinem, who stood a short distance away. So before the clergyman had finished, Nixon interrupted: "Now what you[1] fellas need is *economic* power." Some of the blacks didn't

---

[1] "It was always *your* problem when Negroes were involved," McGinniss realized after listening to Nixon. Roger Ailes, Nixon's tv director, explained, "He's not a bigot. He's just naive."

believe what they'd heard. Speaking rapidly, Nixon, says Steinem, delivered "his high school civics lecture" to blacks fed up with The Man's civics. At long last Nixon came to the end: "You fellas have got to get a piece of the action." The clergyman slapped Nixon on the back and declared that he was a "political independent." After that the Republican candidate became more agitated, repeating endlessly, "Right, right, I see," as the cocky and independent black regained the platform.

"Say," Nixon finally got in, "you must know that fella who was Young Man of the Year, too. You know, the one with a hook for an arm." The black clergyman didn't know the fella with a hook for an arm. Nixon insisted that he *had* to know him. He even gestured to show just about where the hook was attached to the stump of his arm. Before the meeting with the blacks ended, says Steinem, "a possible explanation of Nixon's mental connection became painfully clear. Black skin and a man with a hook: two handicapped men must know each other."

But nobody heckled Nixon much. Hubert Humphrey was a better target. Liberals, Radicals and Democrats couldn't wait to attack him. "T.R.B.," *The New Republic* columnist, mused: "It's funny, sitting in a big hall, waiting for a riot to start . . . Humphrey . . . carries a built-in riot where ever he goes." Nixon was The Plastic Man but Humphrey was The Cowardly Lion; he had stood meekly by while Johnson dictated unpopular policy on Vietnam and had permitted his silence to condone the clubbing of heads outside the Democratic Convention hall in Chicago. He was the *anti-er* hero of the two chief candidates. He became the only major candidate in America who couldn't talk in "lip-sync," his voice going one way, his lips the other. When Democrats were through snickering and jeering at Humphrey, they didn't have much enthusiasm for jeering at a low profile delivering a boring, stock speech.

Nonetheless, the little heckling Nixon encountered in 1968, John Osborne found, "invariably threw him off stride." The hollow resonant Nixon lungs got hoarse and weak, and he cut speeches short so his aides could speed him off one platform and onto another, where well-scrubbed boys, leggy blonde girls and middle-aged ladies would cheer—to cheer him up.

More and more toward the end he couldn't stop straying from the tedious speech. (Three weeks before the election, one of his campaign aides confided, "He is so *damn* bored with that speech, you wouldn't believe it.") His boys would bring him back to the mark. Occasionally he yelled at one or another, reminding them he was the boss, but better them than the public.

It's coincidental, perhaps, but just about the time the speech started fitting like a noose around his throat, George Ball stood up for the Democrats and accused Nixon of lacking the character and principles to bring us safely through real crisis. Word came over the wire. Nixon said he would not dignify Ball by replying to Ball. Instead he replied, in his fashion, to the press, because to him, *all his critics were alike.* Standing on the steps of his campaign plane, posing for pictures, suddenly Nixon looked down and said to the reporters that they had a bad habit of putting words in his mouth. "Of course you boys have a right to put words in my mouth."

Toward the end it got stickier. George C. Wallace, the third candidate, seemed to be hurting both men, yet Humphrey started pulling up in the polls even though he had what "T.R.B." called "the worst case of logorrhea of any modern man." (Humphrey once took forty-five minutes to answer three questions and he wasn't dodging like Nixon; Humphrey just couldn't find a proper place to bring his statements to an end.) "Even a Cowardly Lion with four game legs (Johnson, Vietnam, a divided Democratic Party and his mouth)," said a reporter at the time, "is giving Plastic Man a race." Louis Harris's poll a day or two before the election actually put Humphrey out front.[1]

In 1970, sitting over lunch in a Washington restaurant, Tom Wicker came to the conclusion that "almost any other

[1] Frank Shakespeare, the aide who uncovered conspiracies with more ease than anyone but Nixon himself, said that he always thought the Harris poll was fixed, and if Nixon became President, he'd see to it that Harris was investigated. No investigation was ever announced.

Democrat would have beaten Nixon and any other Republican would have beaten Humphrey much worse." Many Washington observers think that if Johnson had kept his nose out of the race (At the end it looked to a lot of Americans—whether true or not—that the abrupt end of his intransigence over Vietnam was hypocritical electioneering.) or if Nixon just had another two or three days to slide, he would have lost the election.

As it turned out, relatively few Americans, offered the choice they were, cared who became their President in 1968. Nixon won with thirty-one million votes, representing twenty-five percent of the adults in America and two million votes less than he had when Kennedy defeated him in 1960. Ironically, the ones who voted for Nixon believed they had chosen him for "the calm he offered the nation, opting," as White said (muddling the critical distinction between calm and dullness), "for the orderliness which lay at the root of his personality . . ."

CHAPTER ELEVEN

Richard M. Nixon became the thirty-seventh President of the United States of America on January 20, 1969. That morning, small, vocal clusters of anti-war demonstrators met the Inaugural Parade and as Nixon passed, they shouted obscenities. Nixon was "bitterly offended" by the demonstrations, according to Richard Harris in *Justice*, which describes the failings of the Justice Department under the Nixon Administration, and the new President was "determined not· to allow anything that insulting to his office or himself to happen again." Consequently, one of John Mitchell's first official acts after being sworn in as Attorney General was to announce that the Administration would deny permits of assembly to "activists" of the sort who had besieged the new President, although the First Amendment forbids denial of that right simply because somebody in government fears that the applicant *might* not be peaceable.

"Nixon lusted after power," wrote Pete Hamill, the outspoken columnist for *The New York Post*, "and when he got it there were still men who refused to give him proper respect." The Nixon who was his own reason for politics, it seems, quickly became his own reason for government.

That evening the new President casually reminded jubilant Republicans at each of the seven Inaugural Balls that his slogan was "Bring Us Together." Cramped as they were, they enjoyed a good laugh, but he was conscious of the theme's more serious meaning too and at one ball he said: "This honor now beckons America, the chance to help lead the world at last out of the valley of turmoil and on to that high ground of peace that man has dreamed of . . ." It was the cognitive wish, beautiful, sincere and worthy of the moment.

At another of the balls he remarked that to prepare himself for this, the biggest day of his life, he had "read a book about all the inaugurations of the past and how each man prepared his speech, and you learn what not to do and to do, at least you hope so, and, uh, I learned for example, there was probably only one President who really was unhappy when he became President. *He was unhappy because he felt that it . . . honor should have come to him earlier in life."* Quick to remember Nixon's career, celebrants chuckled. "And, ah, that morning as he . . . just before he went down to the Inaugural Pa . . . Parade [sic] . . . this was Buchanan, James Buchanan in 1856 [sic], he turned to a friend and he said that . . . as he looked at that day, *all the enemies he hated and wanted to punish were now his friends,* and that all of his friends that he loved and wanted to reward were dead . . ." "Oh, no," moaned his daughter Tricia. Quickly Nixon added that those crowded into the ballroom with him didn't have to worry; they were all his friends.

(A man who frequently boasts of his mistakes by repeating them, Nixon told the same story the next morning, on his first full day in office, to Republican workers gathered for a brief victory celebration in the East Room of the White House. Was this the inappropriate and emotional wish to punish all those people, Republicans mainly, who had deserted him in 1960, 1962 and 1964 and who returned only now that he had belatedly reached the high ground *by himself?*)

Nixon and Buchanan had much in common. Buchanan too came to the Presidency late; he was also a conservative, a strict constructionist who thought slavery morally wrong but who defended the Constitutional right of Americans to own slaves. A minority President suspected in the North (his home) of southern sympathies, he had campaigned to unite a divided nation. He was also stiff, isolated and stubborn. (The late Allan Nevins, an outstanding scholar of American history, considered Buchanan "obsessive" and "weak-willed" and in probable need of psychoanalysis not available in those days.)

But the one thing the two Presidents did not have in common was the remark which Nixon attributed to Buchanan. Buchanan was confronted with awesome patronage problems, yet no authoritative biography of Buchanan, published or privately printed, no known history of Inauguration Days in the United States, reveals an expressed desire to punish anyone. Asked for the source in 1970, the White House (Margita White of Herb Klein's communications staff), presumably after investigating, could not supply it. Further requests, made directly to the President's office, were answered with silence. One thing is true: Buchanan had been unhappy at his Inauguration (in 1857). It seems the water had backed up in the sewer pipes of his hotel and like other members of the Inaugural Party, he had contracted "the National Hotel Disease." On Inauguration Day, James Buchanan had diarrhea.

But the activists and the Republicans weren't the only people on Inauguration Day who seem to have displeased the new President. His wife Pat, like some Republicans, had not wanted him to run in 1968.[1] In the midst of the riotous acclaim he received at the Inaugural Balls, Nixon seemed to take this out on her, intimating that he had climbed to the high ground *despite* Pat Nixon. At one of the balls early in the evening, he forgot to introduce the new First Lady, breaking a tradition as old as the Inaugural Ball, itself. At the next ball, he first introduced his daughters and his son-in-law, David Eisenhower (who, Nixon once explained with a straight face, had influenced his running in 1968: David "had written me a letter telling me the country needs me") and then he remembered: "I just assumed that everybody knew the lady I was with . . . but at another stop they said, 'Why, introduce Pat.' " With that he introduced her in flowery terms. But in Walter Winchell's phrase, it was onions and orchids all evening for Mrs. Nixon.

The most telling demonstration of Nixon's probably unconscious feeling of resentment toward his wife occurred as he finished speaking. Stepping down, he led the way through the crowd of well-wishers, responding elatedly to their smiles and extended hands. Several seconds later, just as he was about to step into his limousine and go on to the next ball, the new President was reminded by one of his aides that he

[1] Interviewed by Flora Rheta Schreiber for *Good Housekeeping*, Pat Nixon swears that by 1967 she decided that silence was a virtue and, although she still did not want him to run, she stopped arguing against his running (to his face). The interview ran in July, 1968, *before* her husband accepted the nomination in Miami.

had left the new First Lady standing by herself in the ballroom. Nixon dispatched a Secret Service man to fetch her.

Nixon forgot a lot of other things on Inaugural night. He couldn't remember what job he'd given his old foe, the man who had sent the spy in 1966, George Romney: "This is the Secretary of Health . . . no, the Secretary of Housing and Urban Development . . ." He couldn't remember what jazz musician Duke Ellington says: "Duke Ellington says, 'It don't mean a thing if it ain't got that thing . . . no . . . that swing . . .'" His audience was prepared to laugh at every word (Everybody heard he had gag writers.), but his own laugh was special: "Hunh, hunh, hunh, hunh," like an engine that won't spark. At other times it sounded more like a staccato moan. And when he told the same jokes at every ball (e.g., "Believe it or not, all nine Justices were there and this is one time when all were dancing to the same tune"—reportedly written by one of Bob Hope's staff), "Heh, heh, heh, heh, heh," over and over he went, until a few skeptics heard echoes of Joe McCarthy's nervous laughter wafting over the loudspeakers and droning out the happy babble of Republicans back on top after eight years.

Some things Nixon remembered fairly well. At the first ball (where the nine old men had danced to the same tune from their seats in the dress boxes), Guy Lombardo was on the bandstand. Appropriately, Nixon remembered that he and Pat had been in New York, at the Hotel Roosevelt, on V-J Day, 1945, dancing to Lombardo's music. The new resident added, "I hope we're dancing to his music at the end of the next war."

That night, when he said, "We're not going to remember it was cold during the last part of the parade [the part where the protestors made obscene gestures and Nixon turned away, his eyes glazed], we're only going to remember this warm feeling," some Americans were not reassured. They saw Inauguration Day, 1969, as Richard Nixon's first Presidential crisis.

A professor of sociology at Yale who constructed a broad system of evaluating Presidential behavior, James D. Barber, said Nixon had an "unclear and discontinuous self-image" and was continually involved in self-examination and the "effort to construct a 'Richard Nixon.'" Listing the President's "fatalism and pessimism," "the substitution of technique for value, the energies devoted to controlling aggressive feelings, the distrust of political allies, and, most of all, the perpetual sensitivity to the power dimensions of situations," Barber seriously believed that "if Nixon is ever threatened simultaneously with public disdain and loss of power, he may move into a crisis syndrome . . . but in the ordinary conduct of the Presidency (and there are long stretches of that), Nixon's personal relations may interact with his character to produce a different kind of danger . . . that he will commit himself irrevocably to some disastrous course of action, as, indeed his predecessor [Johnson] did . . . Unless there has been a fundamental change in his personality, Nixon has within him a very strong drive for personal power—especially *independent* power—that pushes him away from reliance on anyone else and . . . toward stubborn insistence on showing everyone that he can win out on his own."

Barber saw a President who clung "adamantly" to critically important issues, barring any influence that might moderate his rigid beliefs. "Add hostile reporters, an increasingly independent Senate, a generationally polarized nation, and a set of substantive problems nearly impossible to 'solve'—and *the state is set for tragic drama.*"

But there is another image of Nixon—the image of a crisp, no-nonsense, eminently rational man on view in one of Henry Kissinger's favorite stories about Nixon's executive abilities. Shortly after he took office, the North Vietnamese launched a heavy attack on the South, and Defense and State Department and CIA officials, still geared for the Johnson style of management, called Nixon's new national security adviser to say they were on their way to the White House situation room so that the President could personally direct the tactical response of the allies.

"I said, 'Wait a minute, I'll see what the President wants to do,'" relates Kissinger. "I went to see the President and he asked, 'Is there a decision I can make now that will make any difference to the battle?' I said, 'No.' He asked, 'Is there any risk if I do not make any decision on this now?' I said,

'No.' 'Then tell them not to come over,' the President said. 'I will make a decision when there is a clear decision to be made.' "

Nixon was crisp and logical when he felt no personal pressure, but some things required more complicated responses, and at those points, it appears, his execution grew flabby.

Entering the fourth month of his Administration, Nixon grasped at one excuse after another to postpone action on matters which had been largely defined for him before Inauguration. In the first eight weeks, Nixon sent one bill to Congress, requesting a compromise electoral college reform—letting it be known, however, that this was not the reform he really wanted. (He explained he didn't think the one he wanted would pass Congress.)

By early spring, the White House announced plans to have messages for Congress ready on April 14, the day legislators returned from Easter vacation. But the planned messages were broad statements about broad reforms—in short, messages promising other messages. At one point in the first half of the month, Ron Ziegler, the President's press secretary, denied to reporters eager for some hard news that the President had announced a new Model Cities program and volunteered, "There's been no final decision by the President on this or any other program," confirming for journalists what they had already begun to suspect.

While Nixon made his own preparations to spend Easter at Key Biscayne, he sent Moynihan out of the Oval Office to announce that the President had devised a plan to put over two-hundred-million dollars toward cleaning up riot-torn areas in twenty American cities. Standing outside Nixon's door, his adviser on youth, poverty, welfare and urban affairs repeatedly said, to show that the President had worked out every detail in his short time in office, that these funds were "new money," appropriated by the boss for this explicit purpose. The truth, however, was that the money had been hastily diverted from existing Federal urban programs, reveals Osborne, "in order to make the showing wanted by the President."

Nixon was already blaming Arthur F. Burns, the senior

staff "dignitary," for weakness in the decision-making process and, simultaneously, in another announcement (of an announcement), Nixon celebrated an Administrative reorganization plan, years from completion, that guaranteed to make the White House more efficient. Sensing a "rising unease," Bryce Harlow, the President's original Congressional liaison and one of the few people on Nixon's staff with prior Washington experience, started explaining to doubters that Eisenhower in his early months had achieved less than Nixon. Ziegler, who reflects carefully Nixon's thoughts and feelings, announced that the new President's Administration was "moving along as he intended it to move along."

Nixon, meanwhile, continued looking for something he could hold up as dramatic proof of his leadership. At another time, Vietnam would have been the first place to look. The North Vietnamese were shelling Saigon with outrageous ease. Wisely, however, he averted an increase in fighting in Vietnam because so much was riding on his still-warm campaign promise of "a plan to end the war." And resumption of bombing over North Vietnam or an invasion of Cambodia or Laos so soon after taking office might have also damaged his reputation for truth. Nixon had no conscious desire to raise the nation's blood pressure, yet he was still drawn toward some clear-cut military action that would display America's might now that he was President.

On April 15, 1969, one day after Nixon and Congress returned from Easter vacation, the excuse seemed to explode on Nixon's psyche like a Fourth of July fireworks display: Some middle-level general in the Pentagon notified him, as a matter of course, that North Korea had shot down an unarmed American EC-121 and all aboard were killed. The EC-121 is a reconnaisance plane.

The many unofficial versions of subsequent events all agree on one fact: While others ultimately saw the loss as the risk of cold war, Nixon took the downing of the plane personally. He reasoned that because he had assailed the Johnson Administration for failing to retaliate when the North Koreans captured and imprisoned the crew of the spy ship *Pueblo*, these same North Koreans had *deliberately set out to insult him*, as well as to test the new President's will to retaliate.

Nixon became enraged. The only person who seems to believe otherwise—presumably because he had relied on information from Nixon, since the whole story has never been published —was Arnold Hutschnecker, Nixon's "former" physician, who suggested a few months later that the President's emotional strength and coolness were amply demonstrated during this "impersonal" crisis. Since Nixon felt the North Koreans were testing him, he made up his mind, without extended thought, to meet the test.

The Pentagon functions on "contingency plans," the kind of military options that the Rand Corporation and other "think tanks" dream up. If the Middle East were to explode, the military might give Nixon seven or eight major military options. There are "low" alerts and "high" alerts. The "low" alerts tend to be stand-by programs. As for the plane incident, some watchers at first imagined that Nixon had ordered a stand-by, which means Be Ready But Do Not Act Without Further Orders. But of all the many buttons Nixon could have pushed to implement an emergency program against North Korea, he seems to have selected one from the upper scale of violence, according to the pieces put together from various sources. Within perhaps five minutes (some sources say a little more time elapsed, maybe fifteen minutes), the new President of the United States had decided to bomb North Korea from the sea and from the air and, possibly, from fixed allied ground positions just south of the demarcation line.

So far, the President had spoken to none of his civilian advisers. In fact, the civilians who would normally be most involved in such a decision knew nothing of it until the wheels for massive retaliation had been turning for several minutes —at least one of them found out about it on paper.

The plan selected called for forty American warships (the fleet included three carriers) to steam toward the North Korean coastline. They were scheduled to attack several hours hence, at the same moment a large flight of B-52 bombers, based on Guam, also would begin bombardment. The navy would fire on North Korean shore installations while the flyers would bomb one or both of two military sites farther inland. (Some reporters were told unofficially that the second base was an alternate site, to be struck only if bad weather or heavy ground-to-air fire shut off the primary target, but others heard that the attack was against both at once.) The roles to be played by some thirty thousand American troops and the Army of the Republic of Korea (ROK forces) have never been clarified outside the Administration, but the ground force certainly had been alerted to the coordinated air-sea attack. Within a matter of several hours, maybe forty at most, the United States would be in undeclared war on two sides of mainland China, south and north.

Later, once Nixon's plan had flopped and the horror of journalists had been made plain, the Pentagon whitewashed itself, implying to newsmen that the generals had counselled restraint, says William Beecher, a Pentagon reporter, "on a President inclined toward bold action." But the actual attempts to restrain Nixon appear to have come first and most vociferously from civilians who had been advised belatedly of his "firm" decision to attack North Korea.

News of the emergency is said to have reached William Rogers, the Secretary of State, through "regular" channels. It's said that Nixon's speechwriters, summoned to prepare a statement which the President planned to deliver on television *after* the attack had begun, heard about it sooner than Rogers. The Secretary of State received an interdepartmental memorandum apparently prepared by a White House assistant and teletyped as a matter of form to all parties concerned. Just imagine the Secretary of State picking a paper up out of his "in box" and discovering that his country is going to war. Rogers reportedly rushed a call to the White House but had to go through Haldeman, zealous keeper of the door. Rather than waste several more precious minutes, Rogers hastened in person to the White House to find out what was happening. Evidently what he learned from Nixon frightened him—if he wasn't frightened already.

Bill Rogers is a most unlikely choice to play President Nixon's first internal adversary. Quiet, steady, loyal, a sweet droner of a man, and until then almost ingenuous in his faith in Nixon,[1] Rogers had innumerable questions which Nixon

[1] In 1952, during Nixon's first national campaign, Rogers set a course that was to endear him to Nixon. The campaign train had

allegedly answered with the argument that the Koreans, perhaps with Chinese backing, were trying to make him look ridiculous. Rogers is not known as an incisive speaker—he phumphs a great deal—but he kept pushing, almost begging Nixon to listen to reason. Nixon remained adamant. The conversation has been described as an "agony."

The visit ended in frustration, but the distraught Secretary of State came back for a second visit, apparently after he had worked up the nerve. The Secretary of Defense, Melvin Laird, was reportedly summoned. Possibly responding to Nixon's ardor, Laird, according to Pentagon sources, was "unenthusiastic" about the attack but not adamantly opposed. Sitting on the fence, he left Rogers to flounder alone on the outside.

By now Rogers's feelings were apparently as intense as Nixon's, for he called on the President a third time in a matter of hours, while the warships were steaming toward their destination. Now this last attempt may have been made through a telephone call to Nixon rather than a visit. (All the details of the story may never be known.) If it was a phone call, it soon became a three-way conference call, for Kissinger appeared.

As the resident expert on foreign affairs, he is often looked upon as Rogers's main rival. Surely Kissinger had been informed of the attack by now, for although he had reportedly not been consulted prior to Nixon's decision, he had seen the interdepartmental message. Whether Kissinger was summoned or appeared voluntarily is not known, but he provided the decisive element in calling off the war. If Rogers drones, Kissinger speaks clearly, decisively, wittily. His friends say he can raise the most prosaic point and make it seem new and brilliant, entertaining the President, honestly pleased to have around an authentic egghead who, at the same time, shares Nixon's hard-line.

---

pulled out of a California station while Nixon was still addressing the crowd. Nixon couldn't wait to get at Jack Brown, who was in charge of scheduling the train's movements. He complained that Brown, supposedly a close friend, had committed a "major" blunder. Rogers overheard the candidate sharply warn Brown, "*Never let that happen again.*" Expressing his amazement, he told Nixon, "I thought you planned it that way."

First, according to one account, Rogers talked, then Kissinger, taking turns until Nixon began to wear down. Finally, Kissinger asked, "All right, Mr. President, suppose we do attack North Korea in force. What then?" Not very brilliant for a brilliant scholar and debater, but Nixon, dazed and weakening, ran out of arguments. With evident reluctance, he cancelled his war.

"We are told of crises (by Nixon and his spokesmen) and we are told they won great victories,"[1] Hugh Sidey of *Time-Life* says. "It's kind of dreaming, it's kind of make-believe." But the reasons Nixon had for fighting North Korea were very real *to him* for some hours. That Nixon seems to have acknowledged that he was unable to reason indicates at some level a partial return to reason.

The full story of the Korean incident has never been released—not because it did not happen but rather because it was an embarrassment. Only underlings in various departments outside the White House seem willing to publicize Richard Nixon's aborted war in order to grab credit for their departments and heads of departments for bringing the President to his senses. Had it not been for these tattletales, the White House might have succeeded in bottling up the story entirely.

Oddly, some White House people seem to have talked too much anyway—not about the Korean crisis but about Nixon's mood that spring. John Osborne, one of the more zealous "Nixonologists," was "astonished" when Nixon's aides revealed the President had fallen "into a passing phase of extreme frustration." The word "depression" was introduced into the discussion and, evidently realizing they'd already said too much, Osborne's sources suggested that the word was "too strong for the mood Nixon exhibited."

[1] Frank Holeman, in his mini-biography in 1959, said of Nixon's behavior as Vice-President that "cynics [presumably like Sidey, who was to come upon the scene somewhat later] insist that these much-headlined fireworks do more for Nixon personally than they do for the United States. They even accuse him of deliberately walking into trouble so he can appear to advantage climbing out." Today, however, the cynics are not at all sure that Nixon does deliberately stage all his crises, but if he does, some of them are so fraught with danger no man can be sure he'll walk out safely.

Within a few days the President had become transparently "exhilarated." Later, when the President's behavior seemed to Osborne to have stopped flopping from one extreme to the other, he observed that "A President who suffered from and failed to rise above the weaknesses that [he] seemed to me to suffer from would have been a disaster for the country." Still later, however, Osborne appeared less certain that Nixon's stability had seriously improved.

In 1968, one of Rockefeller's major advisers told a great many people that he didn't think Nixon, the leading candidate for the Republican nomination, had the intellect to lead the country. He was partisan and people discounted what he said, but felt something else was missing in Nixon too. One day early in the campaign, Paul Hoffman of *The New York Post* mentioned to this Rockefeller man that he thought Nixon would be elected because Americans are likely to choose the "safest" candidate rather than innovators like Rockefeller. The Rockefeller man was aghast. With much more than partisan feeling, according to Hoffman, the Governor's aide said, "Richard Nixon is the most dangerous, of all the men running, to have as President."

The Governor's aide was Henry Kissinger.

CHAPTER TWELVE

Many visitors find the inner reaches of 1600 Pennsylvania Avenue reassuring, quieting. They pad in on thick pile carpets, past white-panelled Colonial doors and discreet, stone-faced Secret Service men who seem like scrubbed statues. The deeper in one goes, the more distant the harsh outer world becomes. Typewriters sound like distant crickets and human voices like murmuring leaves. But these rich, protective layers of wool, wood and deferential humanity apparently did not provide for Nixon the same serenity which other Presidents reputedly enjoyed.

At the beginning, he had the same basic problem every President has had—getting used to the complexities of the job. But Nixon had more difficulty than most settling in. After one year H. R. Haldeman, his chief of staff, declared that anyone who believed that any President should—or could—settle so soon into a perfectly suitable "functional pattern" was being unfair to Nixon. But after two years in office, Nixon was still searching for an executive plan into which he could settle comfortably. Meanwhile, he kept adding to the White House staff until his aides were sprouting their own aides; within eighteen months of his ascendancy he had a personal staff of over six hundred men and women and an operating budget exceeding twelve million dollars a year—substantially outdistancing that legendary spender, Lyndon Johnson, in manpower and money. By adding to a system that even he felt did not work well, Nixon virtually institutionalized it.

With so many people tumbling over each other internally, there was confusion, and, as one observer said, staff members found themselves shooting down each other's grand designs. For example, Richard Kleindienst, John Mitchell's chief assistant in the Justice Department (which became practically an adjunct of the White House because of the closeness of Nixon and the Attorney General), announced to Congress during Nixon's first year in office that the President planned the elimination of college deferments in the draft. The same day, a flustered spokesman in the White House proper denied that such a plan existed. On another occasion, George Romney, the Secretary of Housing and Urban Development, was informed by one of Nixon's White House assistants that he had been espousing housing views in opposition to the Administration's. According to John Herbes of the *Times*, Romney was perplexed. "What the hell is the Administration's policy?" Romney demanded. "It changes from day to day and hour to hour."[1]

In the last analysis, the confusion in the Nixon White House stems from Nixon himself. "He delays when he should be decisive, he stands firm when he should equivocate, he equivocates when he ought to stand firm," *The New Republic* summarized. "He commits himself only to reverse himself, or when he ought not to commit himself at all."

In the third year of his Presidency, Nixon, as if to illustrate the point, promised a group of media executives that he would "automatically" invoke the Taft-Hartley act if East Coast longshoremen went out on strike at the same time that West Coast longshoremen were still striking. Exactly one week later, the White House announced that it would *not* immediately invoke Taft-Hartley although there was a strike on both Coasts. Ron Ziegler strained to explain Nixon's change of heart. He argued, "You can't equate 'automatically' with 'instantly' or 'immediately.' "[2] A few days later, Nixon changed his mind, signing an Executive order invoking Taft-Hartley.

[1] Nixon, says Evans and Novak in *Nixon In the White House*, sought to purge Romney after two years because he irritated Nixon with his campaign to integrate white suburbs—"attacking the sensibilities integral to Nixon's dream of a majority Republican Party." But out of fear that the HUD chief would not resign quietly (in the wake of Walter Hickel's messy firing as Secretary of the Interior), the President tabled his plan.

[2] Between Nixon's mention of Taft-Hartley and Ziegler's, the President learned to his surprise, according to A. H. Raskin, an editorial expert on American labor, that the "last thing [employers] wanted was an invocation of the law" because it would upset efforts of union middle-of-the-roaders to subdue union ultra-militants. There is no information as to what made Nixon change his mind the second time.

Other Presidents in history have changed their minds under pressure or recognition of an earlier mistake, but rarely as precipitously as Nixon, or as totally. In the middle of his term, he informed Howard K. Smith of ABC that he had become "a Keynesian in economics." Recalling that the basic economic philosophy of Republicanism in the past was a balanced budget, Smith remarked that Nixon's sudden espousal of Keynes' doctrine of expansionist public spending —allowing for running up budget deficits—was the equivalent of a Christian saying, "All things considered, I think Mohammed was right."

Nixon seems to do such things often for the sake of the impact they have on people. But dramatic impact apart, there are observers in the government and the press who believe that Nixon changes his mind from one extreme to the other because, intellectually, he has no idea where he's been, much less where he's going. This extreme view is shared by writers as respectable as Hugh Sidey, who observes Washington regularly for *Time* and *Life*. "No President has done things as arrogantly and mindlessly." (Sidey has seen the President become so excited by one thing or another that "he steps ahead of himself.") Sidey's argument has basis in fact.

One Saturday morning, some twenty members of the White House staff, along with members of the Cabinet Nixon feels he can trust, received urgent summonses from Camp David, where Nixon was supposedly resting. Expecting a major crisis, they stumbled, bleary-eyed, toward the Maryland retreat. Once he had them around him, the President announced that he was going to support the Family Assistance Plan (to provide a minimum annual income to all disadvantaged American families). The rest of the day, he explained, would be devoted to discussing his decision, a decision most of them already knew that he planned to make.[1]

[1] Many of the men had spent time working on it. Some of the time had gone toward creating a title which Nixon would find palatable. It seems that the President had objected to several names because they sounded "socialistic." As a result, Melvin Laird, who, as Secretary of Defense, has nothing whatsoever to do with civilian family assistance, reportedly spent several hours dressing up the winning name.

However, though talk they would, the President continued, they would "not be allowed" to alter his decision.

When the President goes to Camp David, to Key Biscayne or to the Western White House at San Clemente, two of his motives are the much-discussed need for rest and his even more publicized need for isolation. But Nixon seems ambivalent about both. Though he may need rest, he hasn't got the ability to sit still, and though he needs to be alone, he may fear the silence. Frank Mankiewicz and Tom Braden, who wrote a political column together until Mankiewicz went into politics, remembered the phone call Nixon made from Key Biscayne to Kissinger, his busy national security adviser. Nixon, it seems, told Kissinger to drop everything and fly down at once because Charles de Gaulle was dead. The columnists felt that while one might expect the President of the United States to take in stride the death of a foreigner who had died out of office and out of power, Nixon seemed to take very little in stride. They, like others after them, accused him of showing a notable preference for "motion over action."

Along this line, possibly the most interesting statistics released by the White House cover the amount of time Nixon spends away from his desk. In little more than one year, Nixon spent two hundred and fifty-four days outside Washington. Two trips took him to Europe, one all the way around the world; there fifty-two days at Key Biscayne, eighty-seven at the Western White House and fifty-six at Camp David. The White House says he travels in order to demonstrate his belief in "decentralizing" the government and to remain in touch with the people, but there seems to be very little real contact along the route: he only lights on territory guaranteed friendly to a conservative Republican President.

There may be a more covert reason for leaving Washington, which White House correspondents recognize, to one degree or another, and that could be that the President fears the city itself. William Timmons, once chief of Congressional liaison for Nixon, one day questioned the President's peripatetic travelling, because he had heard considerable "harsh criticism from Republican Congressmen," says Evans and

Novak. "Bristling, Bob Haldeman glared at Timmons, who had inadvertently touched on a sore point . . . Washington was where the enemies were gathered . . . But beyond that, Timmons's question looked to Haldeman like an effort to penetrate the deeply guarded private life of the President, · and he [Haldeman] was not about to permit it."

Haldeman is well known as one of the White House "Germans."[1] The other chief "German" (once they were called the "terrible teutons") is John Ehrlichman, Haldeman's longtime friend and Nixon's chief assistant for domestic affairs. "I think [the two of them] harbor in their minds a real outrage," says Sidey. "They feel like an occupying army and they build up hostilities and fear, and the first enemy is the press, then the 'effete' liberal establishment. And Washington is a Democratic town in their eyes, a town full of colleges." "They are xenophobes," said a network reporter who feels he spends too much time in the Nixon White House to freely permit the use of his name. "No matter how you dress it up, they are xenophobes, and they are dangerous. How do you tell your viewers without sounding a little preposterous?"

Haldeman and Ehrlichman are the mechanics of Nixon's vest-pocket government. They have built what reporters call the "Berlin Wall" around the President. According to Evans and Novak, Haldeman has an immutable mistrust of Congress and Congressmen, apparently extending even to Nixon's liaison people. (So strong is Haldeman's influence on Nixon's thinking that the President reportedly sides invariably with Haldeman in any dispute with his men inside Congress.)

Though the Germans seem to realize that they cannot altogether prevent negative thoughts from reaching Nixon,

[1] Daniel Patrick Moynihan was fully aware of the nickname, and the reputations that gave birth to it. He sent a copy of his book, *Understanding Poverty*, to Ehrlichman, inscribed: "For John Ehrlichman, *Achtung*. D.P.M." Such teasing may have contributed to Ehrlichman's mistrust of the intellectual counsellor. When reporter Mick Kotz published a story about Nixon advising Clifford Hardin, the Secretary of Agriculture, to use "rhetoric" instead of money to feed the poor, Ehrlichman told newspapermen that it was just this kind of story which Moynihan liked to spread "to embarrass the President." Kotz had actually verified the story from a transcript of the meeting between Nixon and Hardin.

they work effectively to keep him from any human contact *they* deem troublesome. They seem to share many of his phobias and to reflect the President so well that reporters in the White House press corps have learned to read Nixon's angers, fears and occasional joys by listening carefully to either or both of the Germans.[1] Often it's not what they say but how they say it.

Haldeman, Ehrlichman and John Mitchell, Nixon's most trusted adviser, seem to have developed a symbiotic relationship with the President, to the point psychologically where they reinforce each other's view of reality—no matter how distorted their vision may sometime seem to the rest of the world. Therefore, if in other respects the Nixon Administration has had trouble completing projects, building a wall was a snap because these key men sensed easily that a wall would please Nixon most.

But this has led to other distortions. The very idea that a man does not work in the White House appears to make him suspect, as if without constant surveillance, he might have alien thoughts. Pierre Rinfret, who had been Nixon's original economic adviser before returning fulltime to his business, after Nixon's election felt he had something urgent to impart to the President. However, six months had passed since Rinfret left and now he could not get past Ehrlichman. In desperation, the economist wrote an article for the bulletin he publishes, figuring that its contents would reach Nixon quickest by indirection and, sure enough, Evans and Novak excerpted Rinfret's bulletin, perhaps because they were impressed by his final sentence: "We accuse the Administration of incompetence." Sitting in San Clemente, a perplexed President looked up from Pat Buchanan's digest of the news and supposedly asked Len Garment, one of his few (relatively) liberal aides, "What's wrong with Pierre?"

[1] Ehrlichman, by all accounts the milder mannered of the two, also seethed over a sarcastic editorial in *The Washington Post* panning the President's veto of an education money bill. A day later, Ehrlichman lunched with the *Post*'s editors—something Halderman would avoid altogether—and, to their amazement, accused them of insulting *the dignity* of the President. Nixon has frequently made similar accusations of the press, reportedly in this instance too.

Haldeman and Ehrlichman have tried, with much success, to lock the door to the outside world in order to rule out dissonance and potential dissent.[1] In case after case, they have overruled some of the more reasonable men on Nixon's team, and Nixon seems to have allowed them to make exclusionary judgments on their own, perhaps because Haldeman and Ehrlichman—despite tactical differences—are most like the President himself.

As a result, though, all they can constructively do for him is feed him his own prejudices and then intensify his difficulties in governing effectively. In the final judgment, Nixon's Administration may prove the danger of selecting, and heeding, aides in one's own image.

But the more serious problem is that this cabal expects the rest of the world to head them too. Richard Whalen, a former Presidential aide, has likened the Nixon regime to a "walled-off Cathay" in which "Germans" Ehrlichman and Haldeman have the view of the outside world that prevailed among Kublai Khan's Chinese: "Anyone who is not inside the White House and subject to its peculiar discipline and ideology, or non-ideology, is an outsider and therefore subject to manipulation."

In the beginning, Nixon voiced the conservative's dream: efficiency and order. He hoped to perfect a committee system which truly made use of experts, to finish off for good the prodigious expense of bureaucracy and, above all else, to prevent "vest-pocket government, no matter who wears the vest." Paradoxically, the President may have created the costliest, most overmanned, least productive vest-pocket government in federal history.

[1] William S. White says that before he became President, Nixon expressed amazement that Lyndon Johnson—in White's words— "kept on men who persistently cut him up." "Nixon assumed office," writes White, "with a firm resolve that nothing like this was going to happen to Richard Nixon. Loyalty to the boss has been made the first and absolute requirement by President Nixon."

CHAPTER THIRTEEN

Max Frankel thought "the jog, the slow and steady trot . . . permitting fairly easy recovery from a stumble" summed up the Nixon Presidency in 1969. It was "hardly surprising" to the *Times'* Washington bureau chief in "a man who spent the better part of two decades acquiring his job and whose greatest internal fear is that the strains of overwork and tension or crisis may overwhelm his judgment."

While it's true that, after the aborted war against North Korea, Nixon locked himself into fairly deep isolation, some observers today would not agree with Frankel that the President was trying to stay out of harm's way. Nor would they necessarily agree that Nixon's greatest internal fear was that his judgment might be overwhelmed by tension or crisis —now that he *was* President. On the contrary, the President went out of his way, it appears, to create crises and his greatest fear may have been that he would lose respect if he did not quickly do something big enough to define his *power*.

He emerged from isolation in June to meet with South Vietnam's President Thieu on Midway Island in the Pacific, where he announced that he would withdraw the first twenty-five thousand American soldiers from Vietnam by August. ("He desperately hoped," say Evans and Novak, "that this evidence of good faith would persuade Ho Chi Minh to begin serious negotiating in Paris.") Nonetheless, the President seemed ambivalent about his own peace posture, for in the same month he addressed the graduating class of the Air Force Academy in order to damn the critics of America's uniformed fighting men as "isolationists" who purveyed a ruinous "unilateral disarmament." If Nixon wanted a reaction, he got it. His address was criticized as irrelevant and intemperate, with one editorial writer deeming the speech "more suitable to a Presidential candidate than a President." But this attack and counterattack ended too quickly to become something big enough by which to define his Presidency.

It seems, however, that the previous March, Nixon had set the stage for another domestic battle when he proposed a "modified" program for dispersal of anti-ballistic missiles "vital for the security and defense of the United States." ("Nixon knew that the battle in Congress over the ABM would be by far his toughest battle of the year," say Evans and Novak, "and, he was convinced, his most important.") Many Congressmen thought even the best of ABM plans a waste of both time and money—shopworn and, like many of Nixon's later proposals, oddly underdeveloped, as if the President felt compelled to say something before he really had anything to say. "He hasn't made a good case for himself," a Capitol Hill reporter heard from a Democratic Congressman, but because the proposal, named Safeguard, resembled the already gutted Sentinel program of 1968, there also numbered among the skeptics a substantial body of efficiency-minded Republicans.

As a result, Hugh Scott, the Senate's Republican minority leader, joined Bryce Harlow, White House chief of Congressional affairs, in urging Nixon to think twice before pressing for his program. Scott begged the President to avoid making a vote on Safeguard a matter of Republican Party loyalties.[1] Either Nixon did not believe that Republicans would defy their President or, as one observer on the Hill said, "he just didn't give a damn for their feelings when *his* were concerned."

In order to appease reluctant Republican Senators, Scott

[1] Of all people, George Aiken, a Republican Senator opposed to Safeguard, was asked by the White House to "talk to" Margaret Chase Smith, another Republican, and persuade her to vote with Nixon. "The visit boomeranged," says Evans and Novak, simply strengthening her resolve to cripple the bill, which is what Bryce Harlow had told Nixon would occur. But White House pressure perhaps more deeply soured Senator James Pearson of Kansas, a fairly independent Republican who was informed by the Agriculture Department that a rural job-development bill he was backing would lose department support.

One day during a staff meeting Bob Haldeman snapped at Colonel Kenneth BeLieu, who had been put in charge of the ABM fight: "You shouldn't be sitting here, you ought to be up in the Senate telling Hugh Scott how to vote." Telling Scott how to vote, Evans and Novak commented, "would have been one likely way of ensuring his opposition."

and Harlow next suggested, purportedly in a more appeasing tone, that if the President worked on it, he could probably have a ballistics dispersal system that pleased Congress and that Nixon himself could support without feeling that he had surrendered the missile lead to Russia. At that, Nixon is said to have flushed, declaring that he opposed the idea of Congress usurping his Presidential "prerogatives."

"Nixon's strong individual views," Joseph Kraft later said in trying to comprehend Nixon's style, were often permitted to "override the concerted opinion of his closest advisers." By demanding a pledge of party loyalty and by ruling out a compromise, Nixon had, predictably, destroyed his options —and in August his ABM program was narrowly defeated in the Senate.

In the intervening days, he tried with an apparent lack of success to relax. Having sought out the breezy insulation of the new White House at San Clemente (after a trip to Rumania), the President surfaced occasionally to stroll on the beach or to play golf. At those moments he seemed somewhat uneasy and peripatetic.

Less than two weeks after his ABM defeat—perhaps unwittingly this time—Nixon created a truly big problem that would define his power, or lack of it. For over three months, there had been a gaping hole on the United States Supreme Court. Abe Fortas had resigned in May after the discovery of an apparent conflict of interest between his private income and his role as a Justice. Prompted by Senator Strom Thurmond, the South Carolina Republican who had helped Nixon win the South in 1968, Attorney General Mitchell selected as Fortas' replacement a South Carolina judge, Clement F. Haynsworth. Haynsworth's nomination was announced from San Clemente on August 18 by press release, but the President did not appear. Reporters were puzzled: earlier in the year, when Nixon announced Warren Burger as his choice for Chief Justice, they remembered it as an impressive ceremonial occasion.

Quickly an excuse was provided. The press secretary explained that Judge Haynsworth, who stammered when he spoke, would have been ill-at-ease in a joint appearance with the President. That may have explained why the nominee remained at home in South Carolina but not why Nixon remained in seclusion just a few yards from where reporters waited to question him. Journalists began suspecting that Nixon was "run down" and could not handle the press.

A second factor may have helped keep Nixon on ice. The President knew very little about Haynsworth's record as a judge, except that he had been certified by Thurmond and Mitchell. The two had purportedly assured Nixon that the nominee had a record of being "hard" on integration, a fact which could be used to undercut George Wallace in case the Alabama racist decided to oppose Nixon for the Presidency in 1972. It was learned later that the first time the President had spoken to Haynsworth at any length was the morning his mimeograph machine announced the nomination. In fact, that may also have been the first time Nixon had *ever* spoken to Haynsworth.

But Nixon's personal evaluation apparently meant less to him than the publicizable fact that the work of selecting a nominee for the Supreme Court had—after so long a delay—been carried out; though others took care of the necessary details, the selection itself was evidence of Presidential progress. Nixon assumed that Haynsworth would be accepted by the Senate as automatically as Burger had been and paid no further attention to his nominee until the desultory selection began generating intense opposition. Not only did Haynsworth's lower court rulings on blacks and labor bother the unions, but, it turned out after investigations by persons outside the White House, that the judge from South Carolina may have been guilty of various breaches of judicial ethics, including a conflict of interest. Observers were amazed that after what had happened to Fortas, Mitchell—and Nixon—had not examined the credentials of their Supreme Court selection more closely.

By October, the mail mounted to some forty-to-one *against* the confirmation of Haynsworth, and a Gallup poll indicated that Nixon's popularity had dropped eight percentage points since the moon landing of July 20. The Gallup poll was released on October 15, the very day that The Vietnam Moratorium and The New Mobilization, two peace organizations working in concert, held their first nationwide demonstration. (Mitchell had informed the President, as he had the public, that these anti-war groups were guided by professional agitators and "foreign" influences, yet the demonstrations, Joseph Kraft reported in *Harper's*, were like the beginning of an "avalanche," with the peace movement embraced for the first time by the middle-class, the middle-aged and the middle-American.) One supposes that it was relatively easy for Nixon, the poll watcher, to relate the spreading anti-war protest to his reported decline. His prestige and popularity seemed to be on the line.

So, on October 20, Nixon took the first step to protect both. Now in Washington, but still reluctant to come all the way out of isolation, he abruptly summoned reporters to his office. There were no cameras or microphones to reveal his mood to the nation in vivid pictures and sounds. During the briefing, with Ehrlichman crouching on a sofa behind the President and press secretary Ron Ziegler standing to one side, the President appeared a bit feverish. His worry lines seemed of late to have grown permanent. His mouth plunged morosely, the corner creases puffing his limp jowls, and he squinted at the forty or more correspondents standing awkwardly in front of his big desk. Nixon stated that he now wished to discuss "the Haynsworth matter."

"I find Haynsworth an honest man," the President said. "He has been, in my opinion as a lawyer, a lawyer's lawyer and a judge's judge . . . I think he will be a great credit to the Supreme Court, and I am going to stand by him until he is confirmed."

John Osborne noticed at the time that the President had control of his hands. In the past, if he was upset or self-conscious, those hands had jerked in inappropriate directions. But he couldn't hide the effect of stress in his words. Instead, the White House stenographer had to do that, later altering the official transcript to delete Nixon's gaffes. Since one of the major items at issue had been Haynsworth's extensive stock portfolio, Nixon said that he'd advise all judges to "own nothing but real estate"—unless it happened to border on a government installation. The jest reflected Nixon's concern about his San Clemente property holdings, which stood conveniently adjacent to a Coast Guard station. Bitter and revealing, those words were omitted from the transcript.

Also, Nixon promised, his head shaking, that if Haynsworth asked that his name be withdrawn from nomination, "I would not let him do it." Perhaps because the statement seemed too pugnacious, too tyrannical for the leader of a democracy, the transcript was changed there, too, to imply that if Haynsworth removed his name, it would be without Nixon's encouragement.

Soon after the press conference, the President left in an unhappy frame of mind for Camp David, there to take care of his other major problem. The peace groups, encouraged by the turnout on October 15, had immediately gone ahead with plans for even larger demonstrations on November 15; and the thrust of their activities would be directed against Nixon. Though he had run for office on the promise that he possessed a secret plan to end the war, he still had not ended it; the best he had done was to promise limited troop withdrawals. Ironically, if he had any intention of fulfilling his pre-election pledge quickly, he had one of the most powerful allies a peace President could have wanted. Shortly after he moved into the White House, the Central Intelligence Agency[1] confided in the President that he could safely remove every last one of the more than five hundred and fifty thousand American soldiers stationed in Vietnam and *"all of Southeast Asia would remain just as it is at least for another generation."* (It was also ironic that Nixon would later apply the last word of the CIA's report to his justification for continuing the war. He did not want to leave Vietnam, he would say, until he was able to assure the boys of America "peace for a full generation.") But Nixon did not need the CIA to tell him this. Even before he took office, he admitted America could not win the war in the presence of his campaign aide, Richard J. Whalen, who in his book, *Catch the Falling Flag*, quotes Nixon as saying;

[1] Despite its reputation as the hard-line, meddlesome "agent of American imperialism," the CIA debunked the "domino theory" on which earlier involvement in Vietnam had been built. In a copyrighted article printed June 25, 1971, The Chicago *Sun-Times* quoted from government documents revealing that the CIA— thought to be behind widening the war in Vietnam to oppose Communism—had actually opposed bombing North Vietnam as militarily and propagandistically ineffective.

on the strength of the military information he already possessed: *"I've come to the conclusion that there's no way to win the war. But we can't say that of course . . ."* Therefore, by October 20 of the next year, Nixon's problem was not how to end the war, but how to convince the public that he *wanted* to end it, in order to cut the heart out of the protests against him and his policies.

There is no doubt that Nixon felt personally threatened by the scheduled protest. With his approval, and (reporters think) with his prompting, Vice-President Agnew was sent out to admonish the "effete snobs" allegedly populating the peace movement and, on Mitchell's information, to associate the Moratorium with Hanoi. Meanwhile, the President labored over a speech on Vietnam to be given over television on November 3. With time out only for one brief campaign visit to nearby Virginia, Nixon spent virtually every waking hour between October 20 and November 3 writing the revising; he put the speech through ten drafts, all written by him, summarily rejecting the proposals of his aides. (According to the *Times*, Nixon poured more time and energy into the document than any since his acceptance speech in Miami, in 1968.) Answering the peace protestors seemed to have become almost as private an affair as writing the last chapter of *Six Crises*. Right up to air time, no one other than Rose Mary Woods, his personal secretary, and Henry Kissinger was allowed to see or touch Nixon's words.

Despite all that effort, however, and with the exception of the word "Vietnamization" (a concept designed to keep American troops in Southeast Asia until the far-distant day when South Vietnam could fend for itself), the President said very little that the nation had not heard before. Using prime television time, he declared himself in favor of "the right way" and against "the easy way" of ending the war, the latter being the militarily feasible option of up-and-leaving that the CIA had given him months earlier.

Like Johnson before him, Nixon spoke of "the humiliation" of being the first President in United States history to lose a war. Perhaps this fear encouraged him to become illogical: after confessing that the *"popular* and easy course" was immediate withdrawal, Nixon, for the first time, appealed to the "silent majority" to support his hawkish line. If there were a silent majority, though, didn't it already represent the *popular* opinion?

Rhetorically, Nixon asked the American people if they had "the moral stamina and the courage to meet the challenge of the free world leadership"? At that moment, he seemed to be questioning whether the nation-at-large had as much courage as he. He also seemed to be urging the American people to leave him alone: "Let the historians not record that, when America was the most powerful nation in the world, we passed on the other side of the road and allowed the last hope for peace and freedom of millions of people be *suffocated* by the forces of totalitarianism." If America did not stay in Vietnam until the free people of South Vietnam could take care of themselves, Nixon cautioned, *"We would lose confidence in ourselves."*

Why those words at that moment? Nixon had heard from the Gallup poll, he had heard from the press and he had, obviously, heard from all the Americans in business suits and respectable clothcoats who had stood outside the White House protesting *his* war. At that point, Nixon's unconscious could not possibly have had any more faith in the silent majority than it had in Nixon, himself.

Lacking confidence, he went on to make a blunder that went largely unnoticed. "I have chosen a plan for peace," he said. "I believe it will succeed." In the corrected text, the next line reads: "If it does not succeed, what the critics say now won't matter." However, the President of the United States actually said: "If it does not succeed, it won't matter." Did he omit "critics" because critics are vocal and he was thinking instead of that damnably silent, silent majority? In any case, in that one line, Nixon let slip a characteristically egocentric attitude: What did peace abroad or peace at home matter when Richard M. Nixon himself was not at peace?

Semple of the *Times* also believed Nixon's speech of November 3 was "very much a personal affair . . . In psychological terms [Nixon had put] his own capacity for leadership to what he considered a deliberate test." Consequently, when network commentators immediately observed that the President had labored long but conceived nothing they hadn't heard dozens of times already, Nixon became, by most accounts, extremely irritated. As the week wore on, his aides reflected his irritation over various rebuffs. One of his assistants belligerently predicted that Nixon would nominate another southerner if Haynsworth was rejected, and Warren Weaver Jr., a reporter, noted that the staffer did not pause to question the President's right to shove more of the same down the Senate's throat, if Senators refused to take their orders from the White House.

On Veterans Day, November 11, Nixon and the First Lady drove to a Veterans Administration Hospital. Making the rounds of the wounded, the President turned to one old soldier wearing an eye patch and in what an observer, John Herbes, referred to as a "philosophical half-joking[1] vein," said, "All you need is one. You see too much anyway."

The next day, November 12, the daily papers carried a story that Nixon's intermediaries had insisted Haynsworth stick it out. A "close friend" of Haynsworth's explained, "They told him that it was important that he stick; he argued, they argued back—and he stuck. At first, the job on the Supreme Court looked mighty good to Clem," said the friend, "but then with all this noise and these attacks . . . he would just like to get back to work and forget it."

But the Senate was ready to open debate on Haynsworth and the President had no desire to look the coward. So he sent Mitchell to see Len B. Jordan, a conservative Republican who invariably voted with his President. Although the Attorney General cleared up many of Jordan's questions, he failed to explain how Haynsworth could have testified in June —prior to his nomination—that he had resigned from *all* business associations at the time he joined the lower bench and then testified in September that, in fact, he had retained one of those business associations *simply because he didn't think about it*. When Jordan remained dumbfounded by the

[1] "Philosophical half-joking" is the kind of description journalists had begun using to convey Nixon's state. The job in the main, though, has proved greater than their ingenuity. "Philosophical" is a safe, vague word they have learned to lean on when unable to pin down the point of Nixon's more bizarre expressions or actions. But "half-joking," on the other hand, manages to reveal by implication just how disturbed he was at the moment of utterance.

138

prospect of a Supreme Court Justice who felt it was okay to maintain a conflict of interest so long as it wasn't public information, Mitchell pressed so hard that he managed to turn Jordan off Haynsworth. "Support of the President," Jordan later explained, "is urged as if it were a personal matter rather than an issue of grave Constitutional importance."

In one sense, Jordan was more fortunate than other Republicans; thinking of him as a proven ally, the Administration at least *talked* to him. But Senators like Clifford Case of New Jersey and Mark Hatfield of Oregon were treated like lepers. To a lesser degree, so were Republicans such as George Aiken of Vermont and John Sherman Cooper of Kentucky. Although Aiken had supported Republican Presidents all but once in his thirty years in Congress on major nominations, and would again with Haynsworth, his saltiness and his shrewdness seemed to intimidate Nixon. And Cooper's "very dignity and formality," explained one wire service reporter on the Hill, "scares hell out of 'em down at 1600."

On November 12, the day after his visit to the VA hospital, Nixon volunteered somewhat petulantly that he would not be affected by anything the peace marchers said or did, and reflecting this, his surrogates grew tougher. On November 13, ten days after Nixon's offhand dismissal by the television commentators, Vice-President Agnew condemned these network men as "self-appointed analysts" with minds "made up in advance" and as a "tiny enclosed fraternity of privileged men" who prevented the public from making up its own mind, inadvertently suggesting that the silent majority listened to Nixon's enemies, rather than Nixon. Also, Dean Burch, a devout conservative appointed by Nixon to the Federal Communications Commission, personally called each of the three networks to request transcripts of the various commentaries. And the peace marchers, who were not going to affect Nixon one way or the other on November 12, began affecting him nonetheless. On November 14, as demonstrators of all sizes, types and ages, from all over the country, poured in, swamping the city, Nixon fled in another burst of motion. He flew down to Cape Kennedy, travelling one thousand four hundred miles to sit for twenty-two minutes in a driving rain for the two-minute lift-off of Apollo 12. Then, as he was leaving the Cape to fly back to Washington, he wiped out the last agonizing thirty days in a gem of a slip. Signing the Cape guestbook, the President wrote his name first and next the date: "October 14."

But there was no turning the clock back. While somewhere between a quarter and a half million Americans collected at the foot of the Washington Monument, three or four hundred yards to the north, Nixon watched football on television, then arrogantly announced the fact. Later that same afternoon, warned by Federal agents that the peace people intended to destroy Washington and kill the President of the United States, he slipped out of town again—this time to Camp David.

On November 21, less than one week after the largest group of human beings assembled in one place for a purely political meeting, the Senate of the United States rejected fifty-five to forty-five Nixon's nominee, Clement Haynsworth. It was the first such rejection of a nominee to the high bench in a third of a century. Calling it "a political setback of stunning proportions," *The New York Times* said, "Ironically, the President could have averted the debacle if he had seen fit, by withdrawing the judge's name once he realized the depths of the opposition it had stirred up."

Yet in his peculiar way, Richard Nixon had again defined himself, perhaps failing because unconsciously he never stopped thinking of himself as a failure.

CHAPTER FOURTEEN

Two weeks after the Senate rejected Clement Haynsworth for the Supreme Court, the President announced that the defeated nominee would continue as the chief judge of the United States Court of Appeals for the Fourth Circuit. With Haynsworth at last by his side, Nixon said, "I must say that after the brutal, vicious and, in my opinion, unfair attack on his integrity, I would well understand why the judge would retire to private life. A weak man would; a fearful man would. The judge is not a weak man; he is a strong man."

But it was Nixon who refused to give up the fight, the fear of being considered weak obsessing his consciousness. "I'm not afraid of [the press]," he said to the press a few days later on December 9, "just as the press is not afraid of me."[1] But the main contest, for the moment, was with the Senate, so Nixon threatened to veto a tax bill then coming to a vote on the floor; moreover, to summon Congress for a special Christmas session if they refused to give him the appropriations bill he now demanded. There was one moment of frank vulnerability during the press conference, when the President unexpectedly said, "I like to be liked, I don't like to say things that everybody doesn't agree with." But it was the only moment.[2]

[1] Asked about Vice-President Agnew's growing criticism of the news media—"broadcasting in particular"—Nixon replied, "The Vice-President does not clear his speeches with me . . . However, I believe that [he] rendered a public service in talking in a very dignified and courageous way about a problem many Americans are concerned about, and that is the coverage by news media and in particular television news media of public figures." In short, Nixon was praising Agnew for damning the network's coverage of himself. Before long, the consensus seemed to be that the man behind Agnew's voice was Nixon. Even some of Agnew's belligerent polysyllables belonged to speechwriters Nixon lent him.

[2] Earlier that day, the President was in touch with Arnold Hutschnecker, putatively about the doctor's scheme to test the infant population for criminal tendencies. Could the President's

Nixon seemed to hold on to his belligerence for weeks and on January 14 went out of his way to praise a New York City policeman for fighting with his superiors over the right to wear an American flag pin on his uniform. It was common knowledge that the pin, worn largely by people in support of the Vietnam war, had also become a symbol of defiance to the peacenik, rather than one of old-fashioned patriotism. In his letter to the officer (which the White House publicized), Nixon implied that anyone who failed to wear the pin on his lapel was somehow dishonoring America. But very soon, many Washingtonians came to the unshakeable conclusion that the President—having associated himself indivisibly with national pride—was demanding that America, his enemies in particular, honor *him* with a demonstration of obedience to his will.

For until January 19, when they received the President's next nominee for the U.S. Supreme Court, even the liberal Democrats in the Senate were eager to heal the wounds inflicted on him during the Haynsworth battle two months earlier. But to have the name of G. Harrold Carswell flung at them seemed deliberately insulting. With Haynsworth, Senators worried about a conflict of interest. With Carswell, they were awed by judicial incompetence topped, after some investigation, by apparent bigotry. In his brief tenure on the Fifth Circuit Court (his first job on the bench, which Nixon had given him not very many months earlier), Carswell had racked up an unconscionable judicial record: most of his decisions had been summarily reversed upon appeal by higher courts whose members frequently demonstrated naked contempt for the man's judgment. Moreover, Carswell, a Floridian, in a 1948 speech had openly espoused white supremacy and in 1956 had participated in the conversion of a city-run golf course in Tallahassee into a private country club so as to circumvent the recent Supreme Court ruling on desegregation of all public facilities. So bad were Carswell's credentials that Ernest F. Hollings of South Carolina, one of the Senators who had led the fight for Haynsworth,

uncharacteristic admission have been a temporary by-product of their communication with each other? One objective of psychoanalysis is to make patients understand and accept their phobias.

142

eventually complained that Carswell "was not qualified to carry Judge Haynsworth's law books."[1]

Had Mitchell known in the beginning how inadequate Carswell was, say some reporters, he never would have sent the name to the Senate. But this opinion does not explain why Mitchell had taken Carswell, whose name had been far down on the Attorney General's list of candidates, and had leapfrogged the Floridian over several better qualified judicial talents. The more common opinion, as variously described by Washington observers, was that the Carswell nomination was "deliberately provocative" and "an act of political aggression against the President's opponents." William V. Shannon of the *Times* said the President lacked "peaceable intentions." This was also the opinion of men outside the press.

Joseph Rauh Jr., a persuasive voice in the civil rights-oriented Leadership Conference, said afterwards: "[Nixon] wanted to defeat his enemies in face-to-face combat. Lots of Southerners would have been confirmed easily, and he knew it. But he chose the *only* man the Leadership Conference had ever opposed for the bench.[2] The White House knew about our opposition, and I believe they actually *hoped* for it." Rauh pointed out that the President appeared anxious to reingage in open warfare blacks and organized labor who had urged the Senate's defeat of Haynsworth, adding, "That's taking on a lot of enemies."

The more enemies and the more awful Carswell's personal and judicial background, the greater Nixon's victory over his enemies might seem. Because he'd been humiliated in November, poetic justice and psychic ends might be better

[1] But feeling politically obliged to support Nixon's "southern strategy," Hollings nonetheless voted for Carswell, as did other Senators who did not like the judge's record but put politics first.

[2] That happened in 1969, when Nixon had proposed Carswell for the Fifth Circuit Court.

Rauh's argument that there were any number of qualified southern judges was strengthened in 1971. When reluctantly (after less qualified choices were ruled unacceptable by the American Bar Association), the President nominated Lewis Powell, a conservative lawyer from Virginia, to fill one of the next Supreme Court vacancies, the Senate embraced him wholeheartedly because of his solid legal qualifications.

served if he could force them to hold their noses and swallow an excessively bitter object plucked from the bottom of the barrel. Carswell's blemishes so thoroughly overshadowed any issues that the nomination was converted into a pure test of power, which Nixon consciously believed he was going to win, on the theory that the Senate would not have the nerve to reject two Presidential nominees in succession. Still working off that assumption some days later, the President became flippant. Discussing Carswell's racist background with members of the press, Nixon said that even if he had known beforehand of Carswell's record, he still would have nominated the Floridian. "If everybody in government who has belonged to restricted golf clubs were to leave the service," he remarked, "[Washington] would have the highest rate of unemployment of any city in the country."[1]

At this time in history, the President found corollary means, it appears, to balm his wounded pride, for he vetoed the nearly twenty-billion-dollar health, education and anti-poverty bill. Although he'd been threatening the veto almost from the day of Haynsworth's defeat, Republicans—as well as Democrats—were "mystified," according to reporter John Finney, "as to why the President chose to veto a bill containing politically popular money for education, medical research and hospital construction . . . A common if somewhat cynical explanation was the President decided that he must draw the line somewhere if only to prove the credibility of his [veto] threats."

In February, the first Senator to go on record against the Carswell nomination was a New York Republican, Charles Goodell. According to Evans and Novak, Goodell was grouped in Nixon's mind with Charles Mathias of Maryland, Charles Percy of Illinois, Mark Hatfield of Oregon and, "most of the time," Hugh Scott of Pennsylvania, Nixon's own Minority Leader—"phony liberals" who "attacked him personally only for personal political gain." The co-authors

[1] Richard Harris, in *The New Yorker* article on the Carswell fight, noted that membership in the club was begging the point, since the accusation had been that Carswell, at the time the government's highest law-enforcement officer in Tallahassee, "had violated his oath to uphold the Constitution by helping to circumvent the Supreme Court's interpretation of it."

offer the testimony of a White House aide who said, "I was amazed at the intensity of his [the President's] feelings against the liberal Republicans." Goodell's opposition to Carswell was the final straw,[1] especially when the Senator refused to change his mind after a visit from Bernard J. Lasker, chairman of the New York Stock Exchange and Nixon's emissary. "Mr. Lasker pursued the possibility of my muting my voice," Goodell recalls, "and adapting to the Administration politically, and conceivably getting support from the Administration."

While Goodell didn't especially like the visit, it seemed legitimate politics. But as Nixon began to realize that victory was slipping away, he and his aides grew politically inept. During the Haynsworth battle, Nixon's Congressional aides had promised Hawaii Republican Hiram Fong that, in return for his favourable vote on the nomination, they would help establish an East-West trade center in Honolulu. Now Fong was told he could have the same reward in return for a favorable vote on Carswell. "That . . . didn't sit well with Fong," noted Richard Harris. "A number of Republican Senators observed that they had never seen such incompetent liaison work by an Administration as there was in the Haynsworth case—until the Carswell nomination." Winston Prouty and George Aiken of Vermont and Marlow Cook of Kentucky, three other Republican Senators who originally pledged to support the President's nomination, faltered after nineteen faculty members of Florida State University Law School—of which Carswell was a founder—publicly urged Nixon to withdraw the nomination. Cook, who had been the floor leader for Haynsworth, said, "I am not enamored with the [Carswell] nomination."

Nixon now began defining his enemies in a series of bizarre actions that often had nothing to do directly with Carswell. In the middle of March, he invited Johnny Cash to perform at the White House, explicitly requesting he sing "Welfare Cadillac," about a shiftless father who relies on

[1] The following fall, in retaliation, Nixon sent Agnew on the attack. The Vice-President called Goodell "the Christine Jorgensen of politics" while the President threw his support to James Buckley, the Conservative. The result was Goodell's failure to win.

taxpaying "fools" to finance his new car. Cash discreetly refused to sing the song, which fed, perhaps inadvertently, off a pervasive prejudice that black men both dominated the welfare rolls and drove shiny Cadillac cars. American blacks were intensifying the pressure against the Carswell nomination, and a week after the invitation went out to Cash, Republican Senator Edward Brooke of Massachusetts abruptly informed the President at a White House meeting on another subject that he was now "working night and day to defeat Carswell." Witnesses say that Nixon grinned "indulgently" and for the rest of the meeting patronized the black Senator.

On March 23, in possibly the most aggressive act at the time, Nixon ordered Federal troops to New York to overcome an illegal strike by postal workers. Explained the President in a special television announcement that day: "We cannot and we will not negotiate while thousands of postal workers are participating in an illegal work stoppage . . . *What is at issue then is the survival of government based on law.*" Though the strike was national in scope, Nixon sent troops only to New York City, capital of the Eastern Liberal Establishment, where so much of the anti-Carswell, anti-Nixon sentiment centered.[1]

White House aides quickly reassured the press that the first peacetime call-up of this type since Lincoln sent Federal troops to break a longshoreman's strike was reached by Nixon without panic, relying on "his own sense of timing and degree." But by the sixth day of the strike, that vaunted sense may have been in disrepair. During a meeting in the President's office, a staff member tried kidding him about how postal workers had probably lost their enthusiasm for Nixon's plan to replace the Post Office Department with a quasi-independent corporation. Abruptly, Nixon turned on the staff member. "Let's stop this horsing around. It's time

[1] The day he moved to break the strike, Nixon moved to break the Russians, too, sending a "tough" note to Premier Kosygin that all but *ordered* the Russians to join international meetings on the resolution of Laotian problems. The missive was described by one source as harsh—"it was a shit or get off the pot kind of thing."

to start talking turkey." After this jarring note, those present say a profoundly uncomfortable chill fell on the room.

When news reached Nixon that Carswell's nomination was in grave danger on the Senate floor, he summoned Deputy Attorney General Kleindienst (in charge of the Justice Department while John Mitchell was vacationing). Then, according to Harris, the President "angrily" told Kleindienst that "since he was officially responsible for screening candidates . . . And for getting him [Nixon] into the Carswell mess, he had better get them all out of it."

In response, Kleindienst allegedly pressured Charles F. Wilson, a black government lawyer, to sign a letter *written for him* by Assistant Attorney General William Rehnquist. The letter, stating in his numerous appearances before Carswell the judge had never been "rude or discourteous to me," became fairly important because it was the only favorable report on Carswell's treatment of civil rights lawyers.

The charge that Wilson had been pressured, levelled by California Democratic Senator Alan Cranston and based on an affidavit from another black lawyer, Vincent Cohen, was immediately denied by Wilson, who said that while he had been aided in writing the letter, the rest was untrue.

That should have ended the dispute, but three hours later Kleindienst, accompanied by Rehnquist, called his own press conference. "The opponents of Judge Carswell," he countercharged, "are not only getting nervous. They are getting desperate. This is an insidious attack on the Attorney General and the Department of Justice." Kleindienst said the Department had nothing to do with the letter, then Rehnquist got up to say that he'd visited Wilson at home to draft the letter for him.

Inevitably, as things got stickier, Nixon began viewing the entire Carswell battle as an insidious attack on Nixon. In a letter to Ohio Republican Senator William B. Saxbe, Nixon defined the attack, "What is centrally at issue in this nomination," he wrote, "is the Constitutional responsibility of the President to appoint members of the Court—and whether this can be *frustrated* by those who wish to substitute their own philosophy or their own subjective judgment for that of the *one person* entrusted by the Constitution with the power of appointment . . . The question arises whether *I* [emphases added], as the President of the United States, shall be accorded the same right of choice . . . which has freely been accorded to my predecessors of both parties . . . What is at stake is the preservation of the traditional Constitutional relationships of the President and Congress."

The Senate's response to Nixon's attitude was uniform indignation. Senator Robert W. Packwood of Oregon responded: "The Senate doesn't like to do very much but it doesn't like to be told that it doesn't have the right to do very much," and Senator Birch Bayh of Indiana added: "This interpretation is wrong as a matter of Constitutional law, wrong as a matter of history, and wrong as a matter of public policy."

Reston of the *Times* commented on both the letter and the President's emotions, characterizing the missive to Saxbe as "full of bad history and bad law . . . The President has taken a chance. He has made the emotional and inaccurate argument that Senators are trying to deny him rights that all other Presidents have had, and that a vote against Carswell is somehow a threat to the Constitution. This could lose him enough votes to lose Carswell." Reston said that it might also make Nixon appear to be "fighting another battle against the professors, the liberals and the Eastern press . . ." Nixon was, but Reston, essentially a man of caution, added that he couldn't quite believe that Nixon had "suddenly become reckless and careless."

Just before Easter, one of Nixon's counsellors suggested to him that they should discuss the President's options if Congress recessed for the holiday without first passing his revised appropriations bill. "There will be no discussion," Nixon stated with what staff members described to John Osborne as "harsh ferocity." "That decision has been made. They [Congress] will have to come back."

On April 6, Sen. Marlow Cook called the White House to inform his party leader that he was voting against Carswell. To soften the blow, Cook added that the President only needed one vote to create a tie on the Senate floor. Immediately, wrote Richard Harris, "Bryce Harlow and his staff got to work—or, as others saw it, they panicked." Harlow, Nixon's

Congressional liaison, ordered an aide to announce that the swing vote, Margaret Chase Smith of Maine, had promised to support Carswell.

On April 8 the United States Senate rejected G. Harrold Carswell, Nixon's second nomination for the vacancy on the Supreme Court, by a vote of fifty-one to forty-five. And the putative tie vote, Mrs. Smith, numbered among the fourteen Republicans who voted no on the judge from Florida.

Several days later, Reston explained why Nixon had failed to withdraw Carswell's name before the inevitable happened. Getting Carswell confirmed had become "such a compulsive and pervasive idea in the President's mind," wrote Reston, "that he didn't have time to consider whether it was a good idea."

That evening of his "disappointment," as the White House press office characterized it, Nixon left for a cruise on the Potomac on the Presidential yacht *Sequoia*. He took with him only two people: John Mitchell and H. R. Haldeman. Symbiotically joining Mitchell, chief architect of the Haynsworth and Carswell disasters, and Haldeman, manager of Nixon's 1962 defeat in California and his most belligerent White House aide, apparently gave Nixon the "strength" he liked to talk about. At noon the next day, he summoned aboard Patrick Buchanan, the most conservative of his speechwriters and author of many Agnew attacks on the media. Buchanan was ordered to draft a strong statement against the Senate. However, the draft Nixon received was said to be "too soft," so the President personally toughened it up.

By three that afternoon, Nixon was back in the White House and there followed a hundred and twenty seconds reminiscent of the "last" press conference of 1962. Then Nixon had strode rapidly into the big hotel room in California and abruptly let fly; now, almost eight years later, he strode into the press room of the White House. Some observers thought he looked determined; others thought he looked disturbed.

The conflict was cleared up the instant Nixon opened his mouth: "I have reluctantly concluded—with the Senate presently constituted—I cannot successfully nominate to the

Supreme Court any Federal appellate judge from the South . . . Judges Carswell and Haynsworth have endured with admirable dignity vicious assaults on their intelligence, their honesty and their character," Nixon said so intensely that the viewer questioned whether the nominees or Nixon, himself, had suffered that assault. And Nixon proceeded to answer that question too: "When all that hypocrisy is stripped away, the real issue was their philosophy . . . a philosophy that I share . . ."

Nixon assured "millions of Americans" that he understood their "bitter feeling" and then he jerkily spun away and vanished from sight, toward the privacy of his office. His next act was to jump on the phone and tell his friends how proud he was of his performance. Then he asked each of them how *they* thought he did.

Shannon of the *Times*, who had not been asked, recorded what Nixon knew but did not want to hear. From beginning to end, Shannon observed, it was "a personal humiliation unprecedented in the hundred years of the Presidency since the Senate repeatedly rebuffed Ulysses Grant's inept nominees for various high offices."

CHAPTER FIFTEEN

If anyone appreciates Nixon viscerally, it's his warlike chief assistant, H. R. Haldeman, who has advised puzzled members of the White House staff that to understand the President's thinking during the Cambodian crisis, they ought to see the movie "Patton." A daringly brilliant, megalomaniacal soldier, General George Patton had rescued trapped Americans during the Battle of the Bulge by moving (in Nixon's awed words) "one million men about a hundred miles in three days." An intrigued Nixon viewed the film for the first time on April 4, 1970, just as the tide of battle was turning against him in his own war with the United States Senate over the Carswell nomination. He saw "Patton" a second time on April 25, three days before the invasion of Cambodia, and a third time in the middle of May, when a hostile world seemed to be closing in on him.

In the midst of a conversation with business leaders meeting at the White House, Nixon unexpectedly asked, "Anybody seen the movie 'Patton'?" (Before anyone could answer, he joked that people who saw the film must have picked up a few four-letter words that not even today's college kids knew.) Secretary of State Rogers told Darryl F. Zanuck, the man whose company made "Patton," that the film came up in "every" Presidential conversation. The real point of Nixon's obsession with "Patton," according to Hugh Sidey of *Time* and *Life*, "was that George Patton had accomplished the impossible." Nixon told people that Patton had won the Battle of the Bulge and saved American men after the other Generals said it couldn't be done. The President suggested that God had been with Patton and that, like this successful General, "you have to have the will and determination to do what is right for America."

Nixon identified with Patton morally but the odd thing is that he may have identified with him professionally as well. Thirteen days before seeing "Patton" for the first time, Nixon had played commanding general and discovered that the role paid relatively handsome political dividends. In March, prior to what a few wits title "General Nixon's invasion of New York City," Gallup found Nixon's popularity sliding; most Americans had decided that he was a "passive President" who, as a young Texan said to a pollster, "just doesn't seem to be getting things done." But after using troops to break up the postal strike, the President's popularity rose, which obviously meant that the exemplary use of force pleased his constituency. It was an object lesson to be remembered.

Five days before Nixon deployed troops in New York, Prince Norodom Sihanouk, the neutralist chief of Cambodia, was deposed by the pro-western regime of General Lon Nol. Because Sihanouk had frequently opposed American wishes, Nixon moved to shore up the new government. On April 16, fearing objections at home, the President secretly initiated the shipment of six thousand captured "Russian-type" rifles to Lon Nol, carefully instructing American intermediaries to circulate the misinformation that the rifles came not from the U.S. but from President Thieu of South Vietnam. In contrast, that same day, an American diplomat in Saigon explained to reporters that he and his embassy would oppose an extension of the war into Cambodia. The talk centered on destroying Communist sanctuaries which, the spokesman emphasized, had existed in Cambodia for five years. The diplomat was convinced that attacks against the sanctuaries situated along the eastern border of Cambodia, near South Vietnam, would serve only to chase the Communists farther into Cambodia, out of reach of allied forces, compounding the military problems of the month-old Lon Nol regime.

Also on April 16, Melvin Laird, seeing greater problems on the home front than in Indochina, advised Nixon to placate the American public by announcing the return home of another fifty thousand GI's by August. This created a conflict because Creighton Abrams, cautious commander of U.S. troops in Indochina, urged the President to delay further withdrawals in case of trouble, particularly in the area of Cambodia. Each man pressed his case, but the President hesitated to give an answer.

The next night, on April 17, a formal "Evening at the

White House," the President gave leather-faced singer Johnny Cash a gratuitous lecture: "You've had some hard knocks in your life, but always remember—true, strong character is built and formed during times of adversity. It's the hard knocks and the hard times that are making you the man you are now. You're reaping the rewards of having realized the mistakes you've made and profiting from the hard times you've had."

On April 18, amid mounting counter-pressures from Laird and Abrams, news reached the President that Apollo 13 would have to abort the latest moon mission in mid-flight; immediately, the President and Mrs. Nixon flew off to the Pacific, to where the astronauts were to splash down. The next day, after the safe return of the astronauts, Nixon huddled with Admiral John McCain Jr., commander in chief of all U.S. forces in the Pacific, who briefed him on a contingency plan for invading Cambodia. The President had actually seen the same plan on April 1, when Abrams forwarded it to Washington. So Nixon already had had time to consider its two principal options: either to permit South Vietnamese troops, on their own, to run harassing operations inside Cambodia, or to use American and South Vietnamese soldiers jointly against Communist supply bases, located in Cambodian sanctuaries. Before boarding Air Force One for the return flight from Hawaii to the Western White House in San Clemente, Nixon and the First Lady attended the Little Stone Church in Honolulu. Although the President did not seem too concerned, he asked Admiral McCain to come along on Air Force One so that he could brief Kissinger the next day on conditions in Cambodia.

Even by the next day, the deterioration in the Cambodian tactical situation was still unimpressive. Two Communist attacks that day against Cambodian cities were rather like earlier attacks in that they did not seriously affect Lon Nol's security. In fact, Kissinger thought so little of the attacks, he barely discussed them with Nixon. However, evidently afraid of potential danger, the President decided in the course of the day to take Abrams advice and delay troop withdrawals until October.

In the apparent absence of a compelling military crisis,

Nixon retired to his quarters at San Clemente to write a speech which he delivered there at six o'clock that evening on television, to comfort the American public about the general situation in Southeast Asia. During the address, he proclaimed "Vietnamization" a success and emphasized the need for flexibility in the search for a *political* settlement of the war in Vietnam. "We finally have in sight the just peace we are seeking," he said. In passing, though, Nixon warned he would take "strong and effective measures" to deal with any escalation of enemy activity originating in Laos or Cambodia. Intent, however, on his first objective, the President camouflaged the withdrawal delay by announcing his "far-reaching decision" to pull out a total of one hundred and fifty thousand troops by May, 1971. On the whole, therefore, his mood was peaceable, and although Nixon's speech on April 20 contained nothing especially novel or enlightening, more than one liberal observer was pleased by his apparent willingness to seek a political settlement.

After the bitter reaction to the invasion of Cambodia, spokesmen for the White House, chief among them Henry Kissinger, deluged the press with ploddingly detailed background information to prove the President's decision neither irrational nor precipitous. Pentagon and State Department sources managed to fill in some more gaps, so that a composite picture was developed, and day-by-day, hour-by-hour and (in the case of *Look*) minute-by-minute accounts appeared in half a dozen or more major news outlets. All of them seemed in agreement that the significant details began on April 20—almost immediately after President Nixon's televised peace speech.

He did something unusual for him afterwards. Though Nixon dislikes arriving places in the middle of the night, he decided to begin the five-and-a-half-hour flight to Washington at once. Noticing that her husband was "wound up," Mrs. Nixon told people later it was because he was "really excited" by the safe landing of the astronauts. But because two days had passed since then, she apparently thought it more honest to characterize the source of his nervousness in general terms: "Well, I think he just wanted to talk to somebody." Reporters, too, noticed that he was anxious to talk, even to them.

Although Air Force One was on a tight departure schedule, the President dallied on the runway virtually to the moment of take-off. Everytime the correspondents accompanying the flight made a move to board, he beseeched them to stay, Bob Semple remembers, with "a lifted eyebrow" or he'd find something, often inane, to say. Avoiding more substantive subjects, he commented, for example, on how beautifully he felt the minister in Honolulu had performed yesterday. As a result, there was awkward shuffling by everyone, but Nixon did not stop finding things to say until roaring jet engines muffled his voice. Airbound, he called many of his friends on the Air Force One phone for their reaction to his speech. At one point in the flight, presumably running out of people to call, he stuck his head out from behind the curtain over his compartment. The President smiled wistfully, as if he wanted to come out, but popped out of sight like a character in Punch and Judy. One of his staff explained in retrospect that the President's restlessness signified that "something was up." With twenty-twenty hindsight the aide said, "Maybe he sensed a big decision coming."

By 7:15 a.m. on April 21, Nixon arrived in the Oval Office. At 7:35 he walked into the Roosevelt Room where the usual staff meeting was taking place. Nixon interrupted to muse, according to *Look*, "about how day-to-day struggles to get something done were important enough, but that the staff should not lose sight of the long run, that the important thing about any program or decision was the end result, not the difficulties encountered along the way." After a meeting on Cambodia with Kissinger and Richard Helms of the CIA, the President ordered the National Security Council to meet within twenty-four hours. That afternoon he talked again with Kissinger. Nixon's behavior on Tuesday, April 21, said an admiring White House aide, showed an increased alertness and charisma, as if he had developed those fabled "extra glands" that enabled Lyndon Johnson to function so well in crises.

At the NSC session on Wednesday, Nixon, chairing the meeting, called for a discussion about the use of South

Vietnamese troops to wipe out the Cambodian sanctuaries. There was no discussion of using Americans, apart from the usual number that generally supported the South Vietnamese as "advisers" and suppliers of food and ammunition.

The next day, at Nixon's behest, Kissinger convened a pet body called the Washington Special Action Group, created after the EC-121 was shot down over Korea in 1969. Sources feel that Kissinger had "conned" Nixon into organizing WSAG to act as a check against any more precipitous Nixon wars, but within the year the group seemed merely to supply operational details to help the President carry out decisions he had already made. Nixon remained in touch with Kissinger for the rest of that Thursday, calling him several times. Most of the calls were made that evening. During one of the phone conversations, the President asked if it was worthwhile letting South Vietnamese soldiers invade a section of Cambodia called "the Parrot's Beak" that jutted into South Vietnam about thirty miles from Saigon. Then he called to ask if the South Vietnamese were capable of carrying it off without help from American combat soldiers. In the final call of the night, Nixon asked the national security adviser for a plan to cover that contingency.

Nixon went to bed, taking along a blue loose-leaf book that brought him in contact with the outside world. It was—as the gold letters on the cover declared—"The President's Daily News Briefing," a digest of fifty or sixty news outlets for Nixon's eyes only, which speechwriter and factotum Buchanan prepared each day with the help of a small but energetic staff. In bed, Nixon learned that *The New York Times*, a newspaper he believes treats him unfairly, much of the time, had revealed that *he*—and not President Thieu— was the source of rifles to Lon Nol's Cambodian army. That night or first thing the next morning, Nixon ordered top officials of the State Department to prepare *written oaths* swearing that they had not leaked the story. By this time, the President considered the Department of State excluding Secretary Rogers, a hot-bed of anti-Nixonites.[1]

[1] In turn, State Department officials below Rogers were incensed. Virtually the only serious attention in the sixteen months since Nixon had become President arrived in the humiliating form of an

Now there was a second irritant. Richard L. Ottinger, a Democratic Congressman from New York, was charging in print that the CIA—with Nixon's explicit approval—was running a military operation in Laos "that could well plunge the U.S. into another major, bloody land war in Asia in this decade." After spending several days in Laos, members of Ottinger's staff concluded that "the precise pattern of hidden involvement which had entrapped us in Vietnam" was being duplicated in Laos, where the war had already "escalated staggeringly" *under Nixon*. The CIA which had informed Nixon in early 1969 that he did not have to keep fighting in Asia was now apparently fighting *his* war very hard, leading and supplying a forty-thousand-man mercenary army in which each volunteer was receiving up to a thousand dollars a week from the United States government. (Bafflingly, the American press paid no attention to the war in Laos after giving only passing notice to Ottinger's charges.)

On the morning of April 24, Nixon advised Kissinger there definitely *would* be some kind of military operation inside Cambodia, even if only to send South Vietnamese soldiers into "the Parrot's Beak." There's no way of telling whether Ottinger, the *Times* and the State Department—individually or collectively—added to Nixon's determination to fight, but no sooner had the President decided that some fighting would be necessary when he gave a strong hint that some might not be enough: he asked Laird to provide a more ambitious contingency plan, to cover a military invasion of "the Fishhook," a second sanctuary located on the Cambodian side about seventy-five miles from Saigon. Evidently sensing that the President was—in Hugh Sidey's term— "stepping ahead of himself," the politically-sensitive Secretary of Defense stalled, advising Nixon to seek the reaction

accusation that they were expected to deny in essay form, as if they were delinquent schoolchildren. A year later, Nixon still looked upon the State Department as an internal enemy and ordered the FBI to conduct a series of investigations to find information leaks. In September, 1971, State Department spokesman Robert J. McCloskey said the latest investigation had been prompted by a fear that "stories harmful to the national interest" were being disclosed by unauthorized persons. Officials were asked to take lie-detector tests.

of Congress before making such an awesome decision. So Nixon made the gesture: he summoned John Stennis, a conservative Democrat from Mississippi and the Senate's premier militarist.

The President, according to a news team from the *Times*, seemed on April 24 to be "pushing the process of making decisions." Although Rogers is less political than Laird, the Secretary of State seems to have shared the Defense Secretary's reservations about invading Cambodia and said so to the President. Somewhere about this time, again according to the *Times*, Nixon became "irritated that the enemy appeared complacent." Nixon instructed Abrams to send him a final attack plan within twenty-four hours. After issuing orders for a secret gathering of the National Security Council within forty-eight hours, Nixon left for Camp David.

Abrams' final attack plan was brought to the Maryland retreat the next day by Kissinger, who stayed for lunch, at the President's insistence. Charles (Bebe) Rebozo, close friend and millionaire who had guided Nixon's Florida real estate investments in the 1960's, was also present. One is told constantly in press reports that Rebozo's role in Nixon's life is fairly clear—he listens while the President talks and talks. But these seemingly one-sided conversations, the White House puritanically footnotes, never involve official business. So after lunch, it seems that Nixon and Kissinger retired to another room to discuss Abrams' attack plan. The meeting could not have lasted very long, though, because the President, reportedly in somewhat of a jumpy mood, went to the phone to arrange a cruise down the Potomac for later in the afternoon. He called Rogers, who had a prior commitment, but Laird and Mitchell were able to meet him aboard the yacht *Sequoia* by 4 o'clock. By 8, the President was back on shore, heading toward the White House, "eager" to see "Patton" again.

Waking on Sunday (April 26), Nixon reviewed the attack plan with the Security Council. The President did not indicate to the group as a whole that a full-scale invasion of Cambodia—involving American combat troops in significant numbers—was imminent. Rather, Nixon seemed to be playing out the decision-making process, discussing with General

Earl Wheeler of the Joint Chiefs, Laird, Mitchell, Rogers, Helms and Kissinger *only* the use of South Vietnamese troops in "the Parrot's Beak." The use of *any* troops reportedly struck one or two in attendance as being unjustified, since the military situation between the last meeting of the Council on April 22 and this one, on April 26, had remained basically static.

On April 27, Nixon informed a few key aides and members of his Cabinet that he was "leaning toward" a double invasion of "the Parrot's Beak" and "the Fishhook," using Americans not as support troops but as combat soldiers. Again Laird and Rogers, reportedly now joined by Kissinger and even Haldeman, were first concerned about the reaction of the Senate Foreign Relations Committee, if the President ordered an invasion of technically neutral territory without first asking its members' consent. (The Senate Foreign Relations Committee was to learn of the invasion when the rest of America did—after it began. The same seemed to be true of Lon Nol, chief of the country to be invaded, although that morning, April 27, the President had made up his mind according to *Look*, to go on television once both aspects of the assault were launched and announce it to the world.)

One of the men in the room was apparently less concerned about the reaction of the Senate than about the reaction of the country. "Mr. President," he said, "I don't know much about domestic affairs but if you do it, in my opinion, the campuses will go up in flames."[1] Nixon retorted, "I want to hear that now, but if I decide to do it, I don't want to hear of it again. *If I decide to do it, it will be because I have decided to pay the price.*"

Nixon continued playing out his role as decision-maker for the rest of that day. He himself worked over the wording of cables to Ambassador Ellsworth Bunker and General Abrams in Saigon, asking them for advice about where to invade, adding that because he had not made up his mind, their counsel would "weigh heavily," as David Maxey later reported in *Look*. That same afternoon, Nixon called in

[1] Though unidentified, William Rogers may have been the only man to speak with that peculiar diffidence and then modestly pin it on his ignorance of domestic matters.

John J. Williams of Delaware. Williams, the fifth-ranking Republican on the Senate Foreign Relations Committee (and evidently the only one informed, in the strictest secrecy), reportedly did not view the invasion favourably. Unwilling to accept that, Nixon, toward evening, turned elsewhere for guidance. He discussed the strategic situation with Haldeman and Ehrlichman, among others, and the spiritual situation with Norman Vincent Peale, who like Billy Graham was both a minister and a Nixon fan.

After this mixed reception, Nixon retired to the hideaway he keeps in the Executive Office Building across from the White House and doodled on a yellow legal pad. Preserved for posterity, the pad reads: "time is running out." Nixon wrote, on the one hand, that "failure to act" might tempt the Communists to attack Phnompenh, the capital of Cambodia, and install a puppet government. He wrote, on the other hand, the willingness to act (i.e., an invasion) might simply make the Communists mad enough to attack Phnompenh and install a puppet government. He went back and forth several times: An invasion of "the Fishhook" "*may*" (Nixon's emphasis) lead the Reds to talk seriously over the negotiation table in Paris about a Vietnam settlement; by the same token, the Paris peace talks could collapse. While an invasion might ease American troop withdrawal, said the pad, the Communists might reciprocate by breaching the Demilitarized Zone between the two Vietnams.

While nowhere did the pad show an inclination against *some* action, it did seem to conclude that limiting the action to "the Parrot's Beak" would do virtually nothing to speed "Vietnamization." That lump of land bordering on South Vietnam was *not* a major sanctuary but rather a refuge for transient guerrillas. Also, Nixon had been told by his generals that "the Fishhook" held large enemy supply caches and was home base for the Communist Central Office for South Vietnam (COSVN). The generals had cautioned the President, however, that COSVN, consisting of an estimated two hundred cadre, was too mobile to locate, much less capture. Even so, the value of the caches alone had made room in Nixon's mind for action in "the Fishhook."

On Tuesday morning, the President met with Mitchell,

Haldeman and Kissinger and at exactly 9:32 a.m. told all of them that he had decided on incursions against both "the Parrot's Beak" and "the Fishhook." Although General Abrams had asked for seventy-two hours' notice in order to mount a proper invasion,[1] Nixon indicted that phase one, an attack against "the Parrot's Beak" with South Vietnamese soldiers, would begin that night, April 28. The more important phase, against "the Fishhook," would begin on April 30 with American combat soldiers leading the way. Having made up his mind, Nixon said, he would assume "full responsibility" for the decision. Shortly before noon, Nixon told Rogers, Laird and perhaps one other member of the Cabinet that the time for discussion was past.

Now that he had announced his decision, the President grew elated, as he had on other crucial occasions. Nixon began coaching his staff that under no circumstances was anyone to say that this was an operation to save the Lon Nol government. (Nixon did not want the public to imagine that he was unilaterally interfering in internal Cambodian affairs.) Instead, said he, seemingly rehearsing the speech he would write, the United States is going to go into Cambodia to undercut an enemy who is plaguing American troops withdrawals, to destroy their supplies and, if all went well (despite the cautions of his generals), *to capture their leaders*. There can be no doubt, as a result, that Nixon, perhaps like Patton, was determined to accomplish the impossible.

One or more of his aides cautioned Nixon to be practical and, according to the *Times*, to treat the invasion "in low key" when he appeared on television. When they were discussing the domestic dangers of such a policy, Nixon, according to Stewart Alsop, picked up his yellow legal pad and pointed to where he had written the words "deep divisions" and said, "Believe me, I've considered the danger."

After what was described as a "pep talk" to the members

[1] With all the psychic hints that Nixon had given to everyone prior to the actual announcement of his decision for a twin invasion, General Abrams would have had to be deaf and dumb not to prepare his troops in anticipation of the inevitable green light. Either that, or Nixon had told Abrams what he had told no one else.

of WSAG late Tuesday afternoon, Nixon started dictating his speech to Rose Woods, his secretary. The rest of that evening and all of Wednesday, April 29, he wrote alone, permitting no editing or modification of the speech by aides, who wanted him to tone it down. He polished the language in the Lincoln Sitting Room until 5 a.m. Wednesday, interrupting the writing to authorize a preliminary announcement, in which "The United States" on April 29 declared that *it was giving combat advisers, tactical air support and medical evacuation teams to South Vietnamese troops* attacking Communist bases in "the Parrot Beak" at that moment. The government would supply no details of American troop involvement other than to say that the number of Americans was "in the low hundreds.".

At 9 p.m. on April 30, with American soldiers already fighting in Cambodia, Nixon went on the air. "Ten days ago," he said, reminding the public of the single warlike aspect of his peace speech, "I warned that if I conclude that increased enemy activity in any of these areas [principally Laos and Cambodia] endangered the lives of Americans remaining in Vietnam, I would not hesitate to take strong measures to deal with that situation. Despite that warning, North Vietnam has increased its military aggression in all these areas."

("Areas" hissed like a sudden wave. Nixon had recently adopted in his public appearances a new mannerism. His "s's" assumed a deep sibilance, almost like a resonant Castillian *sedilla*. As he progressed, Nixon would forget to use this bit of staginess, but if he got nervous, it would crop up again.)

"To protect our men who are in Vietnam," he continued grimly, "I have concluded that the time has come for action. American policy . . . has been to scrupulously respect the neutrality of the Cambodian people . . . North Vietnam, however, has not respected that neutrality. For *the past five years*, as indicated on this map . . . North Vietnam has military sanctuaries all along the Cambodian frontier with South Vietnam. Some of these extend up to twenty miles into Cambodia. The sanctuaries are in red," he said, searching with his finger for the right marks on a visual aid. "They are used for hit-and-run attacks on American and South Vietnamese forces in South Vietnam . . . *Even after the Vietnamese Communists began to expand these sanctuaries four weeks ago*, we counseled patience to our South Vietnamese allies and imposed restraints on our own commanders . . . In contrast to our policy the enemy in the past two weeks has stepped up his guerrilla actions and . . . *are* [sic] *building up to launch massive attacks on our forces and those of South Vietnam*," Nixon said, although there was no such intelligence available to him. "North Vietnam in the last two weeks has stripped away all pretense of respecting the sovereignty of the neutrality of Cambodia . . . *Cambodia as a result of this, has sent out a call to the United States*," he said.

After this fiction, he listed his various options—one, to "do nothing," an option he had not seriously considered; two, giving aid in arms to Cambodia; or, three, "to go to the heart of the trouble, and that means cleaning out major North Vietnamese and Vietcong-occupied territories, these sanctuaries."

Although one day earlier the "United States" had announced the use of a small number of American troops; Nixon promptly told another lie: "The attacks in several areas, including 'the Parrot's Beak' are," he said, losing his tongue, "*excloosely* [sic] *South Vietnamese ground operations*." It's easy to suppose that a man misrepresenting facts might suffer a psychic impulse to confess he was using "exclusively" *loosely*. "The action I have taken tonight is indispensable for the continuing success of [our] withdrawal program . . . ·*American* and South Vietnamese units will attack the headquarters for the entire Communist military operation in South Vietnam. This key control center has been occupied by the North Vietnamese and Vietcong for five years in blatant violation of Cambodia's neutrality."

It was his most dangerous lie, the fulfillment of which his military and civilian aides had emphasized was on the borderline of fantasy.

"Let's look again at the record. We stopped the bombing of North Vietnam . . . We have announced the withdrawal of over two hundred and fifty thousand of our men . . . The answer of the enemy has been intransigence at the conference table, belligerence at Hanoi, massive military aggression in Laos and Cambodia and stepped-up attacks in South Vietnam designed to increase American casualties.

"*This attitude has become intolerable*," Nixon stressed, his eyes furrowed in pain; "attitudes" always seemed the most "intolerable" forces he had to face in life: ridicule, contempt, indifference. "We will not react to this threat to American lives merely by plaintive diplomatic protests. If we did, credibility of the United States would be destroyed." Without hesitation, Nixon mouthed the incredible: "The action I have announced tonight puts the leaders of North Vietnam on notice that we will be patient in working for peace. We will be conciliatory at the conference table, *but we will not be humiliated* [the emphasis is Nixon's]. We will not be defeated. We will not allow American men by the thousands to be killed by an enemy from privileged sanctuary . . . My fellow Americans, we live in an age of anarchy, both abroad and *at home.* We *see mindless* attacks on all the great institutions which have been created by free civilizations . . . Even here, in the United States, great universities *are* being systematically destroyed.[1]

"*If, when the chips are down, the world's most powerful nation—the United States of America—acts like a pitiful helpless giant, the forces of totalitarianism and anarchy will threaten free nations and free institutions throughout the world. It is not our power but our will and character that is* [sic] *being tested tonight.*"

[1] As Nixon wrote his speech on April 28, he apparently worked at least in part from the same misinformation that Agnew was at that moment using in another speech. The Vice-President charged a conspiracy of violence in American universities, a "criminal left that belongs not in the dormitory but in a penitentiary." Agnew was suicidally specific. He said that at Cornell University students, "wielding chains, beat a dormitory president into unconsciousness." *A full day before Nixon had finished writing his speech,* Dale Corson, president of the university, replied, "No such incident has ever occurred at Cornell. It's incredible that the Vice-President of the United States should make such a public statement for which there is no basis in fact. The damage you do through such irresponsible and widely publicized statements," Corson said directly to Agnew, "is irresponsible." Nonetheless, in more general terms, Nixon reiterated the misinformation.

It was Nixon's will and character, above all others', which were being tested—by Nixon. He made "mindless" attacks on himself, telling one lie, then another. The "anarchy" of his own mind so incapacitated him that he lost his place in the text for an embarrassingly long time. His finger ran up and down the page; when he still couldn't find his place, he turned back and forth among the other pages before locating the words. He said, unhappily, "There has been a great deal of discussion with regard to this decision that I have made. I have noted for example that this action I have taken means that my party has lost all chance of winning the November elections," he mumbled, "and others are saying today that this move against enemy sanctuaries will make me a one-term President."

The President proceeded to lose his place at the moment he confessed there were people in his own ranks who thought he was wrong to invade Cambodia.[1] What had seemed so clever in the preparation now became painful in the delivery. Forswearing these "counsels of defeat," Nixon continued, using the war club of his head for disjoined emphasis: "To get peace at any price now, even though I know that *a peace of humiliation* for the United States would lead to a bigger war or surrender later . . . *I would rather be a one-term President and do what I believe was right than to be a two-term President at the cost of seeing America become a second-rate power and to see this nation accept the first defeat in its proud one-hundred-and-ninety-year history.*"

The *Times* reported that some of Nixon's aides remained upset for weeks by the grandiosity of the speech they'd wanted him to play down. Nonetheless, some of his people, at any rate, tried to make his dream come true. Not long after the President went off the air, his Secretary of Defense reiterated Nixon's most implausible dream in an anxious cable to General Abrams in Saigon: "Dear Abe, In light of the controversy over the U.S. move into Cambodia, the

[1] *Time* said it was an "instant of complex psychology." "There was the acute embarrassment and sympathy for the speaker who had fluffed his lines. There was also, for some, an eccentric half hope that if he could not continue, an absurdist, McLuhan logic would apply: 'The U.S. was about to move into Cambodia, but the President lost his place in the script.'"

American public would be impressed by any of the following evidence of the success of the operation: one, high-ranking enemy prisoners; two, major enemy headquarters; three, large enemy caches."[1]

On the day of the telecast, Nixon's Attorney General seemed to take a psychically related action. On April 30, Mitchell ordered four thousand American soldiers into New Haven in connection with the murder trial of Black Panther chairman Bobby Seale. It was, sources in the Justice Department ominously explained, *the eve of May Day*.

There was no violence, not in New Haven.

Appearing the next night as a guest on the Dick Cavett Show, NBC newsman Sander Vanocur said, "I can only explain what's going on now as either conspiracy, which I don't believe in; stupidity; or madness." Vanocur paused before the last word. *The New Republic* expressed a reaction akin to terror: "He is driven, disorderly, secretive but powerful and therefore dangerous . . . a rash blunder," and *Newsweek* may have been the first to sound an alarm echoed everywhere: "To some viewers, [Mr. Nixon] appeared during his tv address to be a beleaguered man who had suddenly come to regard foreign challenges as a test of Presidential manhood."

In the New York *Times*, Semple wrote that virtually nobody was satisfied by the President's reasoning. "The maneuver," said the White House correspondent, enlarging on the *Newsweek* theme, "*has been interpreted psychologically as a personal response by a man who did not wish to appear weak* [emphasis added]." In the same newspaper, Reston presented a variation on Semple: "Powerful men in Congress and even in President Nixon's own official family feel the Cambodian decision was reached with undue haste and carried out by deception." Reston, a Scotsman by birth, burning briefly with Calvinist zeal, also said, "The problem here is not strength but weakness. [Nixon] is not determined about anything. One day he is persuaded that peace is within our grasp, the next he is convinced . . . that his whole command will be in danger unless he expands the war." With glib objectivity,

[1] This was a secret cable quoted by *Newsweek*.

Time noted that Nixon's purpose had been to "get the country's pride back up," adding, "But the manner in which he did it seemed deliberately designed to divide the country further."

These assaults on Nixon's emotional stability gained strength from May 1 on, when Vietnam experts outside the White House expressed flat-out bewilderment as to what military crisis the President had been responding to. The President, himself, in his speech of April 30 had said that the problem of the sanctuaries was five years old. As for Nixon's argument that American soldiers in South Vietnam were endangered by "increased enemy activity," the fact was, noted the experts, that *American casualties had been diminishing* until April 28, the day of the invasion. And one of the reasons was the Communists had been steadily disengaging for days.

As for any threat to Lon Nol, there were never more than 5,000 Communists fighting inside Cambodia. The Communist problem may have been real, but it did not threaten his government with imminent collapse. Even Kissinger did not think the attacks on April 20 against the cities of Snoul and Takeo were high-alarm problems.

Thus, exhausting more imaginative explanations, government propagandists began to suggest that President Nixon had been compelled to take action, as one put it, because "everything [started] hitting him all at once." In its broadness, this excuse struck closest to a truth, but the "everything" had practically nothing to do with a military crisis.

Semple thinks it had everything to do with Nixon's senses of "theater and symbolism," while John Osborne thinks that Nixon recognized the past and future failures of his Vietnam peace negotiations and of Vietnamization, itself, "and the recognition was more than he could bear . . ." Since these programs had been designed to appease American discontent, their failure weakened Nixon's reputation at home. It had weakened in other respects, too, in April. The Senate had repulsed his Carswell nomination and when he cried out in rage that the lawmakers were flaunting his prerogatives, the intelligentsia, the students, the Eastern liberal establishment, the blacks and organized labor cheered the Senators. On top of that, his sympathetic silent majority did not respond to his humiliation in numbers sufficient to soothe these psychic wounds.

But if the compelling reasons for enlarging the war on foreign soil were cultivated on home ground and shaped by Nixon's emotions, there may be a single reason why war sprouted from Nixon's head when it did. First of all, the President did not decide to invade Cambodia on April 24, though he did decide to use South Vietnamese on that date; nor did he decide on April 27 or on the morning of April 28, although he may initially have decided then to use American soldiers. The President decided on *April 20* or in the pre-dawn hours of *April 21*, after consoling the American public with the hope of a negotiated peace. We have Nixon's own words for the approximate date.

Asked on or about May 3[1] when he had decided to go to war in Cambodia, Nixon answered, "Two weeks ago." Everything from then on was reinforcement to help him define the precise kind of war he wanted to wage. From that point on, it seems, the President played the role of a man in the process of making a decision, acknowledging *pro forma* his assistants' advice on whether or not to fight as if he truly sought it.[2]

If there was no apparent military crisis, why did Nixon make up his mind on April 20? The one clue ignored by political analysts was the speech the President had made that day. He had prepared it for rational political reasons: not

[1] One source explains that the remark, to an associate, was made on May 4. Whether on May 3 or 4, the President still gave a pretty good time fix on when he decided to invade some part of Cambodia.

[2] In hopes that Stewart Alsop would answer charges that the President had been irrational, disordered and isolated in reaching his decision, his White House sources gave the influential political columnist a copy of the doodles Nixon wrote on April 27. And when Alsop had finished examining them, as well as listening to the outpourings of the day-by-day accounts given him of Nixon's activities up to that date, he was convinced that the President had been cautious and reasonable and, above all, thoroughly committed to hearing out his advisers. Alsop argued, "The President would have been mad not to consult the military. He would have been mad also not to consult his chief civilian advisers." Technically Nixon had done both.

many days before, the polls indicated that for the first time a *majority* of Americans wanted an end to the war, so the President gave them what they evidently wanted to hear. It was not what he wanted to say, however, for negotiation meant compromise and Nixon, in terms of his ego, had already been compromised at least once in April.

Furthermore, many of the victors in the Supreme Court battles were presumably the same "radic-libs," intellectuals and political moderates who felt that by his delay, Nixon had made the war in Vietnam *his* war. Therefore, if he allowed them to force him into the peace settlement he had resisted for his fifteen months in office, they would be compromising —humiliating—him once again. *Emotionally, Nixon could only go so far toward appeasing them at a time when it was Nixon, himself, who needed the appeasing.* Thus, the speech itself seems to have become the source of a deeply personal crisis.

Though he may not have considered it consciously, Nixon's decision to invade Cambodia could be counted on to quiet the anxieties stemming from his own ambivalence and to increase the anxieties of his domestic enemies. The way things turned out, however, the solution *for him* was temporary.

While the President had all but guaranteed a violent domestic reaction, once it occurred, according to Reston, Nixon was genuinely shaken and, characteristically, began backing away from his own boldness. Earlier, he had promised Abrams and the field commanders more than they had hoped for, giving them permission to penetrate fifty miles into Cambodia (even as he implied on television that American troops would go no more than twenty) and to continue their sweep until all enemy supplies of food, clothing and ammunition were destroyed.

But on May 8, the President announced, "The action actually is going faster than we anticipated." With a pretended heartiness, Nixon promised, "The middle of next week, the first units, American units, will come out. The end of next week, the second group of American units will come out. The great majority . . . will be out by the second week of June and all Americans of all kinds, including advisors, will

169

be out of Vietnam [sic] by the end of June." (Few missed the gaffe.) A defensive President told reporters that he expected the South Vietnamese to leave Cambodia "approximately at the same time that we do."

"Startled and bewildered" were the words used to describe the reaction of the field commanders in South Vietnam. As they and the President knew, their problem was that the Communists had fled the sanctuaries, taking along up to fifty percent of their supplies. As a result, the commanders deemed it imperative to stay on in force indefinitely if they wanted to put the Communists out of operation. American troops began charging about, attempting to achieve nearly everything that Nixon had promised they would in the pitiful amount of time he had left them.

Nixon's South Vietnamese allies were unhappy too, as illustrated by Vice-President Ky's response to Nixon's May 8 press conference. Known as "South Vietnam's Agnew," Ky bluntly described any proposal for a simultaneous withdrawal of American and South Vietnamese troops as "a silly argument of silly people."[1]

There was one other thing Nixon said on May 8 which attracted attention. Justifying the entire war in Indochina, the President said with apparent fervor: "If we withdraw from Vietnam and allow the enemy to come into Vietnam and massacre civilians by the millions, *as they would*—if we do that, let me say that America is finished . . ." Tom Wicker, perhaps the most relentless and perceptive of all the *Times* men, frightened by the implications of Nixon's Cambodia decision, noted that the President's argument for the invasion, and for the entire war, was a "blood bath" that had never occurred. Wicker felt that Nixon's obsession with death stemmed from "something stronger than evidence. It is as though he *wills* [Wicker's emphasis] it to be true even though

[1] In the land next door, General Lon Nol was behaving like a woman robbed of her virginity but afraid to abjure her immensely powerful and wealthy violator in public. The Cambodian wouldn't renounce or acclaim the foreigners fighting on his soil. U.S. government sources began saying that Lon Nol had been warned of the invasion in advance. If the Cambodian chief had been warned, it was apparent from Asian sources that his advance notification couldn't have been more than minutes.

170

it isn't, both to justify the war and his policy and to confirm the anti-Communism on which he rests so much of his public life. Believing perhaps has made it so."

After Richard Nixon was where he had always hoped to be—in the White House—he still had little control over one of his especially unsettling foibles: the grotesque urge to make capital of the dead. To demonstrate forcibly that he was not immune to the death of American boys in Vietnam, he mentioned to a magazine writer that the President's family had not gone untouched by tragic loss. Daughter Tricia, he told his interviewer, had *once dated* a young American, Lt. Gary Granai, who was killed soon after in Vietnam, fighting for his country. Tricia's having dated the young officer may have been a rather tenuous basis for claiming loss —especially as she had a more serious boyfriend at the time— but the President's regard for Granai was nonetheless moving.

After his statement appeared in print, it was learned that the dead soldier Tricia had *dated once* was very much alive. Not only that: Granai was married and had never served in Vietnam.

Expressing respect for the dead can have distinct political advantages. On the other hand, there may be political disaster ahead if voters get the idea that the President is cynical enough to use the dead in vain. But attuned watchers feel that the President may be less cynical than morbid. Nixon seems compelled to continue playing morbid games with his own reputation. Richard Harris, in *Justice*, recognized that Nixon does not merely "stretch the truth to meet political expediency." Instead, Harris intimates that the President tells "outright lies, which can boomerang with disastrous consequences."

One of Freud's chief ambitions was to illuminate and explain the nature of self-destructive behavior: the psychological longing a human being has for things he dreads most because his fears then "can lead to what he fears coming true." A functional definition of neurotic suffering is "self-inflicted punishment" that appears in a vicious circle: guilt produces a compulsion to suffer and, as Paul Roazen said in *Freud: Political and Social Thought*, "the suffering permits the gratification of forbidden impulses as an exchange which only reinforces the initial guilt."

Consequently, a "healthy" politician will be able to avoid most situations that, for whatever the reason, he thinks dangerous. By the same reasoning, axiomatic among depth psychologists, anybody who is sometimes unstable, including Prime Ministers and Presidents, could conceivably seek out the things he fears, so that he can prove to the world he leads, and to himself, that the danger is an illusion. "The unbearable fear of tension of expectation," says Dr. Helene Deutsch, one of the world's most formidable analysts, "can become a motive for suicide."

Because there are few more incontrovertible proofs of abnormal behavior than a successful suicide, we see clearly what can happen when the unconscious mind of a politician can, as they say in the trade, no longer resolve its conflicts. James Forrestal, who sat in the Roosevelt and Truman Cabinets and was generally considered tough and sane, killed himself, shocking everyone and prompting an understatement from Roazen: "It would seem that the normal politician's gap between the inner and outer man became so great as to smash the inner citadel completely."

Many Americans agreed with Forrestal's politics when he lived, but once he had taken his own life, it's unlikely they regretted his never having become President.

CHAPTER SIXTEEN

The morning after declaring war on the Communists in Cambodia, Nixon, many observers think, declared open season on college students. On May 1, arriving at the Pentagon for an early briefing on the fighting, he looked haggard: he hadn't fallen to sleep until 5 a.m. on the day he delivered the news and not until 2 a.m. the following day, when he was up again at dawn.

Inside the Pentagon, Nixon paused in the midst of employees milling in a corridor and addressed them impulsively: "I got down to the conclusion—and y' say, well, the usual thing you ask for support for the President and all that guff." The President had summoned up an accent nobody could recall hearing on any other occasion—perhaps because the people around him were clerks, typists and messengers from lower employment echelons. Nixon was speaking to them out of the corner of his mouth, dropping final consonants in a gutteral hint of Humphrey Bogart.

"And you finally think of those kids out there. I say kids," the President snorted. "I've seen 'em—they're the greatest. Y'know, you see *these bums*, y'know, blowin' up the campuses —listen, the boys that are on the college campuses today are the luckiest people in the world, going to the greatest universities, and here they are burnin' the books, I mean stormin' around about this issue. I mean, you name it—get rid of the war, there'll be another one. And then, out there," Nixon reverberated in reverent tremolo, "we got kids who are just doin' their duty, and I've seen 'em, and they stand tall, and they're proud. I'm sure they're scared. I was, when I was there, but when it really comes down to it they *stand up*. Boy, you gotta talk up to those men, and they're going to do fine. We gotta stand back of 'em."

On May 4, an extended volley of gunfire from National Guardsmen, who had been issued live ammunition after the President's remark about bums, killed four students and wounded several others on the campus of Kent State University in Ohio. None of the students was armed. Two of the dead had been mere bystanders observing the campus anti-war protest.

"You should not be surprised when they are shot through the head and the chest by National Guardsmen," wrote columnist Pete Hamill. "Nixon is as responsible for the Kent State slaughter as he [was] for the anti-integration violence in Lamar, and for the pillage and murder that is taking place in the name of democracy in Cambodia. Is he proving his masculinity," Hamill added, picking up a now-familiar theme, "at the expense of the Asian peasants? Is he showing what a *macho* he can be by unleashing the ugliest barroom instincts in Agnew, Mitchell, the National Guardsmen and the American populace? We should know because we simply can't afford two-and-a-half years of a President who might have those problems. We don't need therapeutic foreign policies..."

Hamill, a gut fighter, may not have been taken seriously outside his circle of devotees, but not everyone who blamed the shootings on Nixon was a professional polemicist. Recognizing that any President's casual statements have a powerful if ramdon influence[1] (particularly on suggestible individuals who justify their own aggressions by heeding the antagonisms of higher authority), Joseph Rhodes Jr., the youngest member of the Nixon-organized Scranton Commission on Campus Unrest, reported, "The first thing we found out was that these campus unrest abstractions result in people being dead, and that is a reality . . ."

Twelve years before, Nixon had used the word "bums" in reference to the mobs which attacked him in South America. Presenting a "psychological history" of President Nixon to the Group for Applied Psychoanalysis in Boston, M.I.T. Historian and scientist Bruce Mazlich said of that occasion, "If one's [Nixon's] opponents are 'bums,' then one is clearly justified in fighting them *without quarter* [emphasis added]."

[1] Specifically of Nixon's November, 1969, speech on Vietnam, his counsellor Daniel Patrick Moynihan said, "I would hardly argue that when a President [says] something very clear, that this does not have its consequences."

Though Mazlich's analysis five months before Kent State all but predicted what might happen, Nixon, himself, as far back as 1954, indicated what he felt the honorable elements of society should do in crushing lower life forms if they became troublesome. Speaking over television of alleged subsersives in America, Nixon drifted easily into verbal violence. "I heard people say," he reminisced, " 'After all, they are a bunch of rats. What we ought to do is go out and shoot 'em.' Well, I agree they are a bunch of rats, but just remember this, when you go out to shoot rats you have to shoot straight . . ."

After the shootings at Kent State, evangelist Billy Graham, Nixon's confidant, explained that the President had not meant his remark to be overheard. Nixon's Communications Director Herb Klein confirmed this: "It was not a statement the President meant for general reference." Until the shootings, however, the President's associates seemed quite proud of it. In fact, the White House mimeographed the "bums" statement and sent it around to members of the press. As for Nixon, himself, he could not have failed to notice as he entered the Pentagon on May 1 that reporters were dogging his steps, holding microphones under his nose to record every word he spoke. By afternoon, predictably, the airwaves reverberated with "bums."

The day of the shootings, Nixon offered his condolences through Ron Ziegler before expressing the peculiar thought that the campus deaths "should remind us once again that when dissent turns to violence, it invites tragedy." The President of the United States was turning tragedy up-side down—blaming the victims instead of the killers. Within hours, out on the hustings, Agnew reiterated this theme.

That afternoon, the Senate Foreign Relations Committee assailed Nixon for sending American soldiers into Cambodia "without the consent or knowledge of Congress" and prices on the New York Stock Exchange plummeted nearly twenty points. The next morning, a fearful James Reston decided that while nobody could be certain what motivated so "complex" a man as Nixon, nonetheless his "wild contradictions" of recent days and the "tragic consequences of the university campuses" were indivisible from "the character and personality of the President."

A few of Nixon's own people were fearful, too, or angry, the foremost being Walter Hickel, his Secretary of the Interior. On May 6, unable to reach the President in person, Hickel sent a letter to the White House, simultaneously releasing it to the press. He began by accusing the President of lacking "appropriate concern for the attitude of a great mass of Americans—our young people." Hickel thought there was hope if the President would sit down with members of his own Cabinet once in a while to "gain greater insight into the problems confronting us all."

The following day, Thursday, May 7, Justice Department officials reluctantly agreed to permit anti-war demonstrators to march in Washington on Saturday, two days hence; but marchers charged that officials were seeking to "insulate" Nixon by keeping the protestors too far away from the White House. The Republican Governors Conference, scheduled to start Thursday evening, was abruptly cancelled; the Governors feared student uprisings. "We feel a deep responsibility," said Governor Raymond Shafer of Pennsylvania, their spokesman, "to keep our avenues of communication open with our home communities." Also on May 7, Averell Harriman, a Democrat, questioned Nixon's capacity for leadership.

During this period, President Nixon ordered the resumption of bombing over North Vietnam.

His agitation mounting, Nixon began striking out in yet another direction. Suddenly, he was angry all over again with his old foe, Russia, warning petulantly that if they refused to pull out of Egypt voluntarily, he'd have to expel the Soviet presence there. He would pick up on this theme again, as he needed it. (The warning in May was issued through Kissinger at a background briefing for the press.)

At the height of the closely related Carswell, Cambodia and Kent State crises, Washington's gossips seemed to talk only of Nixon's seclusion. Like Hickel, they assumed that the President's isolation led to his ignorance of the facts and that, in turn, led to the crises. But the isolation was only a symptom.

Standing tall, Nixon called a press conference. The day was May 8, and operating on the theory that there were more people in America interested in basketball than in the state of the nation, Nixon thoughtfully adjusted the start of his nationally televised conference, setting it back from 9 to 10 p.m., following the final game of the National Basketball Association championship. At 10, the President entered the press room in the White House where, by custom, the press was already on its feet. Nixon raised his hands, beckoning them to stand, and said, "Would you be seated." (Such inappropriate gestures had become fairly commonplace during this period. For instance, he also pointed at the audience and said "I," then pointed at himself and said "you.")

For the first five minutes of the press conference, he spoke slowly, struggling for control of his tone. His eyelids drooped as if to protect him from being stared at. There were long, embarrassing pauses not only between sentences but between words. "No," he said ever so slowly to the press, "I have not been surprised by the intensity of the protest." Initially, he clung as much as possible to familiar ground, trying, sometimes literally, to catch his breath, speaking of things the men in the press room had all heard before: His aim, like the aim of the protestors, was to bring the boys home and to bring peace in Vietnam—"a just peace."

"Do you believe," asked the second questioner, "that you can open up meaningful communication with this college generation, and how?" It was wooden journalism, college textbook stuff, almost ingenuous and certainly not threatening, but Nixon apparently lost his composure. "It is not easy. Sometimes *they*, as you know, *talk so loudly that it is difficult to be heard.*"

Question: "On April 20, you said Vietnamization was going so well that you could pull one hundred and fifty thousand American troops out of Vietnam. Then you turned around only ten days later and said that Vietnamization was so badly threatened you were sending troops into Cambodia. Would you explain this apparent contradiction to us all?"

Nixon (nervously speeding up): "I explained it in my speech . . . I . . . had warned at that time that increased

177

enemy action in Laos, in Cambodia, as well as in Vietnam, was something that we had noted and that if I had indicated and if I found that increased enemy action would jeopardize the remaining forces who would be in Vietnam after we had withdrawn one hundred and fifty thousand, I would take strong action to deal with it. I found that this action that the enemy had taken in Cambodia would leave the two hundred and forty thousand Americans who would be there a year from now *without many combat troops to help defend them*, would leave them in an untenable position. That's why *I had* to act."

Question: "Mr. President, some Americans believe this country is heading for revolution and others believe that crime and dissent and violent demonstrations are leading us to an era of repression . . ."

Nixon: "Briefly, this country is not headed for revolution. The very fact that we do have the safety valves of the right to dissent, the very fact that the President of the United States asked the district commissioners to waive their rule for thirty days' notice for a demonstration, and also asks that that demonstration occur not just around the Washington Monument but on the Ellipse where I could hear it—and you can hear it pretty well from there, I can assure you— that fact is an indication that when you have that kind of safety valve you're not going to have a revolution which comes from repression. *I do not see that the critics of my policies, our policies, are repressed.* I note from reading the press, from listening to television, that criticism is very, very vigorous, sometimes quite *personal*. I have no complaints about it." (Translation: He was not repressing them; they were oppressing him and that *was* cause for complaint.)

Question: "After you met with the eight university presidents yesterday, they indicated that you had agreed to tone down the criticism within your Administration of those who disagree with you. Yet tonight Vice-President Agnew is quoted all over . . . as making a speech which includes these words: 'that every debate has a cadre of Jeremiahs, normally a gloomy coalition of choleric young intellectuals and tired, embittered elders.' Why?"

Nixon: "Miss Dickerson, I've studied the history of this

178

country over the past one hundred and ninety years, and, of course, the classic and most interesting game is to try to drive a wedge between the President and the Vice-President." (He was showing his temper.) "And believe me, *I had eight years of that*, and I'm experienced on that point. Now, as far as the Vice-President is concerned, he will answer for anything that he has said. As far as my attempting to tone him down, or my attempting to censor the Secretary of the Interior because he happens to take a different point of view, *I shall not do that.*

"I would hope that all the members of this Administration would have in mind the fact, er, a rule that I have always had, and it's a *very* simple one—when the action is hot, keep the rhetoric cool."

Question: "Mr. President, do you believe that the use of the word 'bums' . . . is in keeping with your suggestion that the rhetoric should be kept cool?"

Nixon: "I would certainly regret that my use of the word bums was interpreted to apply to those who dissent. All the members of this press corps know that I have for years defended the right of dissent. I have *always* opposed the use of violence.[1] Now on the university campuses the rule of reason is supposed to prevail over the rule of force. And when students on university campuses burn buildings, when they engage in violence, when they break up furniture, when they terrorize their fellow students and terrorize the faculty, then I think 'bums' is too kind a word to apply to that kind of person. Those are the kind I was referring to."

Question: "Sir, without asking you to censor the Secretary of the Interior, could you comment on the substantive points that he made in his letter?"

Nixon: "I think, the Secretary . . . is a man who has very strong views, he's outspoken, he's courageous—that's one of the reasons I select [sic] him for the Cabinet and one of the reasons that I defended him very vigorously before this press corps when he was under attack. Now as far as his views are

[1] Here is as good a place as any to quote Nixon during one of his early campaign tours after a heckler splintered the mythical cool: "When we're elected, we'll take care of people like you! Okay boys, throw him out!"

concerned, I will, of course, be interested in his advice. I might say, too, that I hope he gives some advice to the Postmaster General. That was the fastest mail delivery I've had since I've been in the White House."[1]

Question: "Mr. President, how do you answer the criticism that the justification that you give for going into the Cambodian sanctuary is hauntingly similar to the reasons that President Lyndon Johnson gave as he moved step by step up the ladder of escalation? He wanted peace too."

Nixon: "Mr. Scali, President Johnson did want peace, and if I may use the vernacular, he's taken a bad rap from those that say that he wanted war. However, the difference is that he did move step by step. [My] action is a decisive move and this action also puts the enemy on warning that if he escalates while we are trying to de-escalate that we will move decisively, *and not step by step.*"

Question: "Mr. President . . . considering the toll in lives and in everything else that's happening now, do you think it will have proved to be worthwhile?"

Nixon: "As Commander-in-Chief I found five hundred and twenty-five thousand Americans [in Vietnam at the start of his term] and my responsibility is to do everything that I could to protect their lives and get them home as quickly as I can . . . However, looking at the whole of Southeast Asia, looking to the fact that we have lost lives there, I would say that only history will record whether it was worthwhile. I do know this: now that America is there, if we do what many of our very sincere critics think we should do—if we withdraw from Vietnam—and allow the enemy to come into Vietnam *and massacre civilians there—as they would—if* we do *that*, let me say that *America is finished* as far as a peace keeper in the Asian world is concerned."[2]

Question: ". . . Could you tell us in your judgment . . . the proper action and conduct for a police force or a National Guard force when ordered to clear the campus area and faced with a crowd throwing rocks?"

[1] It was the only enjoyably spontaneous joke from Nixon in many a journalist's memory, but, ironically, it burst from him in the midst of anger.

[2] See chapter fifteen for Tom Wicker's observation.

Nixon: "We think we've done a rather good job here in Washington in that respect. As you note we handled the two demonstrations of October 15 and November 15 of last year without any significant casualties, and that took a lot of doing because there were some *pretty rough people* involved. Ah, a few were rough, er, most of them were very peaceful . . . I want to know what the facts [regarding Kent State] are. I've asked for the facts and when I get them I'll have something to say about it. I saw the pictures of those four youngsters in the evening [Washington] *Star* the day after the tragedy, and I vowed then that we were going to find methods that would be more effective to deal with these problems of violence—methods that would *deal* with those who would use force and violence and endanger others but at the same time would not take the lives of innocent people."

Question: "Mr. President, sir, after the American troops are removed from Cambodia, there may still be a question as to the future of Cambodia's ability to exist as a neutralist country. What is your policy toward Cambodia's future?"

Nixon: ". . . Both [Cambodia and Laos], as you know, are neutralist countries. However, the United States—as I indicated in what is called the Guam, or Nixon Doctrine—cannot take the responsibility and should not take the responsibility in the future to send American men in to defend the neutrality of countries that are unable to defend themselves. In this area what we have to do is go down the diplomatic trail . . ."

Question: "In your Inaugural address, you said that one of your goals was to bring us together in America . . ."

Nixon (patently resentful): "Don't judge us too quickly."

It was now May 8, 1970; he had been President since January 20, 1969. Nixon bent his shoulders, clasped his hands and took a deep gulp of air.

Question: "Mr. President, is the United States prepared to pursue with equal fervor in Paris negotiations to find a political settlement of this war, including the possibility of discussing with the other side a coalition government?"

Nixon: "We are prepared to seek not only in Paris but in any other forum a political settlement of this war. We are not prepared, however, to seek any settlement in which we, or any one else, imposes upon the people of South Vietnam a government that they do not choose."

Question: "Mr. President, did Secretary of State Rogers oppose your decision to go into Cambodia, or did Dr. Kissinger oppose it?"

Nixon: "Every one of my advisers—Secretary of State, Secretary of Defense, Dr. Kissinger, Director Helms—raised questions . . . And believe me, I raised the most questions because I knew the stakes that were involved. I knew the division that would be caused in this country. I knew also the problems internationally. I knew the military risks. And then after hearing all of their advice, *I* made the decision. Decisions, of course, are not made by a vote in the National Security Council, or in the Cabinet. They are made by the President with the advice of those. And I made this decision. I believe it will work out. If it doesn't, then I'm to blame, they're not."

In answer to the next question, the man who had "no complaints" about criticism aired this one: ". . . I think that people should also have the right to speak out as they do in the House, in the Senate, in the media and in the universities. The only difference is that, of all these people, and I refer particularly to some of my lively critics in the House and the Senate, *they* have the luxury of criticism. I was once a Senator," he said, his pique showing through now, "and a House member, and I thought back to this when I called Harry Truman today and wished him well on his eighty-sixth birthday—some of the rather rugged criticisms that I directed in his direction. *They* have the luxury of criticism because they can criticize and if it doesn't work *they can gloat over it . . . I* don't have that luxury . . ."

Question: "Mr. President, will you see any of the demonstrators tomorrow in the White House? Will you talk to them?"

Nixon: "If arrangements are made by my staff so that they can come in to see me, I'll be glad to. I talk to a great number of people and I will be there all day long." (Translation: "I'm not going to be accused of running away to Camp David *this* time.")

"Thank you, Mr. President."

Nixon (sepulchrally): "Could I ask the members of the press to wait one moment? For twenty-six years a member of this press corps did just what Frank Cormier did then—he was known as the man who said, 'Thank you, Mr. President.' Three weeks ago he met a tragic death, and as we close this conference, I would like to suggest that we all stand for a moment in memory of Merriman Smith."

Smith, a wire service reporter who had always seemed in awe of the Presidency, had, as Nixon said, been dead for three weeks. The unmourned Kent State four had been dead four days.

Before dawn the day after his press conference, after a largely sleepless night, Nixon suddenly decided to go to the Lincoln Memorial to "rap" with the antagonistic students he knew would be gathered there. The President boasts that he "petrified" his Secret Service guards by rushing off to the heart of protest country—"nobody knew I was going." Then after a dazzling hour with surprised students, he drove off to the Mayflower Hotel on Connecticut Avenue for breakfast —his first visit to a restaurant since becoming President. He returned home at 7:30 a.m., called in a reporter from a friendly newspaper and told his story.

He had stayed up until 2:30, he said, taking calls from old friends in Washington and California who had comments to make about his televised appearance. He slept fitfully for an hour and then called his valet and asked if he had ever seen the Lincoln Memorial at night. The valet said he hadn't, and Nixon said, "Let's go." Before leaving, the President remembered, he called Helen Thomas, a reporter for United Press International. She was asleep and his call woke her up. He and she had a conversation about Merriman Smith. Nixon and his valet then toured the Memorial and when they emerged, they met about eight students on the steps. They began to talk.

"On the war thing," Nixon is quoted as having said to the reporter for *The Washington Star*, "I said I know you think we are a bunch of so and sos—I used a stronger word to them [i.e., sons of bitches]. I know how you feel—you want to get the war over. I told them that I know it is awfully hard to keep this in perspective, I told them that in 1939 I

183

thought Neville Chamberlain was the greatest man living and Winston Churchill was a *madman*. It was not until years later that I realized Neville Chamberlain was a good man but Winston Churchill was right. I doubt," he added, "if that got over. They were fine kids from all over the country," Nixon continued, "and I told them, sure, you came here to demonstrate and *shout your slogans on the Ellipse*. That is all right. Just keep it peaceful. Remember, I feel just as deeply as you do about this . . .

"I took them all over the world. I told them about Japan. I tried to tell them how fascinating Asia is. I told them how great I think the Chinese people are. I told them that I am working [with] all my heart for the time when they have the opportunity to know the people of China. I told them about the wonderful people of Indonesia and that India has such wonderful people. I said they would find India barren in spots and its cities dirty, but I told them not to look at the cities but at the people. I told them to go out to the Soviet Union and visit cities in Siberia and see a different kind of people."

Then he told them that the "blacks are separating from the whites" and that they, the students, "must find a way to communicate with them in your universities" and that American Indians are "the most mistreated of all our people" and that some Chicanos are worse off than the blacks and that he was aware that the streets and the air of America were dirty and promised, "We're going to clean up these things," continuing, "But you can clean up all that and have sanitized cities but no color, no warmth, no humanity, no human qualities [because] the real problem is finding some meaning to life rather than just air and water."

Pieced together from him and other sources, here's a second version: Nixon felt elated after the press conference, his aides said, because it was a good conference. At 1 a.m. he spoke to John Mitchell, at 1:30 to Nancy Dickerson of NBC, who had asked him the question on Agnew's rhetoric, to "thank" her because "you gave me a chance to answer it in a forthright manner." Nixon told her, "I really love those kids." He also told her that he had instructed Haldeman and Ehrlichman to bring some kids into the White House the

184

next day, but Mrs. Dickerson told him to go out and see the kids instead. Then *he* placed calls to his friends to talk about his speech.

An hour and a quarter later, the President's buzzer sounded in the rooftop bedroom of Manolo Sanchez, his valet. "All I could think," said Sanchez later, "was that something is wrong with the President. That he is sick maybe. I got scared . . . My heart was up here." Sanchez hopped into his pants, tied his tie on the run, racing toward the bedroom where Nixon normally sleeps alone. It was empty, so he ran to the Lincoln Sitting Room and found the President sitting "comfortably" in his smoking jacket on his favorite brown velveteen easy chair.

Sanchez asked Nixon if he'd like a cup of hot chocolate but Nixon asked him instead if he'd ever visited the Lincoln Memorial at night. The valet "blinked" and followed the President with great effort, since English is not his mother tongue. "Well then," said Nixon, "it's a beautiful night for a drive, so why not go now?" He asked Sanchez to alert the Secret Service that they would leave the minute he got all his clothes on. White House aides said later that the President knew he would run into some kids, even though the largest groups were gathered around the Washington Monument. He felt, they said, it was necessary to "dramatize" his understanding of kids today, and to make sure they understood he wasn't repressive.

The kids spotted Nixon and Sanchez walking up the Memorial steps. "Hey, look, the President," someone shouted. Meanwhile, the nervous agents scrutinized those who wore knapsacks—the likeliest hiding places for weapons. Nobody pulled so much as a stick of chewing gum from his knapsack or pocket. Still, several times Sanchez interrupted Nixon (purportedly at the behest of the Secret Service) to say that the President had a phone call. But Nixon answered, "I want to talk to these people."

Nixon did most of the talking, according to student witnesses. Lynn Shatzkin, who worked in the Washington office of the National Student Association, said, "His sentences just didn't make any sense. I thought he was insane. Near a nervous breakdown. A mess." A girl from Syracuse

University echoed this impression: "I thought he was like a robot. You wanted to think it was an actor playing a goof. He looked thick, terrified. He rambled." Other students found him "depressed."

Nixon vainly tried to establish rapport. When he asked one young woman her age and she replied twenty-four, Nixon brightened. That was a coincidence, he explained; twenty-four was Tricia's age too. When a few of the women said they were from Syracuse University, the President instantly glowed with recognition. "The Orangemen," he said, acknowledging that the Orangemen had a good football team. Nixon also mumbled about "surfing," asking if there were any surfers in the crowd.[1]

At last, a student got a direct answer to a question. Asked if he believed the Black Panthers and Bobby Seale could get a fair trial, Nixon said that even a man who sticks "ice picks" into other human beings deserves a fair trial. He did not reply to any questions about the war which had brought these students to Washington in the first place.

One of several students interviewed by Bob Schieffer of CBS said, "He wasn't making any argument. That was the point . . . If he was making an argument, and at least if we didn't agree with it and it made sense, we would have accepted it, but the thing was he wasn't making *any* sense . . . He was rambling about things that . . . didn't relate . . . It was like a surreal scene. He seemed very tired, and nervous and . . . was all leaning over, and he was looking at the floor, he could not look at anybody . . . and he seemed very scared really."

Another witness remembered, "He didn't take students on a 'world tour.' He was just, like, mentioning a list of cities and sometimes he would stop on a city and say something totally irrelevant . . . and then continue on. Besides, we don't even know what that world tour had to do with anything, except that at the end he said something about, there are a lot of problems in the country."

Schieffer asked the witnesses their ultimate reactions, and

[1] Chancellor Alexander Heard of Vanderbilt University said that for the President to chat with students about surfing and football so soon after the killings at Kent State was like "telling a joke at a funeral."

got these answers: "Total fear. Absolute. I'm really afraid for this country. At first we approached the whole situation, and we were in awe because . . . it's the President of the United States. But not when the gentleman can't come out with an articulate sentence. I'm extremely frightened . . . extremely frightened."

"When I walked away . . . we wondered if it was a dream . . . We couldn't believe that we saw it, and we knew that we couldn't possibly articulate our feelings to someone else, because as soon as we said that the President is crazy, the people who didn't agree with him, said, 'Oh, well, we already knew that,' but we were trying to explain that *we* didn't know that. We didn't mean that he was crazy because he didn't agree with us . . . It's like he needed help."

"He just kept saying, have a really nice day, have a really nice time, and then he said there wouldn't be any trouble, which was a blatant lie, since he gassed all the people at the Monument."

Nixon seemed as reluctant to face painful realities inside the White House. A few days after the scene in front of the Memorial, Secretary of Interior Hickel was at last permitted a private audience (his third since Inauguration) with the President. According to Evans and Novak, the President had already decided that because Hickel had embarrassed him "in his most vulnerable moment . . . Hickel had to go." But when the Secretary bluntly asked, "Mr. President, do you want me to leave?" Nixon threw up his arms and, again according to the two writers, replied, "That's one option I've never considered."

Frankel of the *Times* said, ". . . The crises that were Cambodia and Kent inflamed not only the campuses and distant battlefields. They sent tremors of fear through the White House . . ." And then spread. On May 13, the Illinois Constitutional Convention refused to permit John W. Gardner to deliver a scheduled speech in which the former government official planned to say that no advantage gained by force in Indochina could compare with the damage the war inflicted at home and that Nixon habitually gave "undue attention to advisers who give him a distorted view of reality."

The next day, May 14, thirty seconds of police gunfire left two black students dead and at least nine other persons wounded at Jackson State College, in Mississippi. The local police said that they were responding to sniper fire, although the President's Commission on Campus Unrest would find that there had been no sniper fire and that the police were guilty of an "unreasonable, unjustified overreaction."

The violence extended northward, too, to New York City, where construction workers roaming the Wall Street area under the indulgent eye of New York uniformed policemen beat anti-war demonstrators. An alarmed middle-aged woman who had once lived in Germany was heard to cry, "My God . . . they're here . . . The Brown Shirts are here." Later, a "hard hat" appeared on television and declared proudly, "We are the reactionaries in America."

Former Chief Justice Earl Warren declared that the United States was going through a crisis worse than any "within the memory of living Americans" and he attributed it to "war, inflation, unemployment with resulting poverty" and an "atmosphere for repression."

By May 19, Nixon, working behind the scenes, encouraged Republicans, including Senator Gordon Allott of Colorado, to oppose any move in the Senate to curb his war powers or future military activities in Cambodia. The Cooper-Church amendment had been offered some days earlier to limit his right to supply funds or manpower that would deepen American involvement in Cambodia.

On May 22, in the face of all that had happened, Vice-President Agnew renewed his assault on Nixon's "liberal" critics, after comparing campus rioters to enemy soldiers and demanding they and "hard core" faculty members be expelled from colleges. Agnew blamed the frenzy following Cambodia on editorials which fanned the flames of discontent. He singled out James Reston and Tom Wicker of *The New York Times*; I. F. Stone, the editor and publisher of a biweekly newsletter, and Hugh Sidey of *Life*. He went so far as to quote *The Washington Post* editorial that had called Nixon's Cambodian action "erratic, irrational and incomprehensible." "The *Post*," argued the Vice-President, "may as well have come out and said it thought the President had lost his sanity."

On May 26, President Nixon received leaders of the construction trades in the White House and told them that he found their recent public demonstrations reassuring and "very meaningful."

On June 3, Nixon took again to television to tell America Cambodia had been a triumph. As evidence, he offered a long list of things his soldiers had destroyed there, for example: fifteen thousand two hundred and fifty-one "individual weapons"; two thousand one hundred and fourteen "crew-served weapons"; eight thousand two hundred and ninety-six bunkers; six million nine hundred and ten thousand nine hundred and seventy-two rifle rounds; medical supplies (by the pound), fifty thousand eight hundred; eleven million pounds of rice (his first round number) which, he said, was a three months' supply of food for the Communists; and nine thousand nine hundred and forty-five enemies killed in slightly more than a month of action. It sounded as though, instead of fighting the enemy, American troops had stood about counting.

In summarizing, the President stamped it the "most successful operation of this long and difficult war" and promised, "It will take the enemy months to rebuild." Then he turned to the matter which had *forced* him into another public appearance: "As you all know, when I first announced the decision on Cambodia, it was subjected to an unprecedented barrage of criticism in this country." The President lowered his lids and evidently thought about that. "*Let us understand, once and for all*," he said, "*that no greep* [sic]—group—has a monopoly [on peace]. I pledged a withdrawal of twenty-five thousand in June of 1969, and thirty-five thousand in September the same year, and fifty thousand in December . . ."

Watch his hands, John Osborne reminds us. Punching out for emphasis, Nixon's hand struck the microphone once, then again, punctuating his statistical mythology with a series of resounding clunks. The truth was that in the past month and five days since allied forces moved into "the Parrot's Beak," the President had not begun ending the Indochina war as much as he had begun seriously changing its modality.

Nixon promised to have American troops out of Cambodia

by the end of June and South Vietnamese troops out alongside of them. The South Vietnamese never came out, and the Americans who left Cambodian soil returned to do their fighting from gun ships which skimmed inches above the ground. Eventually the Administration was forced into a new policy of what some called "strange-think." When it became unpopular at home to bomb sanctuaries and supplies in Cambodia, Laird announced that American air power would only be used to "destroy personnel." Though the Defense Secretary resisted the interpretation, reporters insisted that he meant American flyers would no longer bomb objects; they would concentrate on killing human beings instead.

On June 10, after hesitating for three weeks rather than repudiate his frequent assertion of welcoming staff debate, the President fired Commissioner of Education Dr. James E. Allen for publicly criticizing Vietnam policy. And, in time, Robert Finch, the Secretary of Health, Education and Welfare, was caught in a murderous cross-fire over the war between his own staff and the President's that made him physically ill and unable to function.[1]

Vice-President Agnew had remained active throughout this period, accusing "criminal misfits" and "charlatans of peace" with creating, he said, "great national confusion."

One year later, in June, 1971, the United Methodist Church provided the Department of Justice with a report, based on detailed circumstantial evidence which had taken months to gather. The report alleged that eight or nine non-commissioned officers from Troop 6 of the 107th Armored Cavalry, Ohio National Guard—between Nixon's expression of feelings about "bums" and the time of the actual shootings —made careful plans to kill students protesting the war on the campus of Kent State. By prearranged signal, they had fired their loaded weapons directly into the crowd. This report was quietly buried.

---

[1] Faithful to his friend, Nixon took him out of HEW and elevated Finch to a limbo-like job in the White House itself, naming him "counsellor" to the President.

CHAPTER SEVENTEEN

Deserting Washington and its chaos, Nixon returned to San Clemente in the summer of 1970. Because the President was *supposed* to be relaxing, he swam, played golf and strolled on the beach for the camera, his Irish setter yipping at his bare heels. Every President has exercised for publicity but the Nixon who makes believe that he's angry—when he is—seems to have greater difficulty making believe he's happy and relaxed, when he isn't. Nixon was essaying "Jack Kennedy, All-American President," said one reporter cynically. In a windbreaker, Nixon looked vaguely like the solitary figure on the beach at Hyannisport but stepping gingerly at the lip of the surf, the man in San Clemente seemed less thoughtful than worried about getting his feet wet.

The presence of cameras has always made Nixon tense, and his aides began emphasizing that the President was a different man in private—relaxed and attentive, *"believable,"* a *real* person. A couple of years earlier, Nixon explained this putative phenomenon: "I think that when a third person is present, one is distracted, wondering what *his* reaction is. Or people sometimes show off to the third man. But if there are just two of you, you can concentrate totally on each other." However, this self-image is not exactly true of Richard Nixon either, for though he may lose his self-consciousness with certain companions, he never seems to lose his self-absorption. When he's as relaxed as he's capable of being, Nixon slows down, his speech comes more easily, he seems free of piousness and the kind of slit-eyed solicitousness of strangers that, in him, often borders on patronizing. When Nixon is relaxed, it seems he can dwell on himself, without worrying to excess about the other man's reaction. When he's relaxed, one hears, Richard Nixon smiles less.

But there are very few human beings with whom he feels at ease. Charles (Bebe) Rebozo, his longtime companion, is one who may see the unguarded side of Nixon. He seems to be Nixon's sounding board; talking to this silent millionaire may, for the President, be like talking to the wind, which is never critical of human frailty. He may be able to relax to a slightly lesser degree with Donald Kendall and Robert Abplanalp, other millionaires who reportedly talk somewhat more than Bebe but who are apparently neither intellectually nor emotionally the sort to challenge his dominance. One also hears that Nixon's daughters, Julie and Tricia, can make him relax, maybe because his role as a father *is* private and possibly also because it was established long before his girls could have possessed the faculty of independent judgment.

Yet even with these few, Nixon may relax only under ideal conditions—in front of a television set (if he's not seeing himself on the screen) or at a movie where he can sit in the shadows. Garry Wills noticed that in the darkness, alone with one other human being, Nixon "solidified, drew himself together, stopped gesturing." (But because the other person in this case was Wills, a journalist, Nixon did not drop his guard entirely.)

There may have been one moment, the first day of August, 1970, when the right ingredients for *honest* relaxation were available at the same time: the President and Tricia, his elder daughter, sat together, alone, watching a John Wayne movie on television.

But by the following Tuesday, August 3, in place of the "believable" Nixon was the man many Americans now intuitively recognized as *the* Nixon. It was during a quick trip to Denver, Colorado, and there, in the Federal Office Building, he said, "I would like to make [a point] with regard to the responsibility of the American people and also of those in the news media . . . What I say now is simply an observation of the kind of times we live in and how attitudes develop among our young people. Over the weekend I saw a movie—I don't see too many movies but I try to see them on weekends when I am at the Western White House or in Florida—and the movie I selected or, as a matter of fact, my daughter Tricia selected it, was 'Chisum' with John Wayne. It was a western . . . I wondered why it is that the westerns survive year after year . . . One of the reasons is perhaps—and this may be a square observation—the good guys come out ahead . . . the bad guys lose. As we look at the situation today, I think the main concern that I have is the attitudes that are created among many of our younger people and also perhaps older people as well—in which they tend to glorify and to make heroes out of those who engage in criminal activities . . .

"I noted, for example, the coverage of the Charles Manson case when I was in Los Angeles—front page every day in the papers. It usually got a couple of minutes in the evening news." (Manson, leader of a hippie cult, was on trial with several of his followers for allegedly murdering actress Sharon Tate and her friends.) "*Here is a man who was guilty, directly or indirectly, of eight murders without reason.* Here is a man—yet who as far as the coverage was concerned—who appeared to be a glamorous figure . . . to the young people whom he had brought into his operations. And, also, another thing that was quoted was the fact that two lawyers in the case—*two lawyers*[1] *who were guilty of the most outrageous,* contemptuous action in the courtroom [were treated instead as] the oppressed, and the judge seemed to be the villain."

As the President addressed the reporters who had helped upend America's old-fashioned, clean-cut, John Wayne value system, his face reddened and he became relatively incoherent. The President had publicly judged a defendant guilty of murder before the jury had retired to consider the verdict.

As President Nixon left Denver on Air Force One, this was reportedly brought to his attention, yet he refused to believe that he could have said such a thing, insisting for

---

[1] Nixon's unconscious may have been hyperactive on August 3. The "contemptuous actions" seem to have had something in common too with the alleged behavior of Leonard Weinglass and William Kunstler, the two lawyers for seven of "The Chicago Eight," whose trial for conspiracy ended the previous February. When Julius Hoffman, the judge in that case, repeatedly cited the lawyers for contempt, some reporters did make a villain of him. There are other similarities between the Manson trial then going on and the ended conspiracy trial. Two of the defendants were "yippies" Abbie Hoffman and Jerry Rubin, bearded and noisy like "hippy" Charles Manson. Furthermore, Kunstler (since the Chicago trial) had loudly opposed the Administration and thus might be classed as one of the "greeps" who had so recently subjected Nixon to an "unprecedented barrage of criticism."

several seconds that it could not be true, according to reporters who ferreted around for a long time afterwards trying to seize on the details. They are not clear on what made Nixon change his mind—a transcript of his remarks, most probably a tape recording. But if the President had quickly conceded his error—or if a timorous Ziegler had called it to his attention while still on the ground—it might never have reached embarrassing proportions. Several hours later, a statement was issued, written by John Mitchell, (whom Nixon had referred to in Denver as "Attorney General of the United Nations") and by Ehrlichman, suggesting that the press had "misunderstood" the President. Reportedly, Mitchell (who behind his back had earned the sobriquets of "The Iron Chancellor" and "Mr. Tough") insisted that this was the best way to protect the President.

By the first day of autumn, Nixon was ready to intervene in the war that broke out between Syria and Jordan on the night of September 20, when Syrians in Russian tanks crossed into Jordan. The next morning, Nixon took personal charge of the planning and the concomitant diplomatic activity. Backed by Kissinger's Washington's Special Action Group, he ordered the carriers *Saratoga*, *Independence* and *Guam* (with fifteen hundred marines aboard) to the Israeli-Syrian coast; he also alerted two airborne battalions stationed in Germany and the entire 82nd Airborne Division in Fort Bragg, North Carolina, then publicized the existence of this intimidating force. White House propaganda made it clear that the moment President Nixon decided the Russian-backed Syrians had gained the upper hand in the fighting, he would join Israel in a coordinated military action to repulse them.

All the while, the President was alleged to be the least excited man in the White House. One close observer, not one of the usual White House explainers or apologizers, found him cool, almost phlegmatic. Yet Nixon himself later verified that very much the opposite was true: During the Middle East crisis he did not watch television or dwell on the newspaper headlines because, as he put it, he feared a rise in his blood pressure. Maybe he seemed calm only because those around him were too active to pay attention to the President's quirks.

On the other hand, there are moments in which Nixon's exterior is at odds with what's evidently happening inside. He had spoken softly, one hears, as his car was being attacked in South America; he had spoken softly some of the time leading up to the invasion of Cambodia. Such contradictions do exist: Either men force themselves to act calmly (when Nixon does, the strain usually shows) or their ostensible calm may more factually approximate numbness—stunned disbelief of the performer in what he has started. In Nixon, however, it is the words themselves that tip off his more pivotal feelings. For example, on September 21, Nixon reportedly told associates that the Russians (like the North Koreans in 1969) had gotten behind Syria to raise his dander.

However, before he could interfere, Jordanian jets drove out the Syrians.

Within a matter of days, Nixon boosters proclaimed that Nixon's master stroke in "brinksmanship" had chased the Syrians. The President had learned this lesson in power diplomacy from John Foster Dulles, Eisenhower's Secretary of State, his people reminded reporters. That the theory has been discounted by such experts as Charles Bohlen ("Bohlen's law" is that privacy marks diplomacy while making tough sounds in public marks nothing more than propaganda) is almost beside the point, because President Nixon, it soon became clear through sources in the Defense Establishment, had not merely been talking; he had planned to *use* his soldiers, ostensibly in a back-up operation for the Israelis. Nixon himself boasted afterwards of the "pretext" he had decided upon to justify the presence of American soldiers and marines on Jordanian territory: the safety of four hundred American civilians and thirty-nine Americans held hostage by Arabs in the Jordan desert after their airplane had been hijacked several days earlier. (Lyndon Johnson had employed a similar "pretext"—the safety of American civilians—when marines interceded in the civil war in the Dominican Republic some years earlier.)

But if Nixon's "brinksmanship" had bluffed the Russians and the Syrians, it also confused American diplomats as to the meaning of the Nixon doctrine,[1] especially when they discovered the threat was no mere bluff.

Only two days after the badly crippled Syrian tanks packed up and limped home, Nixon had an aborted confrontation with Russia, announcing through a spokesman on September 25 that he had acquired news of a strategic base under construction on Cuba's south coast to service Russian submarines. Disturbed Latin specialists in the State Department told the *Times* that there had been reports of such construction as early as 1970 but they had been discounted as false. For a moment, Nixon evidently tried to make them come true. Nothing further was heard from Nixon about the alleged submarine base in the next forty-eight hours.

On September 27, the President left on an eight-day tour of Europe and the Mediterranean, beginning in Rome, where he established the theme of his trip. "The Mediterranean," he said during a ceremonial meeting with Italian President Giuseppe Saragat, "is the cradle of many great civilizations of the past and we are determined it shall not be the starting place of great wars in the future." It was a thinly veiled warning to Russia.

The next afternoon, Nixon spent an hour with Pope Paul VI.[2] Ostensibly paying tribute to the Pope's "spiritual power," Nixon promised the Pontiff: "I will visit the Sixth Fleet, *a great military force . . . the mightiest military force which exists in the world on any ocean.*" Minutes later, honoring the "power of faith," Nixon lectured the young priests

[1] Before the end of the year, a rare public symposium of officials and government consultants attacked the Doctrine for its many inconsistencies. All the articles, cleared by Rogers's own aides, pointed to the lack of specifics in the Doctrine. One U.S. political officer, quoted by Jerome K. Holloway (a foreign service officer and a member of the symposium, printed in the Foreign Service Journal and published by the American Foreign Service Association for professionals in diplomacy), said, "I was physically shocked when I learned what the Guam (Nixon) Doctrine meant." Some officers at first thought Nixon's doctrine was meant to be dovish; then Nixon made clear it was a baffled restatement of his "hawkish side." The symposium discovered that the confusion was widespread among foreign service officers.

[2] Joseph Kraft quoted Nixon as having judged himself thusly: "I would have made a good Pope."

who were students of the American college at the Vatican. He told them he was "Speaking very humbly as *President of the strongest nation in the world, with more power, perhaps, than any leader in the world.*" Though Nixon kept talking, he made no point more important to him than stress on *his* military power.

He flew from Rome to the carrier *Saratoga* and there too told the sailors standing at attention before their Commander-in-Chief, "Never has American power, I think, been used with more effectiveness than it has been used in the recent weeks of Middle East tension. When power is used in such a way that you do not have to go to the ultimate test," he said, "then it is really effective."

Later, aboard ship, Nixon learned from Haldeman that Gamal Abdul Nasser had died. Walking about the deck, the President seemed dazed and directionless. Peter Lisagor, a journalist who has explained that he dislikes "psycho-analyzing" public figures, nonetheless did a radio show on which he observed that *Nixon's inability to display power* because of Nasser's death *had dampened the President's spirits.*

But *all* the American officials aboard were worried, less perhaps about prospective power plays than about the agenda. They feared that Marshal Tito of Yugoslavia would elect to go to Cairo for the funeral instead of receiving Nixon in Belgrade. Secretary Rogers, after a nerve-racking delay, got through to Belgrade and was informed that Tito would carry out his original plan to greet the President. This generated another problem. At least, Nixon treated it as a problem: since he could not go to the funeral, he needed an emissary. First he decided Rogers should go to Cairo. Fretting in his quarters aboard ship, the President lighted on Robert Finch next. Seventeen hours later Finch was cancelled and Elliot L. Richardson, the man who had replaced Finch at HEW, was selected. The President kept amending the list, adding names—Robert D. Murphy, a diplomat and friend of Nixon's; John D. McCloy, a New York lawyer; Donald C. Bergus, the senior diplomat in Cairo, and Michael Sterner, chief officer for the United Arab Republic desk in the State Department.

Finally, feeling an excuse was necessary, the President (through the spokesman announcing his final list of emissaries) explained that he wasn't going to the funeral so as to avoid angering the Israelis. That was September 29.

The more significant international news that day came from Moscow. "It is clear," noted *Pravda*, "that the furor about preparations in Cuba that supposedly threaten the United States security had been raised for a definite purpose." The Communists flatly accused Nixon of using the Cuban missile base as a pretext to fan a "war psychosis." The Russians had ample cause to scoff at Nixon's new Cuban "crisis" of September 25. Evidently they had checked, just as the Americans had.

Several days after *Pravda*'s accusation, Daniel Z. Henkin, the Defense Department's Assistant Secretary for Public Affairs, had a confession. Reportedly with a look of acute misery on his broad face, he made it clear on October 13 that Russia had *not* been building a submarine base in Cuba. Reluctant to embarrass Nixon, however, Henkin added that there was some kind of permanent installation being constructed in Cienfuegos, on the south coast, its purpose unknown.

Indeed, it was clear that the President of the United States had allowed unsupported rumors of a Russian military site ninety or a hundred miles from the United States to be leaked to the press on September 25. Once this fact was confirmed, American newspapers charged that Nixon had given "no apparent thought" to the impact of such a rumor on the world's nervous system. There may be a simple explanation: with the fighting in Jordan over by the 23rd, Nixon's unconscious could have manufactured a new threat[1] by the 25th, as terrifying, by association, as the Cuban missile crisis of 1962.

But September was not a total failure for Nixon: They loved him in Belgrade. There were thousands of cheering Yugoslavians lining his path. Yet there was also a Nixon tugging a reluctant and astonished Tito (normally outgoing) by the sleeve of his jacket toward the press buses parked near Tito's birthplace. "I have fifty publicity men down there," the President exclaimed, grinning fiercely. "We've got to put this place on the map."

---

[1] Unlike a lie, a delusion cannot always be dispelled by reality. That's because the delusion may not have stemmed from reality in the first place but from an unconscious fear or a negative wish. According to Freud, delusions are morbid.

They also loved him in Spain, his next stop. Nixon openly admired Generalissimo Franco's strength and the Spanish leader openly admired Nixon's.

Nixon reached England on October 3, reiterating one theme with Edward Heath, the new Conservative Prime Minister: Russia. He informed Heath that Russia had violated the Suez standstill by introducing new missiles which could be used against Israel, America's ally. Then he told Heath that in the past week the Russians had also attempted to interdict flights to West Berlin. The last verse of this litany of grievances was that Russia was building a submarine base in Cuba. Nixon insisted that the sub base was the gravest concern of all.

The next stop was Ireland. Most of the reporters who had accompanied Nixon on his whirlwind journey through the Vatican, the Sixth Fleet, Yugoslavia, Spain and Britain had decided that the trip made no sense and had no discernible purpose. When their sentiments reached the President, he invited them to a cocktail party the last Sunday in Europe, in a Gaelic castle which had been converted into a hotel. He said he had "some conclusions" to offer that the press might find helpful. Nixon kept repeating something about his visit to the "Sixth Feet" [sic]. He couldn't remember where he'd been first—to the "Feet" or to Italy and he got befuddled attempting to explain that Middle Eastern radicals might "set in the course of events, the train of events, set in motion— I meant to say—a train of events that would escalate into a possible confrontation . . ."

Some reporters felt that the President was at ease at the party, but an equal number perceived an underlying forced cordiality and felt that Nixon was afraid they wouldn't believe him. He had promised that when they reached Ireland, they'd all take a well-earned rest, he fishing with his friend John Mulcahey, an American living in Ireland. Instead, he held the party, at which he managed to widen the group of cynics around him. He had been intense or had laughed at the wrong places; he grimaced at unexpected moments or he seemed rundown.

When Nixon landed back home in the United States, he turned to the Nixon watchers and said that he hoped everyone "had as relaxed a week as we did."

CHAPTER EIGHTEEN

Kevin Phillips, who had assisted John Mitchell in running the 1968 Nixon campaign, said that it was the President's intention, going into the campaign of 1970, "to smash the power of the Senate Liberal Establishment" because its victories had "infuriated" him. Nixon originally planned it so that Agnew, in Herb Klein's words, would "carry the hard line" and "do a lot of attacking" against liberals including Senators Goodell of New York, Gore of Tennessee and Hartke of Indiana. But changing his mind in October, Nixon began a midterm campaign tour of his own, the intensity and motion of which had never been duplicated by an incumbent President. In the course of the campaign, existential violence may have also reached record levels.

The President warmed to his task in September in sporadic actions. Less than a week after sending the Vice-President out to do battle, Nixon publicly congratulated an armed guard for gunning down a would-be airplane hijacker who had a history of mental illness. One day later, he stood in the giant Kansas State University gymnasium and decried violence in America. Nixon listed "the vicious bombing of the University of Wisconsin" and the attacks on school buses, then proceeded in the present tense to the "courtroom spectator who pulls out a gun; he halts the trial, gives arms to the defendants" and, finally, is responsible for four deaths, including his own; then to the "man who walks into the guardhouse of a city park, pumps *five* bullets into a police sergeant sitting quietly at his desk." Though each case was horrendous, Nixon did not seem so much to be disparaging violence as sensationalizing it. Nixon warned, "Those who bomb, who ambush policemen, who hijack airplanes, who hold their passengers hostage . . . deserve the contempt of every American who values decency [and] human life." The President announced his dedication against persons who used "violence and intimidation to get what they wanted." The crowd roared approvingly, but Nixon stopped smiling when a small group of twenty or thirty began chanting "peace, peace."

He raised the spectre of campus violence at least twice more in the next five days. The *Times* accused the President of carrying on this fear campaign in an attempt to blunt the impact of the forthcoming report by the President's Commission on Campus Disorders.

Otherwise known as the Scranton Commission report, it partly blamed the violence on the "inability—or unwillingness —to end the war and move boldly against social problems at home" and went on to say, "We urge the President to renew the national commitment to full social justice and to be aware of increasing charges of repression [and] not encourage belief in those charges." The Scranton Commission had discovered that the campus crisis consisted of two component crises: a "crisis of violence and a crisis of understanding."

H. R. Haldeman reportedly illustrated just what the Commission had been talking about. The chief of staff was seen to finish the report, commissioned by Nixon, then pound his desk and in a paroxysm of rage scream, "Goddamn it!"

Nixon left for his trip through the Mediterranean before the report was released, leaving the ultimate hypocrisy to Agnew, who assaulted the *"self-appointed* interpreters and translators on the commission." Using Nixon's writers, Agnew blamed the evil in the country on the "radical liberals," or as they had become known, "the radic-libs." When Senator Hart of Michigan criticized Nixon, Agnew in turn accused Hart of condoning "disrespect for American institutions" (i.e., the Presidency). Nixon's enemies became "a little band of willful men" in the Senate or members of the Eastern liberal "elite" groups, who Agnew said looked down their noses at blue-collar workers. "They were raised on a book by Dr. Spock," said Agnew, condemning Spock's baby-care credentials because of his leadership in the antiwar movement, "and a paralyzing permissive philosophy pervades every policy they espouse."

When Agnew became the Vice-President, he recalls he had a "big problem: The first thing I had to establish was that I was human. I went through a little self-deprecating treatment, to show that those accusations of insensitivity and coarseness were . . . not quite fair. But, you know, you come to a different decision—*when do you turn off the self-ridicule and turn to something else?*" Expressing much the same wish Nixon had as Vice-President, Agnew said that he no longer wanted to be mistaken for a "buffoon." Apart from their hoped-for therapeutic value, his polysyllabic attacks were designed to give the Republicans the vast middle ground of voters and the President an "ideological majority of one" in the Senate. But somehow Agnew's appeals were often too extreme for moderates. In a "debate" on television, for instance, the Vice-President kept accusing black student leader Eva Jefferson of advocating the bombing of universities, although she had denied the accusation. Agnew rationalized his ad hominems and violent harangues. "Overemphasis," he explained, "[gets] the public out of its lethargy." But to what end, people wondered: to seat Nixon men in the next Congress or to eliminate opposition entirely?

Even the President's friends were not permitted to dissent. "This is a beautiful country," Nixon said to an audience which was inclined to agree. "*Make no mistake about it.*" He seemed truly angry. Edward P. Morgan observed it was as if, in his head, Nixon had heard someone taking exception.

On October 14, the President announced an intensive schedule of campaign stops, promising to visit nine states between the 17th and the 20th. The polls had soured badly for the Republicans, and when the President's advisers told him he was the only man in the country who could turn the tables, Nixon eagerly took their advice, although his off-year campaign record was abysmal. Evans and Novak say that Nixon "longed to replace Agnew on the trail [without considering] the personal risks to his Presidency of such unprecedented barnstorming." But Nixon must have considered them at some level, in order to rediscover the perverse psychic pleasures of scathing his enemies in order to stimulate personalized counterattacks he has always found so humiliating and running when the chances of winning were so low that the inevitable defeat would be his.

On October 13, he had another potential reason to punish himself, and it may have hastened Nixon's campaign announcement the next day. Sir Robert Thompson, whom Nixon had commissioned as his personal representative to study the situation in Vietnam, handed the President his analysis. The news was disastrous. The British guerrilla expert who had thought everything in Vietnam looked good in 1969 now considered the situation precarious. He believed that the Thieu regime could topple any moment and that Nixon's "Vietnamization" and anti-subversive programs were failures. Articulated by the trusted Thompson, this dramatic reversal may have additionally prompted Nixon to release his fiercest and most feral instincts on domestic enemies.

He opened fire the morning of October 17 in Burlington, Vermont, but so did the enemy. Nixon had no sooner landed to launch the campaign for incumbent Senator Winston Prouty when an unidentified demonstrator threw a "small flat piece of concrete," which reporters estimate was "about the size of a half dollar." It fell seventy-five or eighty feet short of the ramp where Nixon stood and fragmented into a dozen tiny pieces. Charles Colson, a Nixon aide, scooped up two of the pebbles for evidence. "These rocks [sic] will mean ten thousand votes for Prouty," Colson grinned.

Inside an airport hangar, a handful of demonstrators yelled "stop the war," their outburst spurring the President to a passionate appeal for law and order. "You hear *that* night after night on television—people shouting obscenities about America and what we stand for." No neutral observer there had heard an obscenity uttered, but Nixon continued: "You hear those who shout against the speakers and shout them down." It seemed an order, and the sympathetic crowd responded. "And then you hear those who engage in violence. You hear those and see them who shout treason, kill policemen and injure them and the rest. And you wonder—is that the voice of America? *I say to you it is not,*" Nixon shouted, glowering and churning his arms wildly. "It is a loud voice, but, my friends, there is a way to answer. Don't answer with violence. Don't answer by shouting the same senseless words that they use. I answer in the powerful way that Americans have always answered." The remaining words were an anticlimax: ". . . speak up with your votes."

As he flew toward Teterboro, New Jersey, Nixon was

reportedly "elated," and his political aides, acting on the assumption that the President had won the skirmish in Vermont, extemporized the setting for a second triumphant confrontation. Warned by Washington to expect trouble, the Bergen (New Jersey) County police appeared in full riot gear and cordoned off the large hangar at Teterboro, where five thousand cheering Republicans were waiting to greet Nixon's arrival. Distinguished from the crowd of predominantly lower-middle and middle-class matrons and their husbands were a hundred or so shabbily-attired, anti-war youth. The police barred them, frisking many for weapons; one bulge produced an apple. Then, acting on news of Nixon's putative triumph in Vermont, an advance man, Ron Walker, changed the orders so that seventy-five or so of the demonstrators could enter. This group was herded into an area some distance from the platform where they were surrounded and confined by blue-collar families bearing banners for Nixon and Nelson Gross, the Republican Senatorial candidate. Thus, housewives and their husbands became props in Nixon's theatrical performance right along with the demonstrators. When the demonstrators jeered his arrival, the President raised his hand. "Let them alone," he said. "I can handle it."

But he couldn't. He—his aides—had sought this confrontation, yet when Nixon heard the demonstrators' voices, his rehearsed gestures became marred by real emotion. His right arm stabbed outward and retracted, only to stab outward again and again like a piston rod that had thrown a bolt. His swagger-smile froze on his face as his voice slipped and waivered, losing its *sedilla* and its resonance. "We see here a number of television cameras. Watch the treverision [sic]," he said. Some observers sensed that he was marrying the words "television" and "derision." In any case, he tried twice and still could not enunciate the hated noun. "I predict what you will see is not this great crowd. You will see these few people right here." So the housewives obediently raised their Nixon and Gross signs, obliterating the demonstrators from sight. "You don't have to throw rocks at them; you don't have to engage in violence." Nixon spoke of *them* contemptuously, his tone once more suggesting the opposite of his words. Housewives closest to the demonstrators began waving their signs, not upward but outward, in motions that threatened shaggy heads. "One vote is worth a hundred obscene slogans," Nixon concluded.

A reporter for the *Bergen Record* said the President "held the audience in the palm of his hand," leaving them in a state of outrage that continued even after he'd gone. "These nice people from Lodi and Ridgefield," the reporter told me in amazement, "I saw them *deliberately* stand in the way of these kids as they were trying to leave. If Nixon had said, 'Kill,' I think they would have killed."

Nixon had been in control of the crowd but not of himself.

In order to comprehend what Nixon had done probably by accident in Burlington and deliberately in Teterboro, one must know what he thinks of the women who work for the Republican Party. He told Jules Witcover that they were "great workers" and "idealists" but also "emotionalists . . . They're the real haters." To Nixon his audience was a time-bomb: he'd set it and it would mindlessly tick away.

Under these circumstances, which prevailed throughout his personal appearances, it is virtually impossible to believe that the 1970 campaign was a positive effort to build up the GOP.

A few days before the election, the editorial board of *The New York Times* somberly warned Nixon against playing the majority of his audiences against small bands of hecklers: "*It is impossible to say what sparks* [these tactics] *strike in some disordered minds* [emphasis added]."

But, historically, it had already been said. Shortly before the editorial appeared, the Justice Department forwarded to Nixon a summary of the Federal Bureau of Investigation's inquiry into the Kent State killings. The FBI differed sharply from the whitewash handed down by an Ohio grand jury on October 16, 1970. Denied access to the same FBI report by the state attorney but not to Nixon's and Agnew's impressions, the jury had put the "major" blame on the university administration, which, it declared, was guilty of "laxity, overindulgence and permissiveness"—words out of the Agnew phrase book. On the other hand, the National Guardsmen were proclaimed guiltless, because they "fired their weapons in the honest and sincere belief and under circumstances which would have logically caused them to believe that they would suffer serious bodily injury had they not done so." Sent to the White House, the FBI report, on the contrary, stated that the Guardsmen who fired their rifles were *not* in fear of their lives. They fired because they heard other Guardsmen firing.

Toward the end of his personal campaign, the President stopped in San Jose, California. Outside the auditorium on October 29 were roughly a thousand "yelling" and "screaming" dissenters. As Nixon emerged, a thick cordon of worried agents attempted to shield him from demonstrators who had taken up positions on top of cars and buses. Their presence must have incensed the President, for he, too, impulsively climbed to the top of his own limousine, where he remained alone—a perfect target—for nearly sixty seconds. In almost a repeat of his bizarre performance twelve years earlier in South America, Nixon grinned, thrusting both arms out in a twin victory salute. *"This is what they hate to see,"* he said audibly.[1]

Some journalists still had it in them to be astonished: The President of the United States had taken radical measures to taunt the radicals. Was he trying to provoke them with his own body in order to prove to himself that they *were* as violent as he had said they were?

On November 3, the Republicans lost the midterm election of 1970.

The Republican defeat may have been worst where

[1] On Monday, November 2, this full-page ad was carried in California newspapers:

"ANARCHY (in 144 point type)

"The riot last Thursday night at the Murphy rally in San Jose, which threatened the lives of the President, Richard Nixon, and Senator Murphy, ought to make it clear that the decision you will make tomorrow will be between

ANARCHY (48 point type)

or

LAW AND ORDER"

The advertisement, allegedly paid for by Californians for Murphy, is believed to have been written in the White House. Although the Administration later denied this, Hugh Sidey, among

206

American political power is forged: The Democrats won thirteen new governorships that had been securely Republican for many years and gained control of seven additional State Legislatures. And the ideological majority of one which the President sought, and said he got, in the Senate would prove non-existent.[1] Mark Hatfield, a Republican liberal, felt that the outcome of the election was a poor augury for his party in 1972 and demonstrated a "significant drop" in Nixon's popularity.

But Nixon's personal loss may have had a deeper meaning too. Having waged an unprecedented midterm election campaign, Nixon had "squandered," as Stewart Alsop saw it (Alsop's admiration seemed to be waivering), his "most precious resource"—the built-in "majesty" that comes with being President.

On November 4, the day after election, Nixon said he and his Republicans had won. On that turned a debate among professional politicians and political observers. The debate was not about whether Nixon had won but whether the President honestly believed he had. Conventional political analysts like Reston decided that the President was consciously "disappointed and angry" by the outcome and covered up his defeat by proclaiming it a victory. On the other side were those who suspected that Nixon had deluded himself into a victory. At a gathering of politicians in New York on November 13, one Republican told a reporter for the *Times*: "If they [i.e., Nixon and his political aides] really believe that stuff, they are more out of touch with reality than I had thought."

But whether the President consciously felt he'd won or not, people kept saying he'd lost. He heard them, and that may have been all that mattered.

others, claims "reasonable evidence" exists proving its source within the Administration.

[1] Conservatives seated through Nixon's efforts (including James Buckley, who displaced Charles Goodell of New York) would show displeasure at Nixon's more dramatic programs in 1971, including his decision to go to China and his wage-price freeze. For this, said one observer, the President drove the left farther from redemption at the Republican center, the right deeper into reactionism and "poisoned the moat in between."

CHAPTER NINETEEN

On November 12, nine days after the election, President Nixon was on his way back home from the funeral of Charles de Gaulle. "Without question," Nixon said to his companions, "de Gaulle was the only man who could have saved his country from civil war from 1958 to 1962. France as a people, as a nation, would not exist today without de Gaulle." The President felt it was de Gaulle's eloquence and distaste for small talk that had preserved France's unity. Nixon continued, "I have some of that too."

Upon landing, Nixon learned that the North Vietnamese had shot down an American RF-4 reconnaissance plane over North Vietnam. Shortly thereafter, Defense Secretary Laird issued the official position, which was that North Vietnam had no legal right to fire on American reconnaissance planes over North Vietnamese territory. Laird's argument, reasoned out with Nixon, was that two years earlier, the North Vietnamese and the Johnson Administration had reached an understanding: if the U.S. stopped bombing North Vietnam, the North Vietnamese would stop shooting at unarmed American planes.[1]

On November 20, Laird announced the first retaliatory measure: resumption of bombing on the North, with Laos thrown in for good measure. Resorting afresh to the language of double-think, the Defense Secretary declared that these American raids were merely "protective reaction missions" in response to attacks against RF-4.[2] The next day, U.S.

[1] Laird's argument was trebly questionable: one, America's decision to halt the bombing in 1968 had been entirely unilateral; two, Nixon had, if only briefly, recommended bombing at the time of the Cambodian invasion, thereby abrogating any putative agreement; and three, so-called unarmed American reconnaissance planes were escorted at all times by three jets armed with bombs, rockets and cannon which they were authorized to fire if attacked. This information would be revealed by government sources within two or three days of Laird's statement.

[2] Republican Senator Aiken of Vermont said that he knew of no

naval vessels sank a presumed Communist trawler in South Vietnamese waters.

But Laird hesitated a full three days before telling the rest of it. On Monday, November 23, the Defense Secretary announced that one hour before U.S. jets attacked North Vietnam and Laos on November 20, a small force of Army and special Air Force infantry troops landed twenty-three miles west of Hanoi, in order to liberate American prisoners of war. Unfortunately, when this combined rescue team landed in their helicopters hundreds of miles behind enemy lines, Laird explained, they learned that the POW camp was empty. Given a dubious place of honor beside Laird during this announcement was the man who had led the mission, Colonel Arthur Simons. Simons said, "We caught them [the North Vietnamese] completely by surprise."

Because the unorthodox mini-invasion had been a failure, the White House promptly after Laird's announcement insisted that the raid had nonetheless been "bold" and "gutsy." When a CBS reporter asked why the President had been reported to be "obviously nervous" during White House church services on Sunday, he was informed (in the correspondent's words) that "the raid may have been what had their boss edgy." But the raid had already occurred on Friday, so it's just as likely that what made the President "edgy"—or, as he might have put it if the mission were described as one of his *Six Crises*, "keyed up"—was how the announcement would be received on Monday.

His fellow politicians and political observers were astonished that the President had authorized *any* announcement, and in an effort to clear up the bewilderment, a Defense Department spokesman confessed that the raid would have remained a secret, save for the fact that the President had been deeply "concerned" about the government's "credibility."

But after the announcement, credibility was perhaps the least of Nixon's concerns. Impeccably noncommittal CBS commentator Eric Sevaroid shook his head and called the raid "harebrained." A few other reporters wondered if it wasn't a more telling problem—the one they'd been

Congressman who had been consulted by the President prior to the attacks.

on the scent of since the Cambodian affair in the spring.

All this was followed by inevitable background briefings in the effort to prove—probably for government sources as well as the public—that Nixon had been anything but irrational in November, 1970. This story emerged:

Sometime in the middle of the year, the President showed "deep concern" for the health and safety of the POW's, so he asked his generals to bring him some "good ideas" about freeing the prisoners. In August, the Army and Air Force (since both had prisoners in North Vietnam) began training a joint attack team that would take off either in October or November, depending on the weather over North Vietnam. In October, Nixon tried to develop the freedom of the POW's into a campaign issue, but bad weather ruled out the raid that month.

Early in November, after a meeting of the National Security Council, Laird remained behind, according to government sources, to remind President Nixon that if he wanted the raid to take place, he'd have to make up his mind immediately. The impression left by this particle of information was that Secretary Laird was more anxious about carrying out the raid than the President, and there would be no reason to doubt the truth of it, except for the date Laird allegedly persuaded Nixon to go ahead with the assault: November 5, one day *after* the fall election results were in.

In another explanation by government sources, it was admitted that Nixon hadn't really been concerned about "credibility"; if the North Vietnamese had said anything, they reasoned, the President could have gotten away with denying their allegations because the raid itself had seemed "so much like a movie plot." These sources, instead, attributed Nixon's decision to announce the mission to his desire to "demonstrate" his enormous concern for the POW's. That explanation, in turn, generated its own response: skeptics argued that if the President had been concerned for the safety of the POW's, he wouldn't have ordered the raid because of the probability that many of them would be killed, either by the North Vietnamese (whom Nixon considered brutal captors) or by the attacking Americans shooting off their guns in the darkness.

Even more inventive accounts were leaked by the government. The more cynical they were, the more rational Nixon might appear. One that caught fire was that the President knew all the time that the POW's had been evacuated. That way, Nixon could make his point to the North Vietnamese without the loss of any American prisoners: that the U.S. could invade North Vietnam at will and, therefore, the Communists had better think twice before shooting down any more unarmed American airplanes. It was unlikely enough to be true, and even an ordinary disbeliever like Senator Fulbright for awhile imagined it so. But how can occupying the enemy's empty office and leaving before he returns from lunch be construed as meaningful intimidation?

Pete Hamill was quick with the theme: "The whole thing is so incredible that you have to really question whether the people who planned this caper have a very firm grip on reality."

That November and December, the President was upset when the Ninety-First Congress resisted his proposals on a trade bill and social security increases and ignored his loosely-organized measures for welfare reform.[1] Most of the time, the President was peeved at Russell Long of Louisiana, who appeared to be behind the legislative snarl in the Senate, and at Mike Mansfield, the Democratic Majority Leader from Montana, for not doing something about it. But, say Evans and Novak, "Nixon held his peace, venting his anger only privately, complaining to aides that he was unable to get off for a badly needed rest . . . furious at Long's madcap maneuvers and Mansfield's lackluster leadership but not appealing to either of them"—keeping his temper, as always, by keeping his distance. Asked about the legislative snarl which gnawed at him constantly, Nixon said, "If I started thinking about that, my health would be in jeopardy."

A week or so before President Nixon's fifty-ninth birthday in January, 1971, Dr. Walter Tkach, the White House physician, reported the President was in excellent health; yet the doctor was "concerned." Tkach explained that any individual who works as hard as Nixon "can get up tight." Of course, Tkach hastily added, the President was *not* up tight. It's just, said the doctor, "I don't want him to get into trouble."

[1] The lame-duck session would adjourn without enacting any of the three.

CHAPTER TWENTY

Sociologists from the University of California at Santa Barbara simulated the conditions facing John F. Kennedy and his advisers during the 1962 Cuban missile crisis and then substituted Richard M. Nixon and his advisers, taking into account known personality factors. Run through the omniscient computer several times, Kennedy and his men came out opting for a naval blockade, while Nixon and his more hawkish retinue bombed again and again. Thus, working independently of Richard Barber of Yale, who months earlier had determined that Nixon's "crisis syndrome" could lead easily to "tragic drama," these California sociologists also discovered a Nixon who leaned toward hard-line, absolutist solutions. This tendency can be coupled with the fact that Nixon—with or without counsel—in twenty-nine months as President had rarely reached an important decision with coolness or for thoroughly impersonal motives.

The main example was Vietnam. Largely to justify lingering there until he consciously figured out how to keep from becoming the first American President to suffer the humiliation of defeat—and perhaps unconsciously to keep alive his options to make war—Nixon introduced a string of "pretexts," a word he enjoys using when boasting of his cleverness. Nixon's earliest pretext was a "just peace" for the Vietnamese, but the minute he realized that a large portion of the American public had grown apathetic after so many years of fighting for justice for Orientals, Nixon sent a "just peace" into semi-retirement. Thereupon, the President wrenched from his soul a deep desire for a "full generation of peace" for Americans, with the stress on American youth. Nixon had only one basic "business" pretext, which, as a result, he trotted out frequently: GI'S could not safely be withdrawn unless they were first employed to destroy the Communist supplies being used to kill them. A variation of the business motive was used to justify Cambodia, and it also became the one the President used to justify attacking Laos in force on January 30, 1971, purportedly to interdict Communist supply routes.[1]

Missing for Laos, however, was the personal motive, because the White House and the Pentagon failed for once to supply the details of the decision-making process. It seemed unfair[2] if not impossible to speculate on whether the President felt he had suffered a new humiliation before ordering the Laotian action.

But a heavily-creased veteran correspondent, once uneasy about analyzing someone else's head, now found himself going all the way with Freud. He blamed Laos on Tricia Nixon's engagement to Ed Cox. The farthest thing from his cheek was his tongue: a father himself, he reasoned that no father likes losing jurisdiction over his children, particularly his one remaining unmarried daughter. Furthermore, Cox

[1] It was four days before the White House confirmed the attack, the first large-scale military operation since Cambodia the previous spring. On instructions from Washington, the military refused to let American journalists follow the troops into Laos and simultaneously withheld operational details. American newspapers had to rely on unconfirmed reports. The argument given by the government was security, but actually, Administration sources later bragged about another reason. The President, they admitted to newspapermen, was gambling that "he could significantly expand the war" so long as the American public did not believe that American boys were directly involved. When the news embargo was lifted, the government rested its deception on a technicality: nine thousand American airmen and soldiers were helping the South Vietnamese by flying bomber runs, supplying helicopter transportation and manning the gunships conveying the transports, but, added the government's spokesmen, no American soldier *set foot inside Laos.* When the attack was ten or eleven days old, however, Howard Tuchner of ABC saw an American casualty being lugged out of Laos dressed in a South Vietnamese uniform, and one of the actual South Vietnamese combat soldiers told Tuchner that the wounded American GI had been in Laos as long as he had.

[2] For the author's purposes, the absence of detailed information seemed for awhile all to the good: too much neatness can make the best psychological theories suspect. If there were no facts, there could be no theorizing and the Laotian matter could thus stand as the exception which proved the rule. Unfortunately for the author, but fortunately for possible enlightenment, by 1971 others had discovered the theory that Nixon's major aggressions were often related to prior defeats and humiliations.

213

had credentials patently unacceptable to Nixon. The fiancé not only had worked for self-appointed consumer *ombudsman* Ralph Nader (who, to many conservatives, including Agnew, was nothing but a troublemaker) but had interned for *The New Republic*.[1] Since virtually every gossip in Washington seemed to know, the journalist presumed that the President, too, knew of his daughter's plans to marry prior to January 30 and that a muted struggle of wills between father and daughter occurred, reaching its emotional climax before Laos.

This theory seemed thin and excessively Freudian, but as facts about the period emerged, a second theory developed more in keeping with the Nixon standard of eccentricity: In late November or very early December, Nixon sat down with Haldeman, Ehrlichman, Mitchell, Finch, George Shultz (the reputable, efficient chief of the Office of Management and Budget) and Donald Rumsfeld (a smooth, conservative ex-Congressman who had lately become a favorite handyman and adviser) to map out his strategy for the next two years. Prompted by the outcome of his latest political efforts, Nixon promised to stop politicking and instead devote himself to being "President of all the people, in every sense of the word." He would be non-partisan, positive and plan great things for the future of the Republic. If this prospectus was broad and familiar, an aide gave assurances that it was sincere. The President wished "passionately" to be a man for all seasons.

After the meeting, Nixon set out to prove he could be the embodiment of all his promises. On or about December 4, he invited John B. Connally to join the Cabinet as Secretary of the Treasury. Connally was a millionaire, a friend of Lyndon Johnson's and three-time Democratic governor of Texas. Connally was also a man of "Presidential proportions" and aspirations. It took at least two more meetings before Nixon could convince the ambitious Texas Tory that he

[1] Discussing Cox at the June wedding with reporters, Nixon started to say something and changed his mind. "He's very out— he's very independent too," he admitted. The "too" referred to Tricia. But did the "out—" precede -rageous, -landish or -spoken? Outspoken liberals have never appealed to Nixon.

would fare better with the Republicans in the White House than with the Democrats in Texas.[1]

Ten days after their first private meeting, the President announced that the glib, self-possessed Connally was going to join the Nixon Cabinet and, indeed, was going to be the official Nixon economic spokesman. The appointment was described as "a dramatic" and "a masterful political stroke". The Texan's lack of paper qualifications was irrelevant. All that seemed to matter to many Americans was that for the first time, the President had taken the country by surprise without creating immediate anguish as well, so they cheered Nixon's originality. As a consequence, the President wasted little time before trying to top himself in the originality department.

But exercising less imagination the second time, he resorted to words instead of deeds, and implicated himself in another potentially humiliating situation from which he may have tried to extricate himself by invading Laos.

Warming up for his annual State of the Union message to the joint houses of Congress, one of which was the essentially hostile U.S. Senate, the President guaranteed in advance that it would be "one of the most bold and comprehensive *of all times.*" To begin the address itself on January 22, he offered a fulsome tribute to the late Senator Richard Russell of Georgia. Russell, said the President, "was one of the most magnificent Americans of all time." Unerringly, Nixon undermined his epic description by adding that he had "had the privilege" of seeing Russell on his death bed. Then one inappropriate moment led to the next: Nixon went from Russell's recent demise to morbid humor, offering his

[1] At the time of publication, Connally had not changed party affiliations, although he was being mentioned as a middling long-shot for Agnew's job in 1972. There was just as much speculation that if he ran for the Presidency in 1976, he would run as a Republican, because the Democratic party left no room for the higher aspirations of a staunch conservative.
Picking a Secretary of the Treasury from the opposition party was not unprecedented. John F. Kennedy had O. Douglas Dillon, a liberal Republican. But Dillon was hardly as prominent a Republican as Connally was a Democrat. Some experts feel that the Connally appointment, even if Agnew runs again, gives Nixon an excellent grip on Texas in '72.

"condolences" to the many members of Congress who had lost their seats and consequently weren't there. He added, in a baffling joke, "I know how both of you feel."

Death and defeat were familiar components of the Nixon syndrome,[1] but tonight they were mere appetizers for the rich main course. The President proclaimed: "This Ninety-Second Congress has a chance to be recorded as the greatest Congress in American history . . . We must let our spirits soar again . . . It is for us here to open the doors that will set free . . . the genius of the American people. How shall we meet this challenge? . . . *Tonight I shall present to the Congress Six Great Goals . . .*"

Although those goals promised to "change the framework of government itself," the anticlimax arrived quickly. "The first of these great goals is already before Congress," he said, urging Congress to act on "more than thirty-five" pieces of legislation he had proposed last year. One, he wanted welfare reform; two, "full prosperity in peacetime." The third great goal was "to continue the efforts so dramatically begun last year—to restore and enhance our natural environment." Fourth, he wanted "a program to insure that no American family will be prevented from obtaining basic medical care by inability to pay." Health insurance? No—more aid to medical schools and "more incentives" to more doctors and new programs against disease.[2] (By May, he would come out

[1] So was apparent nervousness. He fluffed many lines that night, but just to name a few, "welfare" children became "well-fell," a slip that sounded like high praise for one of Richard III's dead-eye archers; "runaway inflation"—which could not happen under Nixon—became "wun" (or "one") -away inflation." (On January 13, Bethlehem Steel defied Nixon's request to hold the line by announcing a twelve percent hike, which Nixon heatedly decried as "enormous" and threatened, emptily, to "review" because he was "deeply concerned.") And now, eyeball to eyeball with this giant cancer called the Congress, Nixon suddenly remembered that its members had "laid-up" (instead of "laid-in," the more puzzling expression found in the transcript) the thirty-seven point program he had presented in 1970.
[2] Once more it seemed to be a case of shuffling. Later in 1971, the Administration made clear its desire to disband the U.S. Public Health Service's medical corps, in which over five thousand doctors and researchers carried military rank and privileges and, as such, were immune from political pressure. Some of the doctors

roundly against cancer.) "The fifth great goal is to strengthen and to renew our state and local governments . . . a new partnership between the Federal government and the states and localities." Nixon assured both houses that these things would wipe out the "great feeling of frustration" that has crept across this land. "The sixth great goal is to complete the reform of the Federal government itself"—reducing the present twelve Cabinet departments to eight.

Afterwards, John Mitchell asserted, *"This is the most important document since the Constitution."*

Congress popped the balloon the next morning. With a restraint typical of colleagues on both sides of the Senate aisle, Mike Mansfield said politely that he thought the President's address "excellent and hopeful." But Mitchell had also said, "Judge us not by what we say but by what we do," and, following that lead, the Senate Majority leader continued, "I want to see the specifics; it was painted with a very broad brush." There were similarly indifferent rumblings for another day or two, before memory of the inflatus seemed to fade into thin air.

Was the yawning reaction of Congress and Washington as a whole sufficient to goad a President yearning for more accolades into making war in Laos on January 30? Though the answer may never be certain, Nixon stopped speaking with peaceable majesty.

In early February, Hans Morgenthau argued in *The New Republic* that Nixon's policy of "winding down" the war "is not the same as ending it." An influential liberal thinker, Morgenthau believed the President was interested only in

---

felt that Nixon wanted five thousand patronage "plums" to give to Republican M.D.'s and technicians. They based this contention on the little-publicized habit of Donald Rumsfeld's and other Administration officials' pressuring civil servants despite a federal law that assures government civilians tenure. Nixon's people realized early in 1969 that nothing in that law prevented them from phasing out a job and giving it a new name or from keeping a civil servant from advancement. One acting unit chief in HEW had been kept waiting for a promotion for over a year. Perhaps it was a coincidence, but six working days after switching his registration from Democrat to Republican, he became head of his unit and received the overdue pay raise.

changing the color of the corpses. Morgenthau feared that Nixon would rely finally on nuclear bombs to defeat Hanoi.

Hastily the President summoned the White House correspondents. (He had lately skirted them, taking his case to editors and publishers instead.) In the Oval Office, a bitter Chief Executive told them, "I am not going to place *any* limitation upon the use of air power, except to rule out a rather *ridiculous* suggestion made from time to time—I think the latest," he said, transparently affecting offhandedness, "by Hans Morgenthau—that our air power might include the use of tactical nuclear weapons. I would use the power of the United States and particularly its power in the air to the extent that I consider it necessary to protect our remaining forces in South Vietnam . . . I will *not* allow those forces to be endangered by a massive North Vietnamese incursion, if one should be undertaken. I think the very fact that the North Vietnamese *know* that I intend to take strong action to deal with that incursion *means* that they are not going to take it. If they do," said the President forbiddingly, "*I can assure you that*—" He broke off, remembering that his conscious purpose today was not to raise fears but lower them. "I don't want to assure you," he said lamely, "I simply want to have the record clear that I would not be bound, of course, by any so-called understanding which they have already violated at the time of the bombing halt."

By middle February the "strong action" in Laos concluded in tragic defeat. The Communists had the South Vietnamese pinned down for three or four consecutive days, and every time the Saigon-directed troops raised their heads, the Hanoi-directed troops slaughtered them.

"The news of serious South Vietnamese defeats along Highway 9 showed yet again the egregious quality of Mr. Nixon's strategic and military judgment," said Townsend Hoopes, former Under Secretary of the Air Force, in *The New Republic*, which ran Hoopes's piece under the pointed headline: "THE PRESIDENT IS THE PROBLEM." The magazine was seen in Washington on March 3 and was presumably digested in the news summary handed to the President that night.

On March 4, again forsaking the more reassuring presence of editors and publishers (who cannot always be rounded up on an instant's notice), Nixon turned on the ubiquitous White House correspondents: "I would suggest that you ladies and gentlemen always pretty much underestimated what I am capable of doing in terms of withdrawing forces and so forth . . . *Night after night* after I announced the decision to go into Cambodia on television, it was indicated that the decision would have the opposite effect, that it would increase American casualties and that it would mean that it would prolong the war." Nixon arched his brow, then squinted, then arched his brow again, sighed, hesitated, fluttered his hands and stabbed a finger at members of the press.

As Nixon vented his emotions, the South Vietnamese began to retreat from Laos, soldiers breaking from their units and running away. Stragglers returned to South Vietnam leaderless and alone, often deserting arms and equipment. Those left in Laos tried to pile onto evacuation helicopters, clutching to the landing rods when the ship was full. Many fell to their deaths from the sky, while others had to be pried loose when the copters couldn't rise.

Also that month, American GI'S stood in front of network television cameras not far from the battlefield and boldly criticized the war. Toward the end of March, two platoons of American soldiers collectively defied orders to advance down a border road along which the Communists had inflicted heavy casualties earlier in the day.

Agnew argued that nobody had the right to call the South Vietnamese withdrawal a "rout." On the contrary, the Vice-President insisted, it was an "orderly retreat." White House aides employed the term thereafter, and on April 8, Nixon concluded that his attack on Laos had hurt the Communists. "Consequentially," he said with an air of pontifical finality, "I can report that Vietnamization has succeeded." Eight days later, he spoke up again, "Without any question [the North Vietnamese] have been the most barbaric in handling of prisoners of any nation in modern history," he declared, in his passion overlooking the record of Germany and Japan in the 1930's and 1940's. Nixon promised to bomb the Communists until the prisoners were released, but perhaps only his critics saw the irony: most of the prisoners had been captured on bombing missions.

Pressed for answers by Congress shortly thereafter, Secretary Laird admitted that "withdrawal" *never* meant that the United States intended to pull out every GI; the President planned to keep American boys in South Vietnam until the South Vietnamese could fend for themselves.

In a press conference on April 29, President Nixon confirmed that Americans would remain in Southeast Asia "no matter how long it takes." In response to Hanoi's implication that all prisoners could expect early repatriation if Nixon set a firm withdrawal date, he refused until he received "not just the promise to discuss the release of our prisoners but a commitment . . . [because] a promise to discuss means *nothing* from the North Vietnamese."

Even as the President was drawing this fine distinction, another enemy was gathering outside his door. Anti-war pickets, capping several days of demonstrations, were trying to march on the White House. The President attempted to laugh them off: "Washington is somewhat in a state of siege." But Nixon was not amused, bitterness compelling an expression his aides had begged him never to use again. *"Well, let me make one thing very clear,"* he said, *"the President is not intimidated."* On tv his features were a composition in inappropriate activity. During the session, he sighed and hesitated, the frequent pauses followed by a listless monotone.[1] "This government is going forward. It doesn't mean that we're not going to listen to those who come peacefully but those who come and break the law will be prosecuted to the full extent of the law."[2]

---

[1] George Herman of CBS made a point of saying after the telecast that he thought the President that night had been, if nothing else, "extraordinarily relaxed," which may be one of those instances where a journalist either cannot distinguish between slowness and calm or is so intimidated by what he sees that he says almost the opposite of what he may think—certainly the opposite of what is apparent to anyone who knows Nixon.

Nixon's disturbed manner, from time to time that spring, became unusually apparent. At a meeting of the President's Council on the Arts, he was seen twitching and, seemingly, out of touch with his surroundings. The political columnist for *The Village Voice* reported that his behavior had led to gossip in Washington that the President had a drinking problem.

[2] On direct orders from the Attorney General, the Washington

Hampered by slippery Vietcong, mocking North Vietnamese, incompetent or uncaring South Vietnamese, defiant radic-libs marching on 1600 Pennsylvania Avenue and by the cynical press (whose presence he repeatedly requested), the President once again demonstrated what side he was on and just how strongly he was on it. A military court had recently convicted Lieutenant William Calley of murdering civilians at Mylai in South Vietnam, and in an extraordinary extralegal maneuver, the President, unasked, intervened to announce that he would personally review the court's decision. When the press asked for an explanation of his action, the President fidgeted and referred to Calley as "Captain" Calley—not once, but three times. Perhaps he personally identified with the soldier as a comrade in arms or even as a fellow prisoner; Calley was under house arrest and figuratively—with the enemy at the door of the White House—Nixon was too. So the President inadvertently promoted Calley in his mind, affording him an esteem denied those who opposed his "principles."

At the same press conference, Nixon renewed the pretext he had used to raid the empty North Vietnamese prisoner of war camp the previous November and to justify bombing that country on April 16. He made it clear on April 29 that he was fighting in Vietnam *only* because prisoners were over there—to which his critics replied that the prisoners were over there only because Nixon was fighting in Vietnam. He raised the POW pretext time and again, so that it became the limb on which he hung everything.

On July 1, Hanoi sawed it off. The North Vietnamese publicly guaranteed the release of all American prisoners in North Vietnam before the end of 1971, provided all American, Australian, New Zealand and South Korean troops also left by then. At the same time, the Vietcong withdrew one of their most nettlesome demands: their right to dictate the

---

police swept up citizens in wholesale numbers, locking them up without charges in order to prevent threatened disruption of government agencies. Many people, including newspapermen, were arrested and detained up to forty-eight hours in overcrowded jails, temporary pens or fenced-in fields, although preventive detention violates the Constitution.

make-up of the Saigon government prior to a truce. The dual enemy offer was widely interpreted as the "commitment" sought by the President.

Though he had made the welfare of American prisoners an urgent concern until now, Nixon did not reply. Instead, he found a new and stronger limb.

Nixon had long harbored a romantic dream to see China. He had hinted of it to the anti-war students in May, 1970, when Henry Kissinger may have been laboring at its fulfillment for some time. Finally, in a secret meeting in Peking in July, 1971, Nixon's national security adviser worked out the broad terms of the visit with Communist Chinese Premier Chou En-lai.

When the President announced from San Clemente on July 15 that the Communists would receive him on the mainland before the spring of the next year, the applause was thunderous. After over twenty years of Cold War, here was the conservative President of the United States, a man who had built his career on baiting Communists, holding out the branch of peace to the world's most populous nation, one which the United States still did not officially recognize. It was a blockbuster which Walter Lippmann figured no liberal could have pulled off without appearing to have sold out to Communism.

The President flew back to Washington on July 18 in a "mood approaching euphoria," it was reported in the papers. But on the morning of July 19, he seemed a different man. Perhaps it was the "let-down" that he says comes to him after a crisis, or it might have resembled the worry entertainers suffer after a hit: "What do you do for an encore?" In either case, Americans were expecting an encore the morning of the 19th. Responding to a Presidential invitation, optimistic Congressional leaders arrived at the White House thinking Nixon was going to hint broadly, in that special theatrical way of his, that with all that was going on in Peking, how could the world's number one convert miss the chance to call off the war with Hanoi?

But a defensive President quickly disillusioned them. Though he had treated Asian Communism as a dangerous monolith for a whole generation, Nixon now suggested that the Chinese Reds were in no position to negotiate for the Indochinese Reds. That was both true, and, as observers later said, beside the point: the world wanted to know how Nixon—and not Peking—would answer Hanoi's latest peace offer.

"My fear," said Clark Clifford not long afterwards, "is that Mr. Nixon is using his trip to China as an excuse for not trying to find a settlement in Vietnam." So Lyndon Johnson's former Secretary of Defense, like a modern Paul Revere, rose up "to sound the alarm."[1] Clifford was not alone. It's had to say precisely what had gotten under their skins, but before the end of July, men who had been at the White House meeting seemed jittery. House Minority leader Gerald Ford endorsed a move in the sister Senate to restrict a President's war-making powers. Though the endorsement was equivocal, it was at odds tonally with Ford's recent staunch loyalty to the Republican Party's leader.

A day or so before the meeting with Nixon, Hugh Scott, Ford's Senate counterpart, predicted that American ground forces would be out of South Vietnam by May, 1972. However, a week after the White House meeting, Scott said nothing but legislation could curb the Executive Branch's prosecution of the Vietnam war. The White House had run the war in secrecy "to the point of suffocation and isolation," he charged, basing his argument on the revelations of "The Pentagon Papers," which had recently exposed the previous Administration's deceptions to enlarge the war. Yet coming when they did, the Minority leader's comments reflected oblique defiance of Nixon's oft-spoken desire for

[1] Without speaking of the President, Clifford had previously written an article (appearing only days after Nixon had announced the first troop withdrawal) suggesting that the United States bring home one hundred thousand men by the end of 1969 and the rest in 1970. Nixon took it personally. "I noticed Mr. Clifford's comments in the magazine *Foreign Affairs*," said the President in one of his press conferences, "and naturally I respected his judgment [but] the full year in which he was Secretary of Defense, our casualties were the highest of the whole five-year period . . . I would hope that we could beat Mr. Clifford's timetable—just as I think we have done a little better than we did when he was in charge of our national defense."

total flexibility in prosecution of foreign and military affairs.

On August 5, Nixon summoned the press to say, "I will only say that as the joint announcement [with Peking] indicated, this will be a wide-ranging discussion of issues concerning both governments. It is not a discussion that is going to lead to instant detente . . . We [He mentioned the Soviet Union and the U.S. but, perhaps thinking ahead to another announcement, he was confusing Russia with China.] have moved from an era of confrontation without communication to an era of negotiation with discussion . . . To speculate about what program will be made on any particular issue—to speculate, for example, as to what effect this might have on Vietnam—would not serve in the interests of constructive talks."

When a reporter asked why the President had not issued a formal response to the Hanoi-Vietcong peace proposal of July 1, the President sighed and thrust his hands into his pockets: ". . . *The Administration is not interested in negotiating a settlement.*"

CHAPTER TWENTY-ONE

At the end of 1970, a few weeks after Nixon's raid on the empty POW compound in North Vietnam and his stunning appointment of Democrat John Connally to the Republican Cabinet, Daniel Patrick Moynihan, another Democrat and the President's counsellor on education, youth, poverty, welfare and urban affairs, decided to go back to teaching before Harvard took away his tenure. Moynihan's valedictory contained praise for the President's "remarkable" record in the White House. His counsellor described a Nixon who had ended urban violence, calmed civil disobedience, quieted ugly racial rhetoric, fed the poor, cured the ill, virtually ended the war in Southeast Asia and exhibited an understanding of government "the likes of which had not been heard in Washington since Woodrow Wilson." But a more provocative Moynihan statement that day was the following: "Time and again the President has said things of startling insight, taken positions of great political courage and intellectual daring only to be greeted with the silence of incomprehension, even in our own ranks."

Even a year later, at the end of 1971, there was no question of Nixon's daring, though some called it recklessness. Nor was there any question of his startling insights: he swiftly perceived his enemies and knew intuitively how to bewilder and sometimes hurt them. This alertness to danger and opportunity, coupled with his endless talk of power and tactics, is often construed as a sign of high intelligence. However, the dangers and opportunities are not always real, and while this may basically be a problem of emotions, it is also a problem of intellect.

Chet Huntley, the former NBC commentator who spent a lot of time with Nixon, said once (He later regretted saying it so publicly.[1]) that he was overwhelmed and frightened by

[1] Huntley was quoted by Thomas Thompson, a staff writer for *Life*, who claims the newscaster unequivocally criticized the

Nixon's "shallowness," and Ramsey Clark claimed the Nixon "hatred style of politics" developed—in part—because Nixon "doesn't know enough about the subject." In this case, the subject was law and the critic a Democrat, but Paul (Pete) McCloskey, Nixon's opponent for the Republican nomination, worried about the quality of Nixon's intelligence in areas as diverse as defense planning and voting rights. "T.R.B." of *The New Republic*, along with one or two of Nixon's economists, wondered if "Nixonomics" were not only the product of nineteenth-century liberal thought but of "oversimplification." Nixon was an excellent student— he remembered things, some of them no doubt outdated— but as Lou Fuller, one of his law professors at Duke, had said, Nixon was not very "profound or terribly imaginative."

Yet if he does not have the profundity to understand or follow through his programs, Richard Nixon does have the imagination to announce them. A sharp, dramatic announcement appears to minimize the necessity of taking meaningful steps beyond the announcement stage. A declaration of, say, a war on Cambodia hurt and outraged but a declaration of a peace initiative, such as a trip to China, numbed the world with its daring. And the magnitude of such an announcement lives on, often long after a comprehensible program has failed to materialize.

With the heroic announcement of his trip to the People's Republic of China, President Nixon began governing the United States by proclamation and at times thereafter by *fiat*. Because the world responds to drama, not logic, every major statement from mid-July through mid-November— except the last—seemed designed for shock value. Uttered in pique, the last was perhaps the most shocking of all.

On August 3, abruptly doing an about-face, the President ordered school busing held "to the minimum required by law," a mini-blockbuster which jolted America's blacks and disrupted his own Administration. Civil rights specialists in

President's intelligence. Though Huntley later denied it, seemingly fudging a bit as he did so, a network news department source explained that Huntley felt that, at the moment he criticized Nixon, he was talking off the record.

HEW and the Justice Department had devised a plan—with his approval—to bus students in Austin, Texas, in compliance with a recent Supreme Court ruling. By August 4, HEW and even some Justice Department conservatives were in an uproar: how did the President expect them to minimally apply the law of the land without virtually ignoring it?

On August 11, faced with a revolt which carried with it rumors (later denied) of Elliot Richardson's threatened resignation as Secretary of HEW, the President issued a private, followed by an unprecedented public, warning: Any government employee who exceeded his authority in the matter of busing would be transferred or fired. His press office could not explain why Nixon had found it necessary to wash his dirty linen in public.

Probing for Nixon's motives in reversing himself on the busing plan, John Osborne found them "tainted with more than a touch of the paranoia that is increasingly evident at and near the Nixon White House." It seems that Nixon's political advisers (Speculation from other quarters is that Mitchell and Haldeman were key figures) had discovered a plot against the President and ominously informed him that a Lyndon Johnson-appointed Federal judge allegedly realized that the government busing plan was too liberal and, consequently, he and a Democratic crony who sat on the district school board in Austin, Texas (where the plan was to be tried first) eagerly approved parts of it to embarrass Nixon politically in the South. Osborne feels that the byzantine and amorphous plot may have existed only in the minds of Nixon's aides. Nonetheless, the President believed their story. Then when his own staff refused for days to recognize the *political realities* behind his new busing order, Nixon grew angry. Perhaps by August 11, he was so angry that he was unwilling—or unable—to keep his anger to himself.

On August 15, one month to the day after the China announcement (There seemed to be some rigidity to the proclamation technique.), Nixon delivered the second major blockbuster. He declared that he was imposing a wage-price freeze and taking the United States off the gold standard.

They were spectacular moves, but what made them all the

more so was that they were another total reversal of ancient Nixon principles. For weeks—some say months—Nixon's economic advisers had pressed him to take positive steps to stave off a depression they feared would rival 1929, but the President argued vehemently that wage-price controls of any kind were undemocratic and floating the dollar free of its once-solid gold moorings was, as images go, a mark of American weakness.

Twenty-four days after announcing the wage-price freeze, Nixon anxiously announced that he was going to discontinue it at the end of ninety days and invoke some other system "to see that America is not again afflicted by the virus of runaway inflation." Speaking to a special joint session of Congress which expected to hear more than it did, the President advised that "hard work is what makes America great" and that "there would be no more dangerous delusion than the notion that we can maintain the standard of living that our own people sometime complain about . . . without hard work." These Nixonian verities, however, did not keep the address from seeming directionless. As Secretary Connally divulged in his exegesis soon afterwards, the President had no precise idea what he would substitute for the wage-price freeze.

On September 16, Nixon reaffirmed an earlier announcement that the U.S. would vote to seat Peking in both the United Nations' Security Council and General Assembly, "in order to affect the realities of the situation." At the same time, he warned that he would fight against the expulsion of Nationalist China.

Still following some kind of schedule (He may have changed the date slightly as a result of teasing about an "Ides complex."), Nixon announced a third blockbuster on October 12: He was going to Moscow in May, 1972. It came nowhere near topping the drama of the China announcement, but since Nixon felt that Moscow had betrayed him in the Middle East, the Russian trip was important news. Twelve days after the Moscow declaration, he cautioned: "We go [to China and Russia] with no false hopes and we intend to leave behind us in America no unrealistic expectations." There were no such reservations reflected in either of the original announcements.

228

In September, the White House already knew what November's blockbuster would be, spokesmen there hinting broadly about number four to favored newsmen, including Stewart Alsop. On November 12, exactly one month after auditioning the Russian trip, President Nixon announced his plans to double the rate of withdrawal so that only one hundred and thirty-nine thousand GI's would be left in Vietnam by February, 1972. The purpose of such a "residual" force, he explained, was to protect the Vietnamese until they could fight their own war or until there was a negotiated settlement with Hanoi and the Vietcong. In other words, the President was personally admitting for the first time that "withdrawal" had never meant *full* withdrawal. Moreover, he had already ruled out his two conditions for "totalling out." Four months earlier, in a burst of anger, the President had admitted that he had no intention of accepting a negotiated settlement. And if "Vietnamization" were the success Nixon declared it after Cambodia, the Vietnamese should have been fighting their own war for the past year and a half.

Still fond of the Ides, on November 15, the President authorized the White House to leak that the "residual" force might go as low as thirty thousand men by June, 1972, provided the Communists made no serious trouble.

Official or otherwise, all of these announcements were dramatic and created their own strong reactions. His economic announcement, for example, was greeted at home with relief, first, then confusion and in world trade markets with confusion first, then anger. The Japanese, among the hardest hit by Nixon's economic edict, complained that while they understood the "logic" of his efforts to defend the dollar, they failed to understand the President's timing or his style.[1]

But timing and especially style—those sudden dramatic displays of power and the ability to manipulate feelings—have always meant as much to Richard Nixon as logic. They are emotional outlets. Logic, on the other hand, displaces emotion, saps power, takes leaders out of the limelight and

[1] It was the second time Nixon had surprised the Japanese: the *detente* with Red China was the first.

active leadership roles and buries them in the ivory towers where effete intellectuals dwell.[1]

A President learns that today's logic can be refuted tomorrow, and the world will still move to his commands. A President can negate his anti-Communism or his budget-balancing principles as often as he chooses, and then negate the negation, and still leave admirers breathless and enemies bewildered and helpless. Sooner or later, even a President who is not sure of his strength discovers that no matter how he contradicts himself, the world shakes just the same. President Nixon, for one, has gained both real and imagined power out of sheer motion. Facing few external restraints as President, he may at last freely convert distortion into reality and self-absorption into a cause.

On November 17, as he signed into law a military procurement bill passed by Congress, the President said he liked the bill. But Congress had also attached an amendment setting forth the policy that all U.S. troops must be withdrawn promptly from Vietnam upon release of American POW's. Nixon explained his position: "[The amendment] does not represent the policies of this Administration," he said. And because Congress's amendment "does not reflect my judgment," the President declared that it had no "binding force or effect" on him.

Therefore, Richard Nixon would ignore the law.

---

[1] Nixon has a sense of inadequacy about his own intellectual capability. Lou Fuller recalls that Nixon was "what today we'd call uptight. There was the suggestion of an intellectual inferiority complex." Therefore, Nixon's inability to fathom intellectuals is easily converted into their *refusal* to understand him.

CHAPTER TWENTY-TWO

The reporter who was too young to be intimidated began, "Mr. President, at a previous news conference you said that what happened at Mylai was a massacre. On another occasion, you said that Charles Manson was guilty. On another occasion, you mentioned Angela Davis by name and then said that those responsible for such acts of terror will be brought to justice. My question concerns the problem of pretrial publicity and the fact that it could jeopardize a defendant's rights at a trial. How do you reconcile your comments with your status as a lawyer?"[1]

Comprehending that it was meant as more than a question, though, Nixon replied, "I think that's a legitimate criticism. I think sometimes we lawyers—even like doctors who try to prescribe for themselves," he said, trying to find some way home, "may make mistakes." There was a deferred flicker and his jaw went slack. "And I think that kind of comment is probably unjustified," he said, so sharply averting his face from the young reporter's that on television, Nixon was frozen in profile.

[1] Though Nixon spoke of a massacre at Mylai as if it were a proven fact at the time, he later made it up to Lieutenant Calley, the principal defendant, by promising to review Calley's conviction. But—after casually tying Angela Davis's name to acts of terror during an attempted prison escape in California—he did her a second legal disservice. In January, not a month after the press conference, the President invited the Russians to come and audit her trial, to prove that American criminal justice is fair. Miss Davis, charged with conspiracy, kidnapping and murder in the escape attempt of prisoners, made no secret of being a Communist; but Nixon allowed the American public to infer that she was one of the Russian variety—i.e., an international conspirator. After discussing this very press conference with the President, which took place on December 10, 1970, Senator Barry Goldwater reflected Nixon's displeasure. The Arizonian said the reporter had stepped out of line by asking the President of the United States for his legal qualifications. The reporter, said Goldwater, was "a bonehead."

Citizens do not demand the President to be a good lawyer —Lyndon Johnson had been a schoolteacher, Harry Truman a haberdasher and Dwight Eisenhower a general—so long as he is advised by good lawyers and by an Attorney General who pursues law enforcement evenhandedly. But John Mitchell was more interested in protecting Nixon than the law and often, Mitchell's anger rose from casual reminders that there are persons out there who did not respond enthusiastically to what Richard Nixon thought was good for them.

When black leaders refused to stand up in public and acclaim Nixon's civil rights record, the Attorney General snapped, "What the hell do you expect them to do with this Administration, stand up and cheer?" When the Ripon Society, an organization of young, progressive Republicans, criticized his advice to the President, Mitchell blurted out that they were so many "little juvenile delinquents." When campus protests were the rage, Mitchell fumed loudly about "these stupid bastards running educational institutions." After the President's own Commission on Campus Unrest indicated that maybe Nixon was as responsible as the stupid bastards running education, Mitchell chastized the Commission "for getting off base in talking about government, particularly the Federal Government." When the anti-war movement was capturing headlines, he articulated the idea that all the leaders of the peace movement in the United States belong to a "militant conspiracy" fed somehow from foreign soil. It was in one of these moments that the Attorney General added with a grim smile, "This country is going so far right you won't even recognize it."

This was not a caution; it was a threat. From his position of power, Mitchell consistently took measures to push the country very far to the right. He matter-of-factly asserted his authority to tap any telephone, bug any home or office without the approval of the courts. He authorized his chief assistant, Deputy Attorney General Richard Kleindienst, to argue against legislation that would inhibit Mitchell's power to collect secret dossiers on American citizens, and to promise that abuses of civil rights, including the right to privacy and freedom from political oppression, would be averted through "self-discipline" within the Executive Branch. And when the U.S. Senate still complained, Mitchell permitted Assistant Attorney General William H. Rehnquist to inform Senator Sam Ervin, the chief complainant, that the President had the Constitutional right to put Ervin under surveillance, too.

Gaining in arrogance and motion, the Attorney General demanded legislation giving his agents the authority to bust down doors without warning. He encouraged local police to make illegal mass arrests, without charging those arrested with a crime, in order to stop violence which has not started. Then Mitchell praised the police for carrying out his wishes. He went to court and requested an injunction forbidding members of Vietnam Veterans Against the War, an organization to which he is opposed, from sleeping on the Mall in Washington; and, after thinking twice about the politics of shooing legless war veterans from Federal property, Mitchell returned to the District Judge who had issued the order for him and asked that it be rescinded. (The Judge, finally fed up, accused the Attorney General of "degrading" the law of the land.)

Mitchell called for drying up "the sea of legalisms" which buoy the guilty, although these legalisms also protect the innocent. He refused to prosecute eight or nine Ohio National Guardsmen on charges of premeditated murder because he did not think the government, federal or local, had sufficient evidence of premeditation to win its case. But the Attorney General also hesitated to recommend to local law authorities that charges be dropped against twenty-four students and one professor accused of conspiring to threaten these Guardsmen, although an FBI investigation patently disputed that there is sufficient evidence of conspiracy to win the case.

This same Attorney General said of Nixon, "He's probably the most informed President there's ever been. He reads everything and remembers it all." The normal edge in his voice sharpened by bitter memories, Mitchell added, "I really can't understand how people can call him isolated. He's aware of everything that's going on."

Nixon is not aware of everything that's going on, although like most Presidents he strives for omniscience. In his case, however, there may be less concern for *what* the public thinks than in controlling *how* it thinks. Throughout his career he

233

has sought to dictate what men should think, beginning a generation earlier with his co-sponsorship of the Mundt-Nixon Bill, aimed at suppressing not just Communistic acts but Communistic thought. Even Thomas E. Dewey, hardly a raving radical, considered the bill an attempt at "thought control," and Congress refused to pass it into law.

But as President of the United States, Nixon has shown that he does not need or want Congress. Though it can perhaps be argued successfully that the current phase of American repression was fathered by Lyndon Jonhson, within months of Nixon's taking office, the Secret Service, which protects him, issued a document requesting information about obvious threats to the lives of the President, the Vice-President and their top aides. The document, labeled "U.S. Secret Service Liaison Guidelines," went well beyond the point of protecting the President's life, though, to protecting his good name, urging Americans to report any fellow citizen who attempts to "embarrass" high officials or who makes "irrational" or "abusive statements" about the President. By the summer of 1970, the federal government had collected political information, according to Ben A. Franklin, a reporter for the *Times*, "on hundreds of thousands of law-abiding yet suspect citizens." The information was microfilmed and computerized by the Secret Service, the FBI and although the material concerned civilian citizens of the United States, by the Army, the Air Force and, for all anyone outside government knows, the Navy and Marine Corps too. Most of the civilians were guilty of things like attending Earth Day festivities or peace parades. Reportedly, other citizens were labeled as "suspicious" for having long hair, attending an eastern university or the funeral of Martin Luther King Jr., or maintaining an unlisted phone number. When Hale Boggs, a leading Democrat in the House of Representatives, complained that his phone was being tapped and blamed it on J. Edgar Hoover, the Attorney General angrily charged Boggs with "slanderous falsehoods and the most vicious kind of name-calling."

It seems almost as if Nixon cannot concentrate for long periods on anything but the abuse he thinks is being heaped on him, whether by Congressmen or *The New York Times*.

Harry Treleavan, a key member of Nixon's campaign staff, was given a special assignment during the 1968 race. He prepared the copy for an advertisement that was to run in the *Times*. It was, in fact, about the *Times* and revolved around two puns. The one placed at the top of the page said, "The Truth Hurts at Times"; the one at the bottom, "In their search for truth, men must rise above the Times!" Treleavan explained proudly to Joe McGinniss: "It was something Nixon himself wanted done and even if it doesn't get us any votes, it's worth it just for the fun of hitting these guys."

That did not stop the *Times*, though, so in his first year in office, Nixon loosed Agnew. The Vice-President said the *Times* was too powerful and had a bad habit of suppressing or subordinating news stories favorable to the President. "When they go beyond fair comment and criticism," Agnew said, also threatening other liberal news outlets (such as the tv networks), "they will be called upon to defend their statements and positions just as we must defend ours. And when their criticism becomes excessive or unjust, we shall invite them down from their ivory towers to enjoy the rough-and-tumble of public debate. I don't mean to intimidate the press or the networks or anyone else from speaking out," Agnew said, intimidating one of the papers by knocking down a straw man: "I'm not recommending the dismemberment of the Washington Post Company."

But since newspapers are harder to intimidate than television companies, which are slyly threatened with the loss of government operating licenses, the *Post* and the *Times* continued to write about Nixon, often uncomplimentarily. In May, 1971, *Post* staff writer John P. MacKenzie rated Nixon's Constitutional legal talents as virtually nonexistent. "It's no answer to say, 'Nixon's a politician first and a lawyer second,'" said MacKenzie, "and it won't do to write off Nixon's law practice as too limited." The author felt the President used the law partly as a "tool for decision" but partly, too, as "*a protective mechanism*." And there's no doubt that Nixon wanted to protect himself from those two newspapers. He could not think of the words they wrote as the product of honest journalism; he felt they were out to torment him.

On June 14, 1971, the *Times* published the first article in a series based on a secret study undertaken in 1967 by Robert MacNamara, Johnson's Secretary of Defense. The study, prepared by government experts, was tantamount to a detailed confession that the war in Vietnam had resulted from a string of blunders and deceits which occurred before Nixon became President. Though it was a self-denunciation by the Johnson Administration and though Nixon and Mitchell *had never read any part* of "The Pentagon Papers," the first significant reaction of the President and his Attorney General was that if it was published in the *Times*, it had to be bad for Nixon. In asking for an injunction from a Federal judge, Mitchell's assistants made clear the President's first concern by stressing that the *Times* had "unilaterally declassified" top-secret documents, thereby usurping an important Presidential "prerogative." "Mr. Nixon's predominant concern," Herb Klein reiterated (and is here paraphrased by John Osborne), "was not any harm that this publication might do *but the harm to the Presidency that uninhibited and unpunished* [emphasis added] dissemination and publication . . . might do."

The court approved a temporary injunction against the *Times* the day the first installment of "The Pentagon Papers" was published. Then, four days later, the *Post* began running material that the New York paper was temporarily forbidden to print, and the Attorney General and the Germans reportedly vied with each other for the Curseword of the Week Award. Quickly the Justice Department obtained a second injunction, but that did not lessen the rage; the feeling inside the Administration was that the *Post* had only done it to make them mad. For once, such paranoia might have possessed more than a grain of justification. The President and Mitchell had flaunted the Constitutional guarantee of a free press by demanding censorship prior to publication of the first unvarnished truth about the war from official sources. It seemed to some editors like a crime against peace and the Constitution at the same time and, although these were the first concerns, the *Post* was flaunting Nixon's wish by standing with the *Times*.

Other newspapers soon carried on where these two temporarily had been forced to leave off, and the President's frustration was thereafter reflected in Mitchell's deepening insistence not on the Constitutional arguments favoring suppression (which were paper-thin from the start) but on the punishable aspects[1] of federal regulations governing exposure of secret documents.

The Supreme Court ruled on June 30, sixteen days after this momentous legal battle began, that the government had "not met the burden" of their own technical argument that publication must be enjoined to protect "national security." By a vote of six to three, the Court held that the historic argument by Nixon and Mitchell to block news articles prior to publication bears "a heavy burden of presumption against its Constitutionality." (Two of the three dissenters on the high bench were Chief Justice Warren Burger and Associate Justice Harry Blackmun, Nixon's appointees: their complex arguments hung not so much on the Constitutional issues as the desire to afford more time to study the case.)

If, say, the *Kansas City Star* and *The San Diego Union* had published "The Pentagon Papers" in the summer of 1971, Nixon and Mitchell might never have tested their power to abridge Article I of the Bill of Rights; the *Star* and the *Union* are pro-Nixon papers. But the articles appeared in *The New*

[1] On June 26, the Justice Department issued a warrant for the arrest of Dr. Daniel Ellsberg on charges that this former government official who had worked on the study had "unauthorized possession of top-secret documents" and that he had "failed to return them." In the days prior to this, Ellsberg made no effort to deny his involvement.

On June 30, after the Supreme Court ruled against the Administration, Mitchell hinted strongly that the guilty newspapers best watch their step because, being unable to suppress them any other way, he just might nail them on criminal charges, from which he assumed they were no more immune than Ellsberg.

On July 4, which celebrates freedom, Martha Mitchell, the Attorney General's outspoken wife, warned the American press might be suppressed after all—somehow—if it continued to reveal government secrets. "I deplore the indiscrete judgment that smells of political implications on the part of the press," said Mrs. Mitchell to a reporter from *The Washington Star* (to her a more amenable daily than the *Post*), "which has reached such an extent that it may result in complete suppression of the press." It's not particularly relevant that Mrs. Mitchell is not an official of government. It is relevant that Mr. Mitchell, who had felt it necessary to condemn stories in advance of publication, did not feel it necessary to disown his wife's public threat.

York Times, which publishes Tom Wicker, for one, and *The Washington Post*, which publishes Herblock, whose cartoons have allegedly ruined whole days for Nixon. At this time, he took to helping them along, ordering Buchanan to remove the *Times* and *Post* from the daily news summaries—not so as to banish them from sight but to take a perverse pleasure in reading them from cover to cover *personally*. It was as if he enjoyed the frustration and suffering they brought. (Nearly a year later, when Anthony Lewis of the *Times*, in a report from North Vietnam, said that the mines which the President had ordered placed outside the harbors of North Vietnam were being removed by the Communists, the President lost his temper. He had one of Herb Klein's assistants lambast the *Times* as a Communist "dupe." The old line had been brought back to attack Nixon's powerful domestic enemy, the *Times*.)

If the *Times* and the *Post* had been less powerful and articulate, the attempt to abridge their freedom might have seemed a mere footnote to other violations of the Bill of Rights by the Nixon Administration. Kleindienst, the man Nixon and Mitchell put in charge of controlling political emergencies, casually bragged to Alan M. Dershowitz, a professor of law, that the Nixon administration did not have to suspend the Bill of Rights. "We wouldn't have to," said the Deputy Attorney General, whose remarks Dershowitz quickly published. "There is enough play at the joints of our existing criminal law—enough flexibility—so that if we really felt that we had to pick up the leaders of a violent uprising, we could. *We would find something to charge them with and we would be able to hold them that way for a while.*"

The hundreds of thousands of Americans carried in political dossiers the summer of 1970 had presumably grown in one year. *Life* reported less than twelve months later that the government now had *political* information in its files on twenty-five million citizens. (Perhaps early reports were underestimated or *Life*'s overestimated, but nonetheless, there did seem to be indications of expansion.)

At this point, well into the third year of the Nixon Administration, The Committee on the Protection of Civil Liberties and Civil Rights of the American Bar Association declared there then existed in the United States "an anti-libertarian climate . . . which properly can be labeled 'repressive.' " Accompanying this charge was a twenty-eight page report compiled over the previous twelve months that found the nation "dangerously close" to a suspension of the Bill of Rights. The investigating lawyers blamed the repression on two underlying factors: a "national stress" engendered by "a highly unpopular war in Southeast Asia" and on "some of our nation's highest leaders."

Some may call him a conservative, but Nixon is a reactionary. First, he is a psychological reactionary. Nixon's relations with others are weak and egocentric; when threatened with some "loss"—which in his case is often—his anxieties mount. Once upon a time, his mounting anxieties led to sore throats and to punishing one man or one group at a time. But today he is President of the United States—the most powerful man in the world, he's quick to tell you, hoping to convince himself in the process—and today he can repress his unconscious feelings of self-hatred by consciously repressing *you*, which makes him a political reactionary as well.

Virtually every act opposing Administration policy (where policy exists) is interpreted by Nixon, and his closest aides, as hostility aimed directly at the President. If that wasn't true originally, his style tends to make that true today, when citizens blame Nixon for more than he could conceivably be guilty of. But the point is that every peace marcher, college student, black man, intellectual, Senator or bureaucrat who does not repudiate his group identity by kneeling publicly and often before the altar of Nixon's Presidency must therefore, in Nixon's head, be a delinquent, a Democrat or another participant in the secret but militant "conspiracy" against the United States of America, a conspiracy that Nixon and his former Attorney General see virtually everywhere, even in the rejection of Haynsworth and Carswell by the U.S. Senate.

In addition, Nixon appears to fear that the Supreme Court itself might become a source of personal torment, unless he can control it. Over a year after losing on Carswell, he sought to place two other under-qualified lawyers on the high bench,

239

claiming they were strict constructionists. One was Mildred L. Lillie, a judicial novice from Los Angeles, and Herschel H. Friday, a bond lawyer and friend of Mitchell's from Little Rock. When the American Bar Association, to whom Nixon had submitted their names for approval, declared them "not qualified," the President became enraged. "Fuck the ABA!" he cried, a curse that I. F. Stone said "reverberated through Washington." Stone realized that Lillie, Friday and the curse were significant "aberrations [which] make up the self-portrait of a man passionately intent on dragging down the level of our highest court. It is as if Nixon will name competent lawyers only as a last resort [because] he fears that men who are well-trained lawyers cannot be trusted once elevated to the Court."

But at least one of his subsequent nominees, Rehnquist, as smart a lawyer as he reportedly was, had qualities that seemed more designed to serve Nixon than justice. William Shannon of the *Times*, among others, felt that Rehnquist is not a "true conservative" who would strictly interpret the Constitution but a rightist radical, "an aggressive ideologue with combative impulses and strong commitment to a harsh, narrow doctrine concerning government and individual." When Nixon's rights were challenged by Sam Ervin, a true conservative and advocate of strict Constitutional construction, it was this same Rehnquist who warned him that the President had the right to put anyone, including the Senator, under surveillance.[1]

Nixon's fear, it seems, creates the very violence and chaos which as President he must then subdue; his reckless or inept management engenders additional fear, violence and chaos which, in an endless cycle, requires additional repression.

Freud argued that by transferring a fear of his father onto some animal, a boy can externalize and thus relieve the inner tension of the socially unacceptable impulse to hate his own flesh-and-blood. As the boy gets older, the terrifying animals

[1] When Rehnquist was confirmed, after a lengthy delay, Ervin voted for confirmation. Ervin was criticized by his own supporters for putting the apparent emotional wants of his southern constituency above his own sense of justice.

of childhood are often replaced by more vaguely terrifying humans or perhaps conspiratorial groups of humans, who then become the boy-man's excuse for externalizing his aggressions, propelling him sometimes into paranoia. Nixon confesses that he feared his father. Virtually the last words in "The Authoritarian Personality," a pioneer collection on the clinical psychology of fascism, read: ". . . Fear and destructiveness are the major emotional sources of Fascism."

One can visualize Richard Nixon's horrified, if not outraged, reaction to any accusation that he has the proclivities of a modified fascist, even though reality is that he has placed his personal opinion of the public's best interests higher than the Fourth Amendment's guarantee of privacy; he has abridged the First Amendment by disrupting peaceable assembly; he has opposed the right of Congress to advise and consent and attempted to undermine the equal power of the Supreme Court. He has done these and more because, it appears, Richard Nixon finds it easier to say that *he* knows best, making as little of his external enemies as his enemy within has made of him.

CHAPTER TWENTY-THREE

Trying to explain Nixon's tediously repetitive aggressive rhythms, two scholars from the University of California suggested in late 1971 that ". . . young Richard was an anal-compulsive character."

While they speculated as to how he became one, and I shall not,[1] anal-compulsive character may be the most clear-eyed way to explain Richard Nixon's impulse—that enemy within—to humiliate himself and then project his humiliation onto the world around him. In *Transaction* magazine, Michael Rogin and John Lottier noticed too that Nixon expressed his "sense of loneliness, bad treatment and impotent rage" in anal terms. They referred at length to a letter from the ten-year-old Richard to his mother in which he imagined himself to be an abused cocker spaniel, accompanying "two boys" on a walk.

When one of the boys accidentally falls on the cocker spaniel, dog Richard loses his temper and bites the boy and receives a kick in return. Farther along, Richard "saw a black round thing in a tree. I hit it with my paw. A swarm of black thing [sic] came out of it. I felt a pain all over . . ." and the "thing" blinded him.

[1] Rogin and Lottier—along with Bruce Mazlisch of M.I.T., in his book, *In Search of Nixon, A Psychohistorical Inquiry*, seem to agree that Nixon should be characterized, at least in youth and early manhood, as an anal compulsive. But these cautious scholars may go too far. After suggesting the fairly obvious *nature* of the problem, they attempt to analyze its *origins*. It could have been his father's angers that made him what he is, or his mother's two-year "desertion" from home (in order to nurse a tubercular brother); it could have been the death of this brother or the other, little Arthur, that made Richard morbidly inclined. It might be none of these has made Richard Nixon what he is, although, more probably, all played a role in his development, but to what degree and in what kind? On the strength of the existing accounts of Nixon's infancy and childhood, it is impossible to say because invariably the accounts are incomplete, even when they are not transparently biased or conflicting.

Rogin and Lottier saw as the central theme of Nixon's early fantasy of self-hate the "black round thing" which punished young Richard with pain and blinding humiliation. "The imagery is anal," note the authors. "Feces retaliate for the attack on the tree trunk's anus."

Fanciful? Probably not; the inferior creature has unjustly bitten one of his superiors, a *real* boy, and as a result finds himself "helpless in the face of punishment." Rogin and Lottier saw loneliness, self-abuse and impotent rage in the Nixon letter to Hannah, which were "too powerful to be of only passing importance."

It's all too easy to recall another time when Nixon, frustrated, alone, impotent, resorted to anal imagery: "Shit or get off the pot," he told Ike in 1952, and ten years later, he accused American journalism of ruining his career by *shafting* him. Moments later, he turned to Herb Klein and, in an effort to save face, bragged, "I gave it to them [the reporters] right up the ass."[1]

To prevent others from in effect using blackmail to censor and dominate his existence, an anal compulsive will try to hide what he believes is his own inner contamination. "A child like Richard tries to keep [his feces] firmly ordered and under control," say Rogin and Lottier. "The central concern at the anal stage is control and autonomy. The individual's intent upon domination by others and control by the self fasten in later life on the principle of 'law and order.' "

Defining the anal compulsive, Erik H. Erikson, author of *Youth and Crisis*, and the leading authority today on the nature of regressive behavior, indirectly defined the habits of Richard Nixon:

"If denied the gradual and well-guided experience of the autonomy of free choice (or, if, indeed, weakened by an initial loss of trust)," Erikson feels, "the child will turn against himself all his urges to discriminate and manipulate. He will over-manipulate himself, he will develop a precocious conscience. Instead of taking possession of things in order to test them by purposeful repetition, *he will become obsessed by his own repetitiveness* [emphasis added]. By such obsessiveness, of course, he then learns to repossess the environment and to

[1] *Time* had it as "in the behind."

243

gain power by stubborn and minute control, where he could not find it in large scale mutual regulation. Such hollow victory is the infantile mode for a compulsion neurosis . . ."

Erickson has also written, "The 'behind' is the small being's dark continent . . . which can be magically dominated and effectively invaded by those [attacking] one's power of autonomy . . . This basic sense of doubt . . . forms a substratum for later and more verbal forms of compulsive doubting [and] finds expression in paranoiac fears concerning hidden persecutors . . ."

It's all there, implied in those few paragraphs: Nixon's self-hatred, his rigid pattern of self-destruction (crisis, followed by humiliation, followed by aggression), his fear of sharing power, his desire to dominate grandly (as America's king—a benevolent king, of course), his obsession with hidden persecutors (intent on examining his bowels).

As he entered his fourth year as President, these traits were more evident than they had been in several months. He seemed to seek renewed psychic comfort in violence and blaming his problems on others. Believing Mrs. Indira Ghandi, Prime Minister of India, had insulted him, he blamed the insult and his problems in India on Russia; when his Vietnamization plan failed a few months later, he again blamed Russia, then sought a military confrontation with Russia almost on the eve of his planned peace visit to Moscow.

Clearly, before the end of November, 1971, he was itching for trouble. He went to visit the AFL-CIO convention in Florida—so that George Meany, the tough, irritable leader of American labor, could insult him publicly. As always, there were those observers—including Meany—who felt that Nixon had deliberately hoped to be insulted in public for strictly political reasons, but in coming to the convention Nixon seemed rather agitated and unsure of himself, not the signs of a man who knew entirely what he was doing.

A couple of weeks later, Nixon put himself into the middle of another impossible situation. For eight months, Mrs. Ghandi had begged the President to ask his friend Yahya Khan, head of Pakistan, to stop the massive and calculated murder of East Pakistani civilians by his soldiers, but Nixon kept his silence. Yet when the Indians began fighting Khan's

Pakistani soldiers, the President suddenly became interested, offering at once to mediate, from his elevated position, a political settlement. It was Mrs. Ghandi's turn to ignore Nixon. He sent notes which she refused to answer. Her silence was galling.

"I asked her to give me *any* response," Nixon explained. "She gave me none whatever." Within hours after saying this, Henry Kissinger was, as he said to members of the Washington Special Action Group, "getting hell every half-hour from the President that we are not being tough enough on India . . . He [Nixon] does not believe we are carrying out his wishes. He wants to tilt in favor of Pakistan. He feels everything we do comes out otherwise."

Although Nixon ordered eight warships and two thousand marines to stand off East Pakistan, where the fighting raged, in hopes of intimidating the Indian army, everything—for him—*did* come out otherwise. After he was ignored by a woman, the most powerful man in the world took the "wrong side of about as big and simple a moral issue as the world has seen lately," wrote John P. Lewis, Dean of the Woodrow Wilson School of Public and International Affairs. Not only had the President, in a fit of pique, sided with a brutal, if minor, military dictatorship against the second largest nation in the world (throwing aside America's "own deepest political values"), Nixon joined a sure-fire loser (Nobody in his defense establishment gave Pakistan a chance against India's army.) and, inadvertently, gave Russia increased influence and power in the Asian sub-continent. Then he said that the Russians had manipulated the Indians into starting the whole bloody mess.

After another humiliation of his own making, Nixon retaliated as he usually does—by increasing the level of violence in another arena: Things had been fairly quiet for some time in the air over Vietnam, but after the Indian affair, the U.S. almost immediately started to bomb Communist positions in South Vietnam. The bombing became more intense after Nixon's visit to China, a visit which seemed to liberate all of his repressive anxieties in their most agitated form.

Before, during and after the trip, his spokesmen in Saigon

and Washington repeatedly and publicly "anticipated" heavy assaults from North Vietnam on the sovereign territory of South Vietnam. The raids did not come, but the bombing of alleged supply routes continued and mounted. Once the raids southward did materialize, quickly and thoroughly destroying the last vestiges of the myth of "Vietnamization," Nixon commanded American bombers—after so long a pause in such tactics—to renew their bombing of North Vietnam. Defense spokesmen announced additions to the number of attacking bombers, until the announcements droned and almost lost their sense of theatre.

To reactivate the drama and his own virility, Nixon significantly altered the level of violence. Instead of continuing the pull-out of troops in any meaningful way, he sent in ships, then ordered the mining of North Vietnam harbors, which had Russian supply ships inside. Simultaneously, he threatened a blockade. Few American military men thought these new and frightening tactics would have any immediate effect on the outcome of the losing war being waged by the South Vietnamese but in the most important sense, for Nixon, it had exacerbated bad feelings at home and potentially broadened the military confrontation abroad—after his peace trip to China.

But why should that trip have become the source of a new humiliation—if indeed it did? After all, nothing untoward occurred to him on the Chinese mainland, unless one counts a theatrically nasty word or two aimed at American reporters who happened to be standing within earshot as the President spoke to Chou. Nixon also seemed slightly fatigued at times during the visit, but fatigue might happen to any human being who has held several meetings with the heads of a foreign government recently considered hostile.

If there is an answer, it may lie in the fundamental reason why Nixon made the trip. Certainly it was not to conduct serious negotiations; Kissinger had done most of the hard work well before hand or Nixon would not have gone, and the trip produced nothing at all unexpected. Nixon instead had gone, basically, to insure his place in history—as the great and fearless peacemaker, and though he was widely praised for just those qualities after the trip, it seems quite clear that the praise was insufficient, as it must always be with him.

He had not been back on U.S. soil five minutes when his ebullience was undermined and he lost his place—symbolically and factually. Cheered by five thousand appreciative Federal employees as he made a brief speech at Andrews Air Force Base, the President faltered the second he heard the all but inaudible jeers of perhaps five or ten persons who presumably believed him wrong in dealing with Communists. He flushed and stumbled in his text. It took him awhile to get back on the track.

Therefore, it was not the visit itself that formed the latest Nixon crisis. It was the aftermath—his famous "letdown"—which was the moment he was forced to measure the response of his fellow man to his acts. Despite the strident acclaim of the majority, Nixon heard the muted voices of his detractors. Wherever there were a few skeptics, he heard them in the midst of strident acclaim. "They" had always known of the hidden contamination and, even though he was now the king, they could still see it. If Richard was to be punished, so must they, the voices of his inevitable judgment. It was they he must answer, and he must answer them always in the same way, even as he punished himself.

But first himself: The next morning, the President very nearly fell into the sea off Key Biscayne. He stepped where no other man would have stepped—on a loose board that protected the edge of the helicopter pad from bumping boats. He stepped blindly, and was barely rescued from hurting himself by his daughter and the very guests he had come to greet.

Two days later, on March 3, he now did the one perhaps disastrous political thing he had previously decided against doing. He and Mitchell, his symbiotic twin who had just quit as Attorney General to direct Nixon's re-election campaign, decided to make Nixon's personality the first—and most target-able—issue. In New Hampshire for the primary there, Republican spokesmen, ranging over the state but orchestrated from Key Biscayne, began stressing Nixon's personal greatness. "The President," said Nelson Rockefeller, speaking from a prepared text, "is a man who has captured the *feelings* of the American people and become the man of the hour." It's almost as if Nixon himself could have written that line.

Having captured their feelings—the wrong feelings—he then almost gratuitously began attacking the ones most easily recognized. People wondered why, at given moments from February on, he abruptly attacked child care plans and anti-abortion laws. The attacks appeared rather arbitrary. The answer is that these were oblique emotional assaults on the liberals and their cherished ambitions. If they could ridicule him, he could hurt them.

Each negative statement from the White House on domestic affairs came at a moment when, anger high, he had temporarily exhausted nasty things to say about the North Vietnamese—and particularly their Russian allies. He always came back to them. The mining of the harbors was aimed at the Russians. The mining, some said, was a bluff to end the war. Others said the mining was only the beginning of the war.

When *Nixon's Head* went to the printer the third week in May, 1972, the Moscow meeting was underway, because the Russians wanted it that way. But no Nixonologist was concerned with how the Russians or the North Vietnamese or even the Chinese might react. They dreaded how Nixon would react if the Russians ignored his minings (or ignored him, in Moscow) or if the North Vietnamese continued ridiculing his new "peace" overtures as he continued to mine and bomb them. One newspaper, in a confessed fit of terror, headed a news summary of May events this way: "No One Knows What He Might Do."

But Nixonologists—whether they had taken to practising psychoanalysis openly or not—were fairly clear on one point: Whatever Richard Milhous Nixon did next, it would ultimately prove dangerous.

He had to find some group, some nation, someone, in addition to himself, onto whom he could project his early guilt.

72111